15288

GEORGE CANNING

Three Biographical Studies

by

P. J. V. ROLO

*Senior Lecturer in History at the
University of Keele*

LONDON

MACMILLAN & CO LTD

1965

MACMILLAN AND COMPANY LIMITED
St Martin's Street London WC2
also Bombay Calcutta Madras Melbourne

THE MACMILLAN COMPANY OF CANADA
70 Bond Street Toronto 2

ST MARTIN'S PRESS INC
175 Fifth Avenue New York 10NY

Printed in Great Britain by Richard Clay and Company, Ltd.,
Bungay, Suffolk

CONTENTS

ABBREVIATIONS

The Rise of George Canning	Dorothy Marshall	D.M.
The Foreign Policy of Canning	Harold Temperley	TEMP
George Canning and his Times	A. G. Stapleton	G.C. & T.
Some Correspondence of George Canning (2 vols.)	ed. E. J. Stapleton	C.G.C.
George Canning and his Friends (2 vols.)	ed. J. Bagot	BAG
John Hookham Frere and his Friends	G. Festing	FEST
Canning's Speeches (6 vols.)	ed. R. Therry	Therry
The Letters of George IV (3 vols.)	ed. A. Aspinall	ASP
The Formation of Canning's Ministry	ed. A. Aspinall	F.C.M.
The Correspondence of Charles Arbuthnot	ed. A. Aspinall	A.
The Journal of Mrs. Arbuthnot (2 vols.)	ed. F. Bamford and the Duke of Wellington	Mrs. A.
The Huskisson Papers	ed. L. Melville	HUSK
The Private Letters of Princess Lieven to Prince Metternich 1820–1826	ed. P. Quennell	L.
The Greville Memoirs 1814–1860 (8 vols.)	ed. L. Strachey and R. Fulford	GRE
The Croker Papers (3 vols.)	ed. L. J. Jennings	CRO
Report on the Manuscripts of Earl Bathurst	(Hist. MSS. Commission)	BATH
Britain and the Independence of Latin America (2 vols.)	ed. C. Webster	WEB

To
HUBERT WYLIE

INTRODUCTION

This book consists of three separate studies of George Canning: the man, the politician and the statesman.

Canning's character and personality played such a decisive part in his struggle for political power, while the qualities and limitations of his mind were so significant in the uses which he made of that power, that a study of the man seems an obvious prelude to any attempt at describing his career or evaluating his achievements. At the same time the union of such talents with such single-minded political ambition is sufficiently rare to be interesting.

My purpose in treating his struggle for political power as the object of a separate study may require more explanation. Although episodes of Canning's political career have attracted the detailed attention of scholars, there is no consecutive account available. I am trying in the first place, therefore, to fill a gap. At the same time I believe that in the process much incidental light can be thrown on an era when the 'wind of change' was effecting a silent revolution as momentous perhaps, although obviously not as spectacular, as the French or Bolshevik Revolutions. In fact the social and economic complexion of England during Canning's political life was completely transformed with results which stretched far beyond England's boundaries. The political structure, outwardly little affected, was inevitably undermined.

In appearance party loyalty, thanks perhaps to Charles James Fox, had somehow survived the virtual disappearance of parties. Parliament, still essentially a Parliament of landowners, was divided into groups based on royal patronage, on family affiliation, on allegiance to an individual leader, on a specific common interest or on a particular matter of principle. From these groups, with the aid of dwindling royal patronage, the Prime Minister was compelled to contrive majorities in both Houses. The prospects of an individual leader did not depend on the number of his personal followers. Canning once rejoiced that his affiliates were few because the plums of office, if available, could be generously divided among them. Liverpool had no personal followers. Peel's talents were particularly appreciated because in the twenties there were no Peelites. In this Parliament of landowners it was personal differences and relics of old loyalties which prevented the establishment of an aristocratic block. Such an alignment would have fatally divorced both Lords and Commons from the social and economic revolutions which were in train. The voices of the new rich, like the elder Peel, were heard only because of the wrangles in the ranks of the aristocracy.

If the character and composition of Parliament was little changed, new forces were in increasing evidence elsewhere. Whereas Pitt for practical purposes could equate the kind of public opinion in which he was interested with the House of Commons, Canning deliberately and realistically recognised that the confines of Westminster were too narrow. Effective public opinion, difficult to diagnose or determine as it always is, had obviously broadened. The Press assisted and at the same time prospered in the process. Fear of offending amorphous, moneyed, literate and on the whole progressive middle-class opinion inhibited George IV and many traditional legislators. The King yearned after Ministers who would make him more popular, or at least less unpopular, and who could govern without too much obvious recourse to royal patronage; by 1827 even the Duke of Wellington found the importunities of the Grenville clan[1] anomalous. Abuses, however currently practised, must be more decently veiled. Canning was one of the first to appreciate the situation and to make personal capital from this intelligence. But he drew no radical conclusions from his observation. He was prepared to cultivate popularity and yet he believed that the old system of Government could remain unchanged.

With hindsight it seems obvious that the King's Government,

[1] Now led by the Duke of Buckingham. Their greed and pretensions were notorious. As Lord Holland commented in 1822: 'All articles are now to be had at low prices, except Grenvilles'. See S. Walpole: *History of England*, vol. 2, p. 42.

old-style, was an outmoded conception. Not only the basis, but the whole functions of Government required reconsideration. The big question was whether any kind of gradual change could contend with the consequences of the Industrial Revolution. If the interests of the new rich and the new poor were to be at all reconciled, Government intervention in ever widening spheres was imperative. The future lay with the expert and the analyst. Awareness of a widening sense of Government responsibility was implicit in the economic and administrative reforms which Robinson, Huskisson and Peel so resolutely promoted during the last years of Liverpool's Administration. Practically, however, the removal of dead wood was more apparent than any new planting. While politicians, including Canning, went through the motions on the old system, its demise was inherent in the policies already being pursued. The political conclusions were eventually drawn not by Canning who remained in outlook a sentimental obscurantist, but by Peel who finally emerged as the Tory master of political transformism.

From a survey of Canning's political career I believe it is possible to illustrate the surviving power of the King and the dwindling resources of the Crown; the surviving strength of party sentiment and the looseness of party affiliation; the surviving element of family connection in Parliamentary groupings and its declining influence on the formation of Governments; the difficulty of holding together any Government at all and the new and growing responsibilities with which all Governments were faced; the broadening of public opinion and the new significance of popularity. I have generally confined myself to an account of Canning's manoeuvres in his own struggle for power, leaving it to the reader to judge the relevance of their contribution to an understanding of the politics of his age.

In considering Canning's claim to rank as a great statesman, I have shown no such diffidence about the exercise of personal judgement. On the contrary, my main reason for attempting an evaluation is that, apart from an excellent brief life by Sir Charles Petrie,[1] there have been no endeavours to make an all-round

[1] Originally published in 1930, but rewritten and reissued in 1946.

estimate of his achievements as a statesman in the light of twentieth-century research. By this I do not mean that Canning has either been neglected or misunderstood, but simply that his career as a whole has not been reviewed. Therefore, on the one hand his fame has tended to be dimmed and, on the other, legends, born of uncritical praise, have enjoyed a lingering survival. This is not the fault of recent general appreciations but can probably be explained by the fact that old text books are cheaper than new.

In his lifetime, because he had opposed the Holy Alliance, Canning was hailed as the enemy of kings and the friend of peoples. A. J. Stapleton, his private secretary and his first biographer, encouraged this 'liberal' reputation. It became well known that he was hated by Metternich, that streets were named after him in Latin America and that Greeks owed him gratitude. Gladstone admired him and it was a small step for him to be registered as the first English friend of small States struggling to be free. In the history of British foreign policy Canning became the hero and Castlereagh the villain. And yet, paradoxically, Canning was also praised for his insularity, for his rudeness to foreigners and for his chauvinism. Had he not seized the Danish Fleet and saved England from invasion? Had he not, before Palmerston, insulted foreign diplomats? Had he not made England respected and feared? Had he not boasted eloquently of his triumphs? All this and yet he was a good liberal too! Why, even at home he had championed Catholic Emancipation; he had backed Corn Law reform; he had discovered public opinion; and he had become, for a hundred days, Prime Minister in the teeth of aristocratic disapproval. Miss Martineau in her *History of the Peace* awarded him the palm of progressive approval by declaring that 'he must be the hero'.[1] It is almost a surprise to be reminded that, although he attacked the Slave Trade, he contrived to defend slavery; that he exercised his wit at the expense of

---

[1] Martineau: *History of the Peace*, vol. 2, p. 145. After a perceptive eulogy of Canning, Miss Martineau did comment regretfully on his opposition to Parliamentary Reform. But she concluded that this 'inconsistency' was an instance of 'waywardness' which proved that even her hero was not exempt from 'human frailty'.

Brougham's propaganda in favour of popular education; that he died an inveterate opponent of Parliamentary Reform; that he had approved tough tactics at Peterloo; and that he thoroughly endorsed the Six Acts. Yet somehow Disraeli could regard him as the father of Tory democracy. In late Victorian appraisals Canning always contrived to be on the side of the angels. Throughout their lives and political tergiversations both Gladstone and Disraeli claimed him as their mentor. No one could have appreciated that kind of joke better than Canning.

In spite of all the readily available contemporary evidence and in spite of all the efforts of scholars such as Professor Temperley, Professor Webster, Professor Aspinall and Miss Dorothy Marshall it is even now difficult to escape from the legend which Canning himself sedulously fostered in so many ways.

On his record in home affairs I can find little to justify for Canning a place among great English statesmen. Although he sponsored Catholic Emancipation, he failed to carry any measure of relief for Catholic disabilities; although he sympathised with Ireland's plight, he lacked the detailed knowledge and the sense of urgency which might at least have made him a hero in a lost cause. During the last years of Liverpool's Ministry he approved but he did not initiate the great economic and administrative reforms for which credit must go to Robinson, to Huskisson, to Peel and indeed to Liverpool himself. As Prime Minister he proposed Corn Law reform on lines prepared by Huskisson, but he failed to carry the necessary measure. Although eventually accepted as a leader by many progressive Whigs he remained, in spirit, a Tory and where Parliamentary Reform was concerned, a die-hard Tory. If he had not died in 1827 it is possible that he might have dominated a Canningite–Whig coalition. The new 'liberal' party which could thus have emerged would have had a greater Tory bias and would surely have known more enemies to the left. The Tories would less easily have survived as a major political party and the course of English history would no doubt have run far less smoothly. While such speculations suggest something of the force which Canning represented in home politics it cannot be maintained that his death interrupted any grand design as a statesman to create a new political party; on the contrary his bargain with the Whigs was an unwelcome necessity.

Even if no material achievements can be claimed for Canning on the home front it might be argued that he showed singular prescience in his understanding of the importance of public opinion. Certainly he displayed tenderness for opinion outside Parliament; certainly he understood the value of educating opinion; certainly he took pride in popularity. In his struggle for political power he was on occasions able to make some capital out of the popularity which he had acquired, but while extolling the importance and cultivating the support of public opinion he drew no significant political conclusions from his attitude. The opinion he flattered was wider than the House but far narrower than the country. The revolutionary implications of recognising even this narrow force were essentially those of an enlightened despot. The support of public opinion was a useful prop to power. If Canning pointed a finger towards popular democracy he did so by chance.

The conduct of foreign affairs was Canning's main objective in his struggle for political power. It is, therefore, not surprising that his most noteworthy achievements should have been in this, his chosen field. He gained his taste for foreign affairs at the outset of his political career as an Under-Secretary to Lord Grenville. But his first opportunity to play a leading part in their direction was when he became Foreign Secretary in 1807. On this occasion he was more interested, not unnaturally, in the successful prosecution of the war than in the routine work of his office. There were signs that he might have proved a war-leader of the class of a Chatham or a Churchill, but in his eagerness to gain complete control of the Government, he disqualified himself, once in 1809 and again in 1812, from any further share in the war-time Administration or in the peace-making at Vienna. He must, therefore, be mainly judged on his second tenure of the Foreign Office from 1822 to 1827. In my opinion, if the interests of Great Britain are accepted as a criterion, Canning proved an outstandingly successful Foreign Secretary. Although he operated on traditional lines and in relatively easy circumstances, his breadth of vision, quickness of intellect and mastery of detail remain unsurpassed among British Foreign Secretaries. In quality he may be compared with a Richelieu or a Bismarck.

It was, however, as a liberalising innovator that Canning gained fame for his conduct of foreign affairs. This was partly because of the methods which he employed to justify and to popularise his diplomacy. By his speeches in Parliament and outside and by his publication of dispatches he contrived to give the impression that he was taking the nation into his confidence. The causes with which his name became associated also helped to strengthen this 'liberal' reputation. Contrast with Castlereagh followed as a matter of course. It was not until Temperley and Webster had applied themselves to studies of the foreign policies of the two Ministers that the habitual contrast was toned down to an essay in close co-operation. Although their methods and temperaments varied, Castlereagh and Canning had the same views of national interests and were equally impatient, apart from loyalty to Pitt's dedication to abolition of the Slave Trade, of all idealistic diversions. But, whereas Castlereagh found it difficult to explain even in the confines of the Cabinet, Canning revelled in public justifications. They were, however, carefully selected and he only believed in showing his hand when it was expedient and convenient to do so. I am not sure whether, when Canning did thus appeal to the public, he was concerned for practical reasons with personal popularity, or whether he hoped, by diverting public opinion from home affairs, to paper the cracks in an outworn but cherished political system, or whether he had come to the conclusion that popular backing was a useful asset in the conduct of foreign affairs, or whether all these motives were in operation. But certainly in his methods of exploiting publicity he was plotting a new course. Similar methods were used by Brougham, 'the old *drum-major* of the army of *liberty*'.[1] It is probable that each learned much from the other and that this may help to explain their mutual respect. But Brougham was a cam-

---

[1] From a tribute in *The Daily Telegraph* after Brougham's death quoted in the preface of *The Life of Henry Brougham to 1830*, by the late Professor New.

B

paigner in 'Causes' which were fought under the banner of 'Liberty'. On the other hand, if I interpret Canning's motives in resorting to such methods correctly, they do not imply the discovery or acceptance of any new or 'liberal' standards in diplomacy. Canning's only 'Cause' was his country. While he may be recognised as one of the founder-fathers of public-relations, I can find no case for presenting him as a herald of Woodrow Wilson. The value of his achievements in the field of foreign affairs is not, in my opinion, thereby diminished.

In attempting these three studies of Canning, I have relied entirely on printed sources. The material available is voluminous. Most important among original sources are *Canning's Speeches* (6 vols.), ed. Therry; *George Canning and His Friends* (2 vols.), ed. J. Bagot; *Some Official Correspondence of George Canning* (2 vols.), ed. E. J. Stapleton; *The Letters of George IV* (3 vols.), ed. A. Aspinall; *The Formation of Cannning's Ministry*, ed. A. Aspinall; *The Correspondence of Charles Arbuthnot*, ed. A. Aspinall; *The Journal of Mrs Arbuthnot* (2 vols.), ed. F. Bamford and the Duke of Wellington; *The Huskisson Papers*, ed. H. Melville; *The Private Letters of Princess Lieven*, ed. P. Quennell; *The Bathurst Papers*, Hist. MSS. Commission; *Britain and the Independence of Latin America* (2 vols.), ed. C. Webster; *John Hookham Frere and his friends*, ed. G. Festing; *The Croker Papers* (3 vols.), ed. L. J. Jennings; and the original material contained in *George Canning and his Times* by A. G. Stapleton, *The Rise of George Canning* by Dorothy Marshall and *The Foreign Policy of Canning* by H. Temperley.

Where interpretations are concerned the historians who have contributed most to my own understanding of Canning are Miss Dorothy Marshall, *The Rise of George Canning*; Professor Webster, *The Foreign Policy of Castlereagh* and his Introduction to *The Independence of Latin America*; Professor Aspinall, particularly his Introduction to *The Formation of Canning's Ministry*, and his article 'The Canningite Party' in *Royal Historical Society Transactions*, XVII, 1934; and Professor Temperley, *The Foreign Policy of Canning*. Professor Temperley's book remains the most impressive single study of Canning. It is theoretically confined to his conduct of foreign policy from 1822 until his death, but the range is in fact far wider.

Although aspects of Canning's life and career have been meticulously explored there is as yet no full-scale biography available. This deficiency is however soon likely to be filled. Mr. C. Collyer has been at work for some time on the Canning Papers in the Harewood MSS. Professor Temperley and Miss Dorothy Marshall have had access to these papers but, according to Mr. Collyer, there remains a considerable amount of new and unexplored material. Certainly, judging from an article which he contributed to the April 1961 issue of *History Today*, it seems that a good deal of fresh light is likely to be thrown on Canning's first tenure of the Foreign Office. Professor Gash has recently shown, in the first volume of what promises to be a definitive biography of Peel, the kind of task which needs to be undertaken. It is encouraging to know that Mr. Collyer has taken the matter in hand. In the meanwhile I hope these three studies will revive some interest in a man regarded by his own contemporaries with abhorrence, respect or adulation, but never with indifference, and now too often either taken for granted or forgotten.

P. J. V. R.

THE MAN

At the beginning of his political career Canning was lampooned as 'a child turning his jacket'. 'To speak honestly,' he confessed, 'I would rather be abused a little, if I had my choice, than have nothing at all said about me.'[1] In this preference he showed little originality. Seldom, however, has a youthful wish been so amply fulfilled and by 1816 it could already be said that 'of all the public men that have appeared in our times there is assuredly not one that ever had so many bitter enemies'.[2]

Canning made his first enemies in 1793 when at the age of twenty-three he obtained a seat in the House of Commons by favour of the Prime Minister. Previously Canning had been at some pains to warn the Whig friends of his undergraduate days that he no longer shared their view of the French Revolution. His conversion to Government opinion seemed too opportune and he was mocked as a renegade. Jibes turned to invective when he was identified as the leading spirit behind *The Anti-Jacobin* and for some years he remained a favourite target for abuse from all revolutionary fellow-travellers and most of the Foxite Whigs.

After Pitt had resigned in 1801, Canning insisted on doing likewise and against his patron's advice launched a campaign of increasing virulence against Addington's Ministry. The rancour of Canning's new victims now matched the still active resentment of the Whig Opposition. By 1807, when he first achieved high office as Foreign Secretary in the Duke of Portland's Ministry, Canning was feared, mistrusted and disliked by powerful elements in both parties. They agreed in considering him self-seeking, impetuous, hot-tempered, a dangerous enemy and a dubious friend. On the other hand, even his enemies conceded his great talents and he had acquired a small but devoted personal

---

[1] *Canning's Journal.* D.M., p. 51.
[2] Lyttleton to Bagot. 27th June 1816. BAG, vol. 2, p. 27.

following in the House. In the country at large his fame was slight and in Europe he was relatively unknown.

During his first brief tenure of the Foreign Office, however, Canning became established as a public figure both at home and abroad. He gained the reputation of being ruthless and flashy, perhaps a man of genius, but hardly one to be trusted. His resignation and subsequent duel with Castlereagh confirmed previous doubts regarding his character. The circumstances of the case were at the time obscure, and sympathy both in the House and in the country was with Castlereagh. Between 1809 and 1812 Canning seemed obviously to be angling for supreme power and not only his enemies labelled him as an unprincipled intriguer. His failure to join in any Administration save on his own terms was interpreted with almost universal disfavour. Such, however, was the power of his oratory that offers of Government office continued to be made.

After 1812, on the other hand, when Napoleon's reverses brought unexpected credit to a weak Government, Canning's tongue ceased for a while even to be feared. His enemies in office could almost afford the luxury of ignoring him. In 1813 he himself formally disbanded his own small group of personal followers and he devoted increasing attention to his Liverpool constituents and to writing for *The Quarterly Review*. Both in his constituency and among his readers he gained a measure of popularity. But when in 1816 he returned unobtrusively to the Cabinet as President of the Indian Board of Control, it was soon apparent that he was still suspected and disliked by former enemies and that he had not acquired any powerful new friends. His support of the Government's repressive policy at home revived the resentment of his old Whig opponents without inspiring real confidence among the established beneficiaries of Tory ascendency. Though Liverpool constituents and readers of *The Quarterly Review* might esteem him highly, there were many in the country who agreed with Cobbett's complaint that Canning made 'a jest of the groans' of the poor.[1] Evidence of the strength

---

[1] During a debate on the Indemnity Bill in March 1818, Canning had referred to 'the revered and ruptured Ogden'. Ogden's case (he had petitioned against

of widespread animosity was forthcoming by reactions to his attitude in 1820 over the question of the royal divorce. 'No greater proof,' noted Greville, 'can be given of the low estimation in which his character is held than the refusal of all parties to give him any credit for a line of conduct which could not fail to be highly disagreeable to those whom it is evidently his interest to conciliate and please.'[1] Chief among these was of course the King, who concluded that Canning 'had strongly manifested by his conduct, what everybody before believed, almost an open avowal of criminal intercourse with the P[rince]ss and thus, while he half acknowledged his treason on the one hand, he added insult to injustice to his sovereign on the other'. 'What confidence, therefore,' George IV protested, 'can I have in a mind so tainted with dishonour and disturbed by apprehensions of guilt?'[2] While Canning's resignation provoked this outburst of royal indignation most former colleagues assumed, uncharitably, that the gesture was merely a characteristic manoeuvre in his quest for power. Even the Prime Minister, who valued Canning's friendship, respected his talents, appreciated the power of his eloquence and was impressed by his popularity among the merchants of Liverpool, began to wonder whether the support of such a trouble-maker was any longer worth pains to secure. It was therefore with some misgivings that Liverpool sought to obtain Canning's return to the Cabinet. The Prime Minister's relief was apparent when his troublesome friend finally agreed to accept the proferred Indian Governor-Generalship. Only the sudden suicide of Castlereagh prevented Canning's relegation to that splendid exile. Liverpool considered that Canning, in spite of his faults, was the only possible successor to Castlereagh at the Foreign Office. Consequently, in the teeth of royal displeasure, mistrusted by most of the Cabinet and described by *The Times*

---

the treatment he received while imprisoned as a political agitator) had been taken up by Opposition speakers. This phrase in Canning's reply achieved considerable notoriety.

[1] GRE, 16th June 1820, vol. 1, p. 96.

[2] *King's Memorandum of 22nd November 1820.* ASP, vol. 2, 875 p. 386. Over twenty years had passed since Canning's alleged affair with the Princess. (See pp. 34, 35 below.) But the gossip had been revived.

as a 'hired advocate', Canning returned to Government service.

In the last five years of his life he succeeded in rousing the liveliest passions of his whole career. While Metternich controlled the strings of Austro–Russian policy it became the duty of Count Esterhazy[1] and Countess Lieven[2] to keep the King's anger at boiling point. Castigated by Metternich[3] as a 'malevolent meteor', 'the scourge of England', Canning emerged as a central figure of international controversy. He became the hero of the legions of Metternich's victims and critics. His praises were sung by Goethe and by Heine. In Latin America he was idolised. Even in England liberals began to applaud and a measure of oblivion for Peterloo was achieved. The Press gradually responded and he rode on the crest of a wave of rising popularity. Nevertheless, old enmities survived and were in some cases exacerbated. Grey and other great Whigs with obstinate memories refused to be mollified. The ultra Tories fumed. The Duke of Wellington soon regretted that he had contrived to convince the King that Canning's presence in the Cabinet, however unwelcome, was a political necessity. Feeling in Government and Court circles against Canning was epitomised by Mrs. Arbuthnot[4] whose diary became a diatribe. In November 1820 she had been 'very glad to hear of his resignation' and she had confessed to her husband that she 'had always disliked Mr. Canning, that he was a tricking, dishonest politician' and that she 'had always detested his coming into the cabinet'.[5] She was shocked and distressed

[1] The Austrian Ambassador.

[2] The wife of the Russian Ambassador.

[3] See *Memoirs of Prince Metternich 1815–1829*, ed. Prince Richard Metternich. Trans. Mrs. Alexander Napier, vol. 4, p. 392.

[4] Daughter of the Honourable Henry Fane, M.P., second son of the 8th Earl of Westmorland. Born in 1794, she married Charles Arbuthnot, M.P., as his second wife in 1815. Charles Arbuthnot, who was then Joint Secretary of the Treasury, in fact and throughout most of Liverpool's ministry, filled the unofficial role of Tory party manager. Through her husband and through Castlereagh and Wellington, with both of whom she maintained very close platonic relationships, Mrs. Arbuthnot was able to gratify her passionate interest in Tory politics. Her diaries covering the period 1820–32 were published in 1950 in two volumes entitled *The Journal of Mrs. Arbuthnot* and edited by Francis Bamford and the Duke of Wellington.

[5] Mrs. A, vol. 1, p. 55.

when in spite of her warnings he succeeded Castlereagh. Early in 1823 she noted with satisfaction that 'the Duke of York has a great horror of Mr. Canning'.[1] She rejoiced that the King 'hated Canning for his hypocrisy, his sarcastic manner, and his tricks of all kinds'.[2] In the crucial month of December 1824 her exasperation was constantly in evidence. 'So,' she protested, 'we are to be driven into a war to give occupation to Mr. C[anning]'s active fancies.'[3] On 10th December she noted: 'Sir Charles Stuart said to me the other day that formerly we had a minister who could neither write nor speak and who exercised influence in every court in Europe. Now we have one who is a master of both arts and we know nothing and are consulted about nothing. It is perfectly true.'[4]

Though Mrs. Arbuthnot and those whose opinions she reflected might rage, Canning achieved his objectives. Metternich's plans miscarried and both at St. Petersburg and in Paris there were significant changes in attitude towards the director of British foreign policy. In England his popularity among the newspaper-reading public was clearly in the ascendent. With deliberation George IV revised his own opinions and in due course Canning emerged as a royal favourite. The 'Ultras' and the Duke continued to disapprove. Canning was accused of plotting with the Opposition to secure the Government's downfall and his attitude over the Catholic Question gave some colour to the charge.

On 18th February 1827 Liverpool was finally incapacitated by a stroke and on 10th March Mrs. Arbuthnot confessed that she 'would almost rather see the Duke die than in a cabinet of which Mr. Canning was head'.[5] Tory peers importunately pressed the King to exclude Canning from the Premiership, but after many hesitations, George IV called upon his new favourite to prepare plans for a reconstructed Ministry on 10th April. The spate of resignations, including the Duke's, which followed showed the extent of pervading hostility. 'There never was anything,'

---

[1] Mrs. A, vol. 1, p. 223. [2] Ibid., p. 262.
[3] Ibid., p. 361. [4] Ibid., p. 365.
[5] Mrs. A, vol. 2, p. 87.

commented Lord Howard de Walden, 'like the bitterness and personality of the Ultras against Mr. Canning.'[1] 'Sooner or later,' jibed Lord Londonderry,[2] 'a tremendous reaction must occur to mother Hun[n]'s[3] offspring,'[4] while the Earl of Clancarty wondered whether England would bear an Administration thus formed of 'Lacklanders' and led by that 'arch schemer'.[5] Deserted by so many Tories, Canning found himself compelled to bargain with the Whigs. Here again old enmities survived and prejudiced the course of negotiation. Lord Grey was irreconcilable and rejected any compromise with Canning, whom he declared disqualified by birth from any claim to the highest office. James Abercromby, who scorned 'to deprecate him with the frailties of his mother', nevertheless insisted that he was 'no defender of the life and character of Canning'.[6] Eventually, thanks mainly to Brougham and the younger generation of Whigs, agreement was reached. Canning now faced the full fury of former colleagues with the wavering support of old opponents. The adulation of his own small band of followers, the general plaudits of the Press and the enthusiasm of liberals in Europe only served to excite the ferment of aristocratic agitation against the 'charlatan parvenu'.[7] A hundred days after his elevation to the Premiership he died, as he had lived, in the midst of passionate political controversy. The Duke claimed that according to medical opinion 'it was Canning's temper that killed him',[8] but Greville accused the Tories of 'hunting him to death with their besotted and ignorant hostility'.[9]

Deprived of the arch-villain in her story, Mrs. Arbuthnot lost much of her zest for writing and she recorded almost nostalgically on 29th November 1830: 'I shall write very seldom now, I

[1] Lord Howard de Walden to Bagot. 10th April 1827. BAG, vol. 2, p. 382.
[2] Castlereagh's brother, the 3rd Marquess.
[3] See p. 20 below.
[4] Londonderry to Wellington. 13th April 1827. F.C.M., no. 107, p. 72.
[5] Clancarty to Londonderry. 17th April 1827. F.C.M., no. 153, p. 102.
[6] Abercromby to Althorp. April 1827. F.C.M., no. 155, p. 105.
[7] Londonderry to Wellington. 12th April 1827. F.C.M., no. 99, p. 66.
[8] C.G.C., vol. 2, p. 325.
[9] 11th August 1831, GRE, vol. 2, p. 182.

dare say, in my book for, except the Duke, none of the public men interest me; I don't feel now the excitement I did during Canning's government.'[1] But though Mrs. Arbuthnot was not prepared to carry controversy beyond the grave, others kept the conflict alive. The Canningites rallied in defence of their late master, goaded by accusations of lukewarmness on the part of his indignant widow. Thus Canning's name, thanks to the violent feelings which he had aroused, continued for many years to kindle angry flames.

Even when passions had cooled, politicians of diverse persuasions were apt in foreign affairs debates to claim Canning as their mentor. With writers of historical text books he rapidly became an established favourite. Comparisons and contrasts with Castlereagh no doubt proved an irresistible temptation. But though Canning's name is still occasionally invoked in debate and remains one to conjure with in class rooms, his fame outside Latin America is growing dim. For many he has now become no more than a recollection of schooldays, a statue in Liverpool,[2] a painting at Christ Church, the coiner of phrases about the New World and the author of a rhyming dispatch.[3]

This eclipse is perhaps due to the fact that Canning is a poor subject for popular biography. In contemporary politics he was sensational; at home a devoted husband who talked politics to a devoted and politically-minded wife. As a personality he is remarkable chiefly because his energies were so consciously and uncompromisingly dedicated to the gratification of political ambition. His private life by popular-biography standards was dull.

---

[1] 29th November 1830, Mrs. A., vol. 2, p. 404.
[2] Now removed for reasons of town planning and not yet re-erected.
[3]   *In matters of commerce the fault of the Dutch,*
       Is offering too little and asking too much
       The French are with equal advantage content,
       So we clap on Dutch bottoms just 20 per cent,
       etc. . . . etc.

The dispatch was sent in cypher on 31st January 1826 to Sir Charles Bagot, Ambassador at the Hague. He did not possess the requisite code and was forced to write to his chief, who was also one of his closest friends, to ask for it. For the full text and further correspondence see BAG, vol. 2, pp. 321–5.

And yet the beginnings were rich with dramatic possibilities. Canning's grandfather, Stratford Canning, occupied the centre of the stage. He was descended from another George Canning who had emigrated from the family seat at Foxcote in Warwickshire to Ulster and had acquired the Manor of Garvagh in London-derry. The family prospered and Stratford Canning was a man of means and consequence. He had three sons, George, Paul and Stratford. Between Stratford Canning and his eldest son George no love seems to have been lost. Usual psychological incompati-bilities were exaggerated by the harshness of the father and the waywardness of the son. A prospective marriage provided the occasion for a decisively violent quarrel. As a result George Canning, without the wife he had hoped to marry, found himself banished to London in 1757 with an allowance of £150 a year. He proposed to read for the Bar but made little progress in this endeavour. He preferred to dabble in radical politics and his prospects in the legal profession were finally blasted when he gained notoriety as a supporter of Wilkes. These radical sym-pathies, which no doubt accounted for many earlier disputes with his father, were accompanied by a taste for writing poetry. Though the quality of his own compositions was mediocre, he had no difficulty in gaining a welcome in literary circles. The pleasures of congenial company proved a strain on his financial resources. He was reduced to writing for profit, but remuneration was meagre. Suddenly determined to be practical and realistic, he made an attempt to set up in the wine trade. The venture proved a costly failure. His father now took advantage of these pecuniary difficulties to persuade him to break the entail on the family estates in return for a settlement of debts. Though the allowance of £150 continued to be paid, George Canning now no longer had expectations. In 1768 he married Mary Ann Costello. It was a romantic match: the bride young, beautiful, well-born and penniless; the groom a radical, an intellectual, a poet and a failure. Stratford Canning in a new paroxysm of rage stopped the £150 allowance. George Canning had now to rely only on his pen to support himself and his wife. In 1770 a son, christened George, was born. Some indication of the household's plight can be gained from a random entry in Mrs. Arbuthnot's journal. 'While Mr. Arbuthnot was absent,' she noted, 'he went to his sister's and there met an old aunt of his of 80 years old who told him a curious history of Mr. Canning's parentage. She was distantly related to Mr. C[anning]'s father, who had been disinherited for wildness and for having made a bad marriage with a Miss Guydickens.[1] They were consequently reduced to the greatest state of poverty. He was a very clever man, and for some time subsisted by writing articles in the newspapers, but at length was so destitute that he determined to endeavour to get a little money by publishing the *love letters* which passed between him and his wife previous to their marriage. This was felt by the family to be so discreditable that a small subscription amounting to 12 guineas was made in the family and this old aunt of Mr. A[rbuthnot]'s was the person selected to carry it to them. She found them in a wretched garret in Holborn in a state of the most abject poverty and the wife nursing a baby which has become Secretary of State and all but Prime Minister! . . . to those who, like me, think that there is a good deal in blood, it may appear that Mr. Canning's want of principle and high honourable feeling may be derived from the stock he sprang from, while all must admire the institutions of a country where talent and genius can force their possessor to power and opulence in spite of the most adverse circumstances.'[2] Dickens could hardly have contrived a more suitable start for a hero's life.

In 1771 George Canning died and his young widow, with the responsibility of a baby son, was abandoned to her own resources. She was, as the future amply proved, a woman of spirit, and with no asset but her looks turned to the stage for a livelihood. In spite of opportunities provided by sympathetic well-wishers, she failed to make her mark in London and was reduced, in the company of an actor named Reddish, to seeking audiences in the provinces. Their acting partnership was punctuated by the birth of numerous children. George Canning's earliest years were thus

[1] Her maternal grandfather had been a Colonel Guydickens; her own name was Mary Anne Costello.

[2] 11th November 1824. Mrs. A., Vol. 1, p. 354.

spent in cheap theatrical lodgings as the eldest child of the Reddish menage.

Chance eventually intervened. John Moody, a successful Irish actor, who had sympathised with Mrs. Canning's misfortunes and had endeavoured to promote her stage career, was impressed by the parentage of her eldest son. In Moody's opinion young George in his present environment was 'on the way to the gallows'. Drastic action was required. Moody appealed to the boy's uncle, Stratford Canning, who had settled in England and was now a prosperous merchant in the City. Although Stratford Canning had a large family of his own he allowed himself to be persuaded to accept complete responsibility for the care of his young eight-years-old nephew. The financial aspect of the burden was eased when Stratford Canning senior was induced to settle £200 a year, the income from a property at Kilmainham in Co. Kilkenny, on his grandson. George Canning was now to all intents and purposes adopted by his uncle and all connections with the theatrical tribulations of his mother were severed. Her partnership with Reddish, after she had borne him five children including two sets of twins, broke up; he died at York Asylum in 1785; on 11 February 1783 she married Richard Hunn, a Plymouth silk mercer. Five more children, including another set of twins, were born. Hunn failed in business; his wife went back to the stage and persuaded him to join her; their endeavours were heroic but generally disastrous. During these years the only contact between George Canning and his mother was by correspondence. 'On Wednesday last,' she once wrote to him at school, 'I received my sweet boy's *last* proof of a heart unchanged . . . how tell thee what raptures even that anxious *wish* to see me can bestow.'[1] During this time of separation it became one of Canning's ambitions to make provision for his mother and eventually, thanks to him, she was able to retire in some comfort to Bath, where she remained until her death in 1827 at the age of eighty. But before her retirement to Bath and after Hunn's death, she made extraordinary efforts, sometimes with the help of her eldest

---

[1] Rev. J. Raven: 'Some Letters of George Canning'. *Anglo-Saxon Review*, December 1899, vol. III, p. 49. D.M., p. 113.

son, to attend to the wants and vagaries of her numerous Reddish and Hunn offspring. Canning refused to recognise the Reddishes as his half-brothers, but he did endeavour to secure army promotion for Samuel Reddish. He provided pocket-money, jobs, advice and old clothes for Charles Reddish. When William Reddish was ill, Canning met the medical expenses; the illness proving fatal, he proferred sympathy and paid for the mourning clothes of brother Charles. Mrs. Canning was grateful for assistance but she still sought to rely upon her own resources. At one point, ever optimistic, she invented an eye ointment called *collegium* and imagined that her fortune had been made. Sales were disappointing, but eventually cartloads of *collegium* were sent to an unfortunate clergyman, with whom two of her young Hunn children were boarded as pupils, in lieu of payment which was owing. 'God help him,' wrote Canning, 'and her! and me! and all of us.'[1] Nothing, in fact, seems to have been able to quench his mother's indomitable spirit. When she visited him in London in 1794 he noted, 'She is come up on a thousand little matters — and seemed so happy to see me, and looked in so much better health and spirits than I had expected to see her — that I could not find in my heart to represent to her as I had intended, the folly of jogging up and down from place to place — when God knows how she contrives to live in any place.'[2]

When Canning wrote these words he had just become an M.P. and his own life, since entering the Stratford Canning household, had followed the conventional lines which befitted eighteenth-century legislators. He was sent by his uncle to Hyde Abbey School at Winchester and thence in 1782 to Eton. At Eton, with the help of a few close companions, he founded a weekly paper called *The Microcosm*, which gained a certain renown and which, thanks to Fanny Burney, was brought to the notice of the royal household at Windsor.[3] In addition to showing literary talent Canning was prominent in debate. His studies were also highly commended and in 1787 he became Captain of the Oppidans.

[1] *Canning's Journal*. D.M., p. 115.
[2] Ibid., p. 116.
[3] *Fanny Burney's Diary 1778–1840*, vol. 3, p. 121. D.M., p. 10.

Although he took no part in sporting activities he was recognised as an outstanding Etonian.

His interest in politics was aroused at an early age. The combination of his uncle's household, where Fox, Sheridan and Burke were frequent guests, and of the Eton atmosphere, was well suited to provide an incentive. On the other hand, his own circumstances made him pause when considering politics as a career. In 1786 his grandfather died. Canning received a legacy of about £400 a year. This permitted him to make some provision for his mother and to pursue his studies at Oxford. It did not seem sufficient to allow him to envisage taking up politics as a career immediately after the University. He therefore decided on leaving Eton that the law must be his road and he wrote wistfully to H. J. Richman[1] of 'some future day' getting 'to the House of Commons — a field open indeed not so much for *solid pudding* as empty praise'.[2]

At Christ Church his political predelictions were quickened. He became a leading member of a debating society which included Robert Banks Jenkinson, Lord Henry Spencer and Lord Holland.[3] The Dean of Christ Church, Cyril Jackson, warned him that his membership of the society was tantamount to a declaration of political ambition and that this could be dangerous to a professional man. Canning confessed that 'the imputation of Parliamentary prospects, already too much fixed in me, is what, of all others a person in my situation ought to avoid. I am already, God knows, too much inclined both by my own sanguine wishes, and the connections with whom I am most intimate, and whom I above all revere, to aim at the House of Commons, as the only path to the only desirable thing in the world, the gratification of ambition. While at the same time every tie of commonsense, of fortune, of duty draws me to the study of a profession. The former propensity, I hope, reflection, necessity and the friendly advice and very marked attentions of the Dean, will

---

[1] A friend of his Hyde Abbey schooldays.

[2] Rev. J. Raven; 'Some Letters of George Canning'. *Anglo-Saxon Review*, December 1899, vol. III, p. 52. D.M., p. 13.

[3] With these three Canning established close friendships. See p. 28 below.

enable me to overcome; and to the law I look as the profession which in this country holds out every enticement that can nerve the exertions and give vigour to the powers of a young man. The way is long, toilsome and rugged; but it leads to honours solid and lasting; to Independence without which no blessings of fortune, however profuse, no distinctions of station, however splendid, can afford a liberal mind true satisfaction; to Power for which no task can be too hard; no labours too trying.'[1] And he duly resigned from the debating society, to the disgust of its members. He applied himself with even greater resolution to his studies. In 1789 he won the Chancellor's medal for a composition on 'Iter ad Meccam'. Subsequently he was awarded a studentship which 'brings God knows how much meat and drink and lodging in the year'.[2] During vacations he kept himself busy by systematic study of the French language. This purposeful attitude to life at the University was offset by general exuberance of spirits and an irrepressible capacity for making friends. Humour and intelligence created bonds which were cemented by a variety of elaborate and boisterous practical jokes. The lighter side of Canning's nature emerged clearly in his correspondence and explains why among intimate friends he proved such a popular and engaging companion.

On going down from Oxford Canning, after a visit to the Hague and Brussels, settled down to law studies in London. Events, however, soon conspired to give precedence to his own real inclinations. As an Etonian his talents had already been marked by the leading political figures of the day. Oxford confirmed the good impression and while an undergraduate he enjoyed the flattering attention of many prominent Whigs. During the summer of 1789 he paid the first of several visits to Crewe Hall and gained the approbation of Mrs. Crewe. Later, as a clear mark of Whig favour, he was presented at Sheridan's house to the Prince of Wales. There was no doubt that Canning was regarded as a political catch. When the course of the French Revolution began to create a rift in the Whig party Canning soon found himself

[1] J. F. Newton: *The Early Days of George Canning*, p. 24.
[2] Canning to Bessy Canning. 27th December 1789. *Western Letters*. D.M., p. 23.

C

in disagreement with his early mentors, Fox and Sheridan. He established contact with the Prime Minister, and Pitt, whose interest had already been aroused, promptly responded with the offer of a seat in Parliament. Canning was unable to resist advances from such a quarter and on 5th July 1793, when the matter had been settled, he boasted to his aunt: 'I have the honour to represent in Parliament the respectable Borough of New Town in the Isle of Wight . . . and I have come in without a farthing of expense and one farthing's worth of obligation to any person in the world — but one. That one you will easily guess. And if you guess it to be Mr. Pitt you will be near the truth.'[1]

Thus, though Canning lacked the family background which usually was required for such an early start in politics, in his case this proved hardly a handicap. Eton, Christ Church and the friendships which he had gained proved an adequate substitute. There was no need for any struggle. He was not obliged to fight his way into the charmed circle. Nor, having arrived, were there any automatic barriers to promotion. He would have been Prime Minister in 1812 if he had not been too eager to grasp the prize in 1809. It was only many years later, when suspicions and jealousies had become exacerbated, that his enemies began to make spiteful reference to his origins. Not indeed until 1827 was the suggestion made that the son of an actress was unacceptable as Prime Minister and were the 'frailties of his mother' flung in his face. At the outset of his political career Canning was unquestionably accepted by the privileged few as one of themselves. Any disqualification which the circumstances of his childhood might have implied was wiped out as soon as he had joined his uncle's household. From thenceforth his progress lacked the romance which early years had seemed to promise.

He was studious both at Eton and at Oxford. He loved the classics and was a distinguished, but not a dedicated, scholar. Though a prolific writer of verse in classical style, he devoted little time to the reading of any poetry other than Virgil. His own favourite English poet was Dryden[2] and he seems to have

---

[1] 5th July 1793. *Western Letters.* D.M., p. 46.
[2] See *Canning's Journal.* D.M., p. 154.

regarded the efforts of his own contemporaries with a somewhat jaundiced eye. 'What does Mr. Canning know of modern poetry?'[1] complained Wordsworth after a meeting at the Lakes. Beyond an expression of some admiration for the verses of Byron and Scott there is no evidence that Canning took any serious interest in the new worlds of poetry which were unfolding in his generation. Nor did he show any greater appreciation of contemporary prose writings. He did enjoy Walter Scott's novels but otherwise he preferred to re-read the classics and to study official papers. And yet he himself, as his public dispatches, his private letters and his polemical writings testify, possessed outstanding literary ability. The Duke of Wellington once confessed that 'Canning was readier at writing than even at speaking', and added, 'I never in my life knew so great a master of his pen'.[2] But Canning, unlike Disraeli, never seems to have felt moved to write a novel.

If Canning's literary tastes were narrow, he had no time at all for music or for art. In 1826 a certain Mr. Dimsdale misguidedly asked permission to dedicate a song to Canning. His secretary was instructed to acknowledge receipt of the letter and to reply that 'Mr. Canning is so entirely and notoriously unskilled in anything relating to music that he fears that the dedication to him, *by permission*, of a musical composition would reflect some ridicule both on himself and on the composer'.[3] In the following year on declining an invitation to view a picture of 'Alexander and Bucephalus' he noted: 'I am no judge of (1) pictures or (2) horses and have no time for the Fine Arts.'[4] Thus he summed up the attitude of a lifetime.

This philistinism was not accompanied by any passion for sport. He avoided it as a boy and remained uninterested. Although he enjoyed riding, it was chiefly as a means of obtaining air and exercise. If he had a companion, a ride was regarded as a

---

[1] H. Temperley, *Life of Canning*, p. 247.
[2] *Conversations with the Duke of Wellington*. Stanhope, p. 297. BAG, vol. 1, p. 1.
[3] C.G.C. Vol. 2, p. 211.
[4] Ibid., p. 359.

good opportunity for expounding his own views on the current political situation without interruption. Though he occasionally joined hunting parties, his opinion of that sport was summed up in a letter to the Rev. John Sneyd[1] of 17th December 1795: 'To-morrow therefore I must return to town having snatched this little interval of leisure for the pleasures of the chace — those pleasures I mean to which you and I partake with equal satisfaction, as the only things in a hunting life worthy of our consideration — that is to say the good dinner and lounging evening which follows the exertions of the day.'[2] The countryside did afford him some pleasure, although he once confessed that he preferred it to be 'well-tenanted'. But the pleasure was mainly due to the opportunities presented for thinking, working and talking. It was rare for him to write as he did on 14th July 1815 to Bagot: 'Collares and Cintra are as cool as a grotto and beautiful beyond anything I ever saw, except perhaps the lakes; and at the lakes, last summer, Southey told me that he thought them more beautiful than anything that he had ever seen except Cintra.'[3] Shortly after his marriage in 1801 Canning acquired a small property at South Hill near Bracknell and for a brief period he fancied himself as a gentlemen farmer, pondering over manure[4] and watching his hay stacking with satisfaction.[5] But this was a passing interest and Canning, unlike so many of his political contemporaries, was more at home in the House than in the country.

Material possessions seem to have preoccupied him hardly at all. He was in no way acquisitive. His wife's fortune enabled him to maintain a growing family in comfort. Her capital gradually dwindled in the process. The only time Canning seems to have given any serious consideration to the problem of the family's diminishing resources was when he accepted the Indian Governor-Generalship in 1822. But when, after Castlereagh's death, the project was abandoned, Canning seems to have resigned himself without difficulty to further sacrifice of his wife's remaining

[1] One of Canning's closest friends. See p. 29 below.
[2] BAG, vol. 1, p. 53.
[3] BAG, vol. 2, p. 6.
[4] See Canning to Sneyd. 6th July 1801. BAG, vol. 1, p. 182.
[5] Ibid. 6th August 1801. BAG, vol. 1, p. 184.

capital. He did not reject the perquisites of office which came his way, but he took no initiative to improve his financial situation.

At no time was his income sufficient to meet the family's comparatively modest way of life.[1] After Canning's death the pension of £3000 a year, which he had been promised on retirement, was granted by Act of Parliament to either of his surviving sons at the family's choice. As the elder son was drowned in 1828 it was fortunate, as far as family finances were concerned, that the choice had fallen on the younger, who became Governor-General of India and lived until 1862.

Simple in his tastes, Canning found little difficulty in avoiding the fashionable excesses of his time. Gambling does not even seem to have been a temptation. Food and wine he could enjoy. After his maiden speech he spoke exultantly of the 'Bumpers of Port wine' which he had devoured.[2] But in the interest of industry and concentration he became steadily more abstemious. When his health broke down it was but a small sacrifice to be confined to a diet of chops and soda water. In an age of hard drinking and gross over-eating Canning's abstinence was remarkable. It was exceptional to find him recording as he did of a party early in 1794: 'We all seemed to like each other very well, and all agreed in showing our attachment to the Madeira Claret and excellent White Burgundy; so that by eleven o'clock I was perfectly unfit to go to the Duchess of Gordon's but unluckily was incapacitated from perceiving my own unfitness.'[3] 'Beware of drinking' was the characteristic closing phrase of this confession. The injunction was not forgotten.

While an undergraduate Canning claimed that the only dissipation which he liked was 'idle and unembarrassed conversation'.[4] Conversation was to remain his favourite and almost his only form of relaxation. Hence, self-centred as he was, Canning nevertheless enjoyed and cultivated many friendships. Some dated back

[1] For details of the Canning family finances see *Note on Canning's Financial Position*. F.C.M., p. lv.
[2] *Canning's Journal.* D.M., p. 59.
[3] Ibid.., p. 124.
[4] 27th May 1791. *Western Letters.* D.M., p. 22.

to his Eton and Oxford days, but new ones continued to be formed until the end of his life. He retained a gift for bridging the gap of years and establishing friendly contact with younger generations. Apart from the conversations which he so much relished, Canning was a most satisfactory correspondent and his capacity for friendship is very clearly manifested in his letters. They were so obviously a source of pleasure to himself; in them he could without effort give testimony to the warmth of his affections and to the sharpness and humour of his mind.

At Eton Canning's closest companions were John Hookham Frere,[1] Charles Ellis[2] and 'Bobus' Smith;[3] these friendships lasted throughout his lifetime and Frere and Ellis were among the chief mourners at his death. George Ellis,[4] Charles's cousin, also became a close friend and through George Ellis Canning became acquainted with Sir Walter Scott.

During his undergraduate days Canning gained the friendship of Sheridan, who became his first political mentor, and of Cyril Jackson, the Dean of Christ Church, who took a fatherly interest in his progress. Among his contemporaries Canning's closest friends were Robert Banks Jenkinson,[5] Lord Henry Spencer[6] and Lord Holland.[7] To Canning's great grief Lord Henry Spencer died in Berlin in 1795. Lord Holland, in spite of political differences, remained a lifetime friend. With Robert Banks Jenkinson Canning's destiny was to be closely intertwined. At Oxford their politics differed and Canning could not resist teasing 'Jenky'.

[1] John Hookham Frere (1769–1846). M.P. West Looe, 1799–1802. Contributed to *The Anti-Jacobin* 1797–98. Envoy at Lisbon 1800 and at Madrid 1801–04; Privy Counsellor 1805. British Minister with the Junta 1808–09. Retired to Malta 1820.

[2] Charles Roe Ellis (1771–1854). M.P. 1796–1806 and 1807–26, leader of the West Indies interest in the Commons, created Baron Seaford 1826.

[3] Robert Smith, brother of Sydney Smith. Appointed Advocate-General of Bengal 1803 — returned to England 1811. M.P. 1812–18, and again in 1820.

[4] George Ellis (1753–1815). Contributor to *The Quarterly Review*.

[5] Robert Banks Jenkinson (1770–1828), created Baron Hawkesbury 1803. Succeeded to Liverpool Earldom 1808.

[6] Lord Henry Spencer (1770–95), second son of the third Duke of Marlborough.

[7] Henry Richard Vassall Fox, 3rd Baron Holland (1773–1840), Lord Privy Seal 1806–07. Chancellor of Duchy of Lancaster 1830–34.

Although the mockery was not always appreciated, friendship survived. Jenkinson preceded Canning as a young M.P. and became the butt of many jokes. Both secured office under Pitt. However, when Pitt resigned and Canning followed suit, Jenkinson, now Lord Hawkesbury, accepted the Foreign Office in Addington's Ministry. Canning's mockery became tinged with malice. Inevitably Hawkesbury took offence and friendship seemed to have lapsed. They were colleagues again in Pitt's last Ministry. But Canning's sharp tongue provoked Hawkesbury to resignation. Pitt was obliged to intervene in order to patch up the quarrel. But their friendship was still clouded when they both retired from office after Pitt's death. They were again colleagues in the Duke of Portland's Ministry between 1807 and 1809. By now, however, Canning had overtaken his friend in political consequence and relations between them were good. Their friendship survived the intrigues of 1809–12 and throughout his long Premiership Hawkesbury, now Lord Liverpool, retained respect and affection for Canning. During the last five years of Canning's life their old intimacy was completely restored. In January 1827 Canning visited Liverpool at Bath and Stapleton[1] commented: 'We rode on horseback each day, and the dinners were particularly pleasant; for on the plea of amusing me (as a young man) with stories of their early years, they went on amusing each other with recounting all sorts of fun and adventures, which were evidently quite as entertaining to the old as to the young.'[2]

While an undergraduate, apart from the Stratford Canning household and that of his other uncle and aunt, the Leighs, at Ashbourne, Canning also was made welcome at Crewe Hall. During his visits to Staffordshire he met the Rev. John Sneyd[3] who was himself a friend of George and Charles Ellis. Although John Sneyd was Canning's elder by a few years a very close friendship rapidly developed. Laughter was the basis and they shared in enjoyment of keenest wit and most execrable of practical jokes.

[1] Augustus Granville Stapleton (1800–80). Canning's private secretary and biographer.

[2] G.C. & T., p. 579.

[3] The Rev. John Sneyd, younger son of Ralph Sneyd of Keele Hall in Staffordshire. Rector of Elford in that county from 1793–1833.

It was Sneyd who brought together Charles Bagot,[1] his own cousin by marriage, and George Canning. Bagot, who was to be Ambassador at St. Petersburg and the Hague, became one of Canning's most intimate friends and one of his chief correspondents. Also, through Sneyd, Canning met the Rev. and Hon. Edward Legge[2] who, though held in much affection, was to be the victim of their practical jokes, and through Sneyd again, Canning became a friend of Bootle Wilbraham[3] and of Gillray,[4] the cartoonist.

At Christ Church in his last year Canning acquired a new set of friends of whom the foremost was Granville Leveson Gower.[5] Others were Sturges Bourne,[6] Markham and Charles Moore, both sons of the Archbishop of Canterbury, and Boringdon.[7] Through Leveson Gower, Canning was invited to the Stafford home at Trentham where John Sneyd was already an intimate friend. Canning's links with the Staffordshire circle were thus reinforced.

In his early days in London he became friendly with 'Gosh' Arbuthnot,[8] but their relations, though cordial, were never close. The most important friendship of Canning's early political career was with Pitt, and their relationship was almost that of a father and a son. Links of friendship were also formed with Dundas and Lord Malmesbury. Castlereagh and Canning, though

[1] Sir Charles Bagot (1781–1847).

[2] Subsequently Bishop of Oxford.

[3] Edward Bootle Wilbraham (1771–1840). M.P. from 1796 until elevation to Peerage in 1828 as Viscount Skelmersdale.

[4] James Gillray (1757–1815), caricaturist, contributor to *The Anti-Jacobin*.

[5] Granville Leveson Gower, 1st Earl Granville (1773–1846), youngest son of 1st Marquess of Stafford. M.P. for Staffordshire 1799–1815. Ambassador Extraordinary at St. Petersburg 1804–05. Created Viscount Granville 1815. Ambassador at the Hague 1823. Ambassador at Paris 1824–41. Created Earl Granville, 1833.

[6] William Sturges Bourne (1769–1845). Entered Parliament 1798. Joint-Secretary of the Treasury 1804–06. A Lord of the Treasury 1807–09. Home Secretary 1827.

[7] John Parker, Viscount Boringdon and 1st Earl of Morley (1772–1840).

[8] Charles Arbuthnot (1767–1850). M.P. from 1795. Ambassador at Constantinople 1804–07. Joint-Secretary of the Treasury 1808–23. Surveyor Woods and Forests 1823–30. Chancellor of the Duchy of Lancaster 1828–30.

both self-styled disciples of Pitt, were at no time close friends. Their duel in 1809 was, however, largely the result of misunderstanding, and anger soon gave way to a certain mutual respect. As Cabinet colleagues after 1816 their relations were excellent and Canning was able to underline the fact by a defence of Castlereagh's Irish policy in the House of Commons. Lord Binning,[1] who became one of Canning's supporters when he entered Parliament in 1802, remained throughout one of his most faithful disciples. His attitude was typical of the adulation which Canning could so effortlessly command. The combination of his wit, intelligence, personal magnetism and absolute loyalty to those who admired him was a potent force. Among his contemporaries Huskisson, after years of political co-operation and in spite of their dissimilar temperaments, eventually fell completely under the spell.[2] Then they became the closest friends as well as staunch political allies. After Canning's death it was Huskisson who regarded himself as the guardian of Canning's political legacy. The bitterness with which he was assailed by other Canningites, spurred on by Lady Canning, when he was deemed to have failed in any aspect of that sacred trust, testified to the strength of the bonds forged between Canning's disciples and their leader. It was perhaps because Peel was eighteen years Canning's junior that they never became close friends. Although they differed over the question of Catholic Emancipation, their general views on home affairs were in substantial accord. But Peel was too independent minded to become a disciple and Canning too accustomed to being idolised by the younger generation. Thus, although they were congenial Cabinet colleagues and although they manifested mutual respect, warmth and intimacy were lacking in their relations. In Canning's later years he gained the affection and esteem of younger men such as Stratford Canning,[3] Planta,[4]

[1] Afterwards Lord Melros and the 9th Earl of Haddington.

[2] See C. R. Fay, *Huskisson and his Age*, chap. 2, for an account of Huskisson's 'adoration' of Canning and his own relations with the Canningites.

[3] Stratford Canning, 1st Viscount Stratford de Redcliffe (1786–1880), George Canning's cousin.

[4] Joseph Planta (1787–1847). Permanent Under-Secretary at the Foreign Office (1817–27).

Lord Francis Conyngham,[1] Lord Howard de Walden[2] and Lord Dudley.[3] Among the rising politicians, Palmerston and Lamb[4] were his most fervent admirers, but they did not belong to the circle of his close friends.

Though the sharing of political opinions provided a basis for many of Canning's friendships, it was by no means the only basis. Canning enjoyed the company of boon companions; if they could also be associated in public affairs so much the better, but companionship was the essential. And here the inner circle, among whose members Canning could most easily relax, were Sneyd, Frere, the Ellis cousins, Bagot, Granville, Boringdon and Bootle Wilbraham. Other circles revolved around Canning, but this was the closest. It was said of him that he could not make a speech without making an enemy; it might have been said that he could not make a friend without drawing him into a clique. This cliquishness was partly a legacy of school and undergraduate days and partly symptomatic of his own love of laughter and uninhibited self-expression.

In male company Canning was at his ease. With ladies he tended to be reserved and withdrawn. This may have been a result of youthful impressions. His aunt Hetty Canning, who took charge of him at eight years old when he was removed from his mother's care, was a domineering and politically-minded woman. She sought to organise every detail of her nephew's life. She wished him to shine in society and to become a leading politician. When he cast off his Whig allegiance she quarrelled furiously with him, but rushed to his bedside when after his maiden speech he collapsed with a fever. Canning found her solicitude as irksome as her dictatorial manners. After his uncle's death he avoided as far as possible the overwhelming hospitality of his aunt. This was a sad blow to her daughter, Bessy Canning. Eight

[1] Lord Francis Conyngham, afterwards 2nd Marquess. Parliamentary Under Secretary to Canning 1823–24.

[2] Charles Augustus Ellis, 2nd Baron Seaford (1799–1868). Parliamentary Under Secretary for Foreign Affairs 1824–28.

[3] John William Ward, 1st Earl of Dudley (1781–1833). Foreign Secretary 1827–28.

[4] Later Lord Melbourne and Prime Minister.

years his junior, Bessy had, from infancy, worshipped her cousin. She became his confidant and devoted admirer. Canning treated her with affection and, when absent, corresponded regularly, but he does not seem to have fully realised the depth of her feelings and the sorrow which he caused by turning for a home to the Leighs[1] at Ashbourne, where he found an atmosphere of peace and a less exacting aunt.

Apart from Bessy's youthful passion no romance had entered Canning's life when at the close of his University career he began to find himself lionised by the great Whig hostesses of the day. Mrs. Crewe was his first patron, but by the time he started reading for the Bar he was busy on a round of 'Suppers with the Ladies, *the fine Ladies* such as the Duchess of Devon, Lady Jersey . . .'[2] Canning was a handsome young man, and though not very adept at small talk, a lively companion. It was not surprising that he should have enjoyed the flattering attentions of these mature, but yet reigning, beauties. Relationships, however, remained strictly social. The first hint of a romance came in 1794 when he met Lady Sutherland,[3] the wife of Lord Gower.[4] Canning confessed that he liked 'Lady Sutherland mightily — she is very handsome and pleasant and *attentive*'.[5] At Easter he visited her home at Wimbledon and wrote, 'You cannot know how very pretty she is and how very pleasant and very clever and how much I like and admire here. . . .'[6] The friendship with Lady Sutherland blossomed, but nothing seems to have occurred which could have aroused Lord Gower's jealousy. His ill-health resulted in a removal to Bath and,

---

[1] The Rev. William Leigh had married, as his second wife, the sister of Canning's father. Ashbourne Hall in Derbyshire was his home. *Canning's Journal*, which provides the main source of information for his early career, was addressed to the Leighs.

[2] Lady Stafford to Granville. 16th February 1794. *The Private Correspondence of Granville Leveson Gower, 1781–1821*, vol. 1, p. 83.

[3] Elizabeth Sutherland (1765–1839), Countess of Sutherland in her own right since infancy.

[4] Eldest son of the Marquess of Stafford and half-brother of Granville Leveson Gower. Succeeded in 1803 as 2nd Marquess of Stafford and was created in 1833 1st Duke of Sutherland (1758–1833).

[5] *Canning's Journal*. D.M., p. 153.

[6] Ibid., p. 153.

without occasions for meeting, correspondence between Lady
Sutherland and her discreet admirer gradually lapsed. Some years
later Lady Stafford told Lord Granville that Lady Sutherland disliked Canning thoroughly.[1] Perhaps she had been disappointed
in him. In 1795 Canning was seeing a good deal of Lady Elizabeth
Monk, whom he confessed to finding attractive. Her charms, however, cannot seriously have affected him, for she soon ceased to be
mentioned and there were no lamentations of a broken heart. The
household where he now became a frequent visitor was that of the
Malmesburys.[2] Lady Malmesbury seems to have been eager to
capture him as an admirer and Canning, up to a point, apparently
responded. Soon, however, he came to prefer political discussion
with the husband to flirtation with the wife. She resented it and
many years later wrote bitterly to Sneyd: 'I saw Canning pass
through the drawing room last night to Lord M's room, but he
literally did not stop an instant. He is plunged deeper than ever in
politicks and though he has been in conference 20 times with Lord
M, has never entered my room. I hope politicks supply the place
of friends, for they certainly annihilate all affection.'[3]

In the summer of 1799 Canning was involved for the first time
in what promised to be a serious amorous intrigue. 'I am this moment returned,' he wrote in a scrawl to Granville, 'from my visit.
The keeper left us for a few minutes: and the thing is too clear
to be doubted. What am I to do? I am perfectly bewildered.'[4] For
the lady in question was the Princess of Wales; Canning thus
found himself in an awkward predicament. As an unattached
bachelor who had become a close friend of the Princess it was not
easy to resist what seemed to be obvious advances. While Canning
was pondering the problem he visited Walmer and there suddenly
fell in love with a Miss Joan Scott, whom he met there for the first
time. This settled his line of conduct towards the Princess; he explained his attitude to Granville: 'Now to come to that subject
which has not of late been used to be relegated to the very last

---

[1] See D.M., p. 194.

[2] James Harris, 1st Earl of Malmesbury. Minister Plenipotentiary during the
abortive 1796-97 peace negotiations with the French. See p. 66 below.

[3] Lady Malmesbury to Sneyd. 10th March 1803. BAG, vol. 1, p. 131.

[4] D.M., p. 195.

page of my letters. I will confess, Granville, that if *this* impression had not been produced on my mind, I know not how I should have resisted, as I ought to do, the abundant and overpowering temptations to the indulgence of a passion (made up of other elements than those of that which I now feel) which must have been dangerous, perhaps ruinous to her, who was the cause of it, and to myself. I am almost ashamed to confess that with all my good resolutions, and with all the occupation of my mind, the day of the last dinner was not quite so blameless as I promised you it should be. I have had one other interview, in which I took leave for a long time, for the Keeper is going on a visit to friends in the Country and during her absence I have said I cannot possibly call at the r.T.[*sic*] or elsewhere. This gains two or three months. If by that time I am enabled to make a confidence of the actual success of my present views, I firmly believe that It will be the most effectual remedy to all the danger, and that accompanied, as It will be, with the profession and a real feeling of an anxious and lively interest, of a desire to assist and a devotion to serve her, there is quite *mind* enough in her to meet all my sentiments, and even to rejoice with me upon reflection at our escape. Such is my hope and Plan.'[1] So Canning was helped to avoid the temptation of pursuing his intrigue with the Princess, and she eventually became godmother to his eldest son. Gossip, however, labelled him, apparently without justice, though with some cause, as her lover.[2]

The meeting with Miss Joan Scott, which was so fortunate for Canning, took place in August 1799 while he was Pitt's guest at the Castle at Walmer. There he found Dundas, his wife Lady

---

[1] 22nd August 1799. *The Private Correspondence of Granville Leveson Gower, First Earl Granville, 1781–1821*, vol. 1, p. 255.

[2] When, in 1806, allegations against the Princess were brought to the notice of the Prince of Wales, Canning's name was among the list of her reputed lovers. According to Lady Bessborough the Prince claimed that he had himself scratched Canning's name off the list. See Lady Bessborough to Granville 27th June 1806. *The Private Correspondence of Granville Leveson Gower*, vol. 1, p. 204. It seems that fourteen years later the Prince, then King, when receiving Canning in audience, also told him about how he had 'scratched his name out of the informations', adding, 'To be sure it does seem odd that we should be sitting together on this sofa and talking upon this subject.' See *Frere's Diary*, 25th June 1820, FEST, p. 207.

Jane and Miss Joan Scott. She was a ward and kinswoman of
Dundas and the third daughter of General and Lady Mary Scott
of Balcomie. At his death the General had left a considerable fortune and his daughters each inherited about £100,000. The eldest
had married Lord Titchfield, the Duke of Portland's heir. Canning at first took little notice of Miss Scott. As he later wrote to
Granville: 'Never was any human being less bent on falling in love
than I was when I arrived at Walmer . . . the first day of my
arrival I did not know who Miss Scott was. Ly Jane is apt to have
Misses with her; and it was upon my mentioning her in some such
way as this to your sister that I was first apprized of her name. The
only effect of this knowledge, combined with the recollection
which presently suggested itself to me of having always heard her
name coupled with some one or other person who was supposed
to be going to be married to her, or who had proposed and been
refused, was a determination to avoid all possible danger of any
such report being circulated about myself, and accordingly, after
the first day, I carefully avoided sitting beside her at dinner whenever (which was the case on most days) the company was large
enough to afford me the opportunity of escaping, and studiously
contrived to give every officer of the Fleet and Army who happened to dine there the place which, from being one of the family,
one should perhaps most naturally have occupied.' After ten days
thus spent in avoiding Miss Scott, Canning was due to leave Walmer and his chaise was at the door. But he found that he did not
wish to go and he contrived to suggest that Dundas should ask
him to stay another day. So his journey was postponed. And Canning remained in agonies of embarrassment at having betrayed
himself to Miss Scott. 'I took no advantage,' he explained, 'of the
opportunity which this day would have afforded me to make any
distinct declaration of what I felt towards her. The doubt whether
I did in fact feel anything more than a transitory liking, the repug-
nance which one naturally has to putting one's self in a situation
to be refused, and the obvious consideration of the apparent
sordidness and speculation of a proposal to a great *fortune* re-
strained me from doing or saying almost anything that could be
construed attention to her; and I question whether in any of the

most populous days at Walmer I had less intercourse with her than
on this day when we were left almost entirely to each other.'[1] The
next morning Canning, after lingering as long as he decently
could and hoping vainly to see her alone for five minutes, eventually left Walmer. In the evening he visited Lady Susan Ryder at
Dover and to her he poured out his feelings for Miss Scott. In a
letter written to Lady Susan on the same night from the Rose Inn
at Sittingbourne he reverted at length to the same subject, excus-
ing himself for having 'in about ten minutes confessed to you a
passion conceived in less than ten days for a girl with God knows
how many thousand pounds, the sister of one who has recently
blended her name with a Dukedom, and imposed upon you the
task of finding out her disposition towards me'. In spite of apologies Canning made it clear that he still relied on Lady Susan to
fulfil her mission and he emphasised that his own conduct would
depend on her report. 'I am pretty sure,' he added, 'that I am not
born to *die* of love and I am quite sure I shall never be a lover,
according to the rules, and dangle in anybody's train for a whole
season.'[2] Lady Susan pandered to Canning's impatience and at
once sought an interview with Miss Scott. The result was incon-
clusive. Canning subjected every inference to minute analysis. He
was particularly concerned by Miss Scott's references to disparity
of fortunes and the hazards of political careers. His mind at once
turned to possibilities of hastening his own advancement. But a
sudden doubt assailed him. 'It strikes me,' he wrote to Lady
Susan, 'that there may perhaps be another point of view in which
she may have considered the profession of politicks: — that she
may have entertained a fear that she should risque her happiness
as well as her consequence by marrying a man engaged in that profession. I know that she lives much, and perhaps prefers living,
chiefly in the Country. This preference of course is cooped by
political and parliamentary habits. Possibly she may have a dis-
taste to the cares and concerns, the conversation, and manner of

---

[1] 22nd August 1799. *The Private Correspondence of Granville Leveson Gower,
First Earl Granville. 1781–1821*, vol. I, pp. 251–2.

[2] D.M., pp. 202–3. Lady Susan Ryder was Granville's sister; her husband later
became 1st Earl of Harrowby.

life, of public men. If this be so — I have not a word to offer. My
hopes and desires, and taste and turn of mind are bent, I fear, irre-
coverably to public objects: and I should certainly look for, in a
wife, a mind which at least would not revolt from what must form
the subject of my thoughts, the occupation of my time, the foundation of my fortunes, or (what I more value) the reputation, whatever it might be, which I should labour to acquire: I should look
for a companion and sharer in all the anxieties, which political life,
I am afraid, cannot but produce from time to time; for a faithful
adviser in all points (and there are many such) for which the most
feminine character of mind is not disqualified; and I should wish
to be able to treat her not only as the connection most interested
in one's success, but as the most confidential of one's friends. I am
much mistaken if in describing this character I have not described
exactly what her mind is capable of realizing, though I cannot pre-
sume to judge how far her inclinations might lead her to approve it.'[1]

While wondering whether Miss Scott would be prepared to
conform to his ideal pattern of a wife, Canning was also considering the propriety of a rapid return visit to Walmer. He did not
wish to put Dundas, who was Miss Scott's guardian, in an embarrassing position, nor did he relish the prospect of meeting with
a rebuff from Miss Scott herself. But, on the other hand, he was
too obsessed with the need for an answer to wait, and so, in spite of
Lady Susan's advice, he decided to risk all on a second visit to
Walmer. He remained there from 30th August to 10th September
1799. Years later, in a letter to Pitt, Canning wrote: 'Here I am in
the very room in which I first touched my own Love's hand and
put my arms around her, and drew her to me — and she was not
very angry — not very angry I think — though it was saucy of
me to do what I did.'[2] By the end of Canning's visit there was an
understanding that she would consider the possibility of marriage
and consult Lord Titchfield on the subject. In a P.S. to a letter to
Sneyd dated 10th September, Canning wrote: 'Can you tell me
without guessing why I ask the question (or guessing if you will,
but not telling anybody what you guess) whether or no Titchfield
has any violent prejudice against *me*. You may add also whether

[1] D.M., p. 206.   [2] Ibid., p. 210.

or no you have been in the habit of going to Welbeck of late, and
whether you think of going there this Autumn?'[1] The questions
were too cryptic for Sneyd and on 17th September Canning wrote
explaining why Titchfield's good opinion was of such importance
and why a visit to Welbeck was so essential. 'You must,' Canning
insisted, 'make him like me; and make him think it altogether a
good and desirable thing. Will you? There's a good Sneyd. She
knows you and likes you very much and will hear and make Titchfield hear what you have to say.'[2] But in spite of Sneyd's good
offices and those of many other friends, Lord Titchfield hesitated
to give approval to the match and Miss Scott seemed willing to be
guided by her brother-in-law's opinion.

The winter was an anxious one for Canning. But in the New
Year Miss Scott came to stay in the Dundas household at Wimbledon. Since she knew that both Lady Jane and Dundas favoured
Canning as a suitor, he could regard her presence there as an encouragement. And indeed he soon became a regular visitor at
Wimbledon. In April, however, Miss Scott joined the Titchfields,
who had now come to London, and her meetings with Canning
ceased. Shortly afterwards she fell dangerously ill. On her recovery Lord Titchfield found that her own mind was now clearly
made up and he therefore withdrew all opposition. Canning
exultantly reported this to the Staffords as the 'Event most
essential to my happiness that has ever occurred'.[3] On 8th July
1800 they were married at 8.30 in the evening. The ceremony was
performed by the Rev. William Leigh and Canning was accompanied by Pitt and Frere. Frere later commented, 'had Canning
been Pitt's own son, I do not think he could have been more
interested in all that related to this marriage'.[4] And certainly, even
if Pitt had not deliberately contrived the first Walmer meeting,
he had subsequently been active in promoting the match behind
the scenes.

In his wife Canning found everything that he had hoped. She

[1] BAG, vol. 1, p. 154.
[2] Ibid., p. 155.
[3] *The Private Correspondence of Granville Leveson Gower, 1781–1821*, vol. 1,
p. 279.
[4] FEST, p. 31.
  D

fulfilled all the conditions which he had envisaged. They talked endlessly of politics and of his career. Her advice was available at every turn. When they were parted he wrote to her voluminously every day. Neither cared for fashionable society and neither ever seems to have been in the least attracted by any other member of the opposite sex. Apart from mutual devotion to Canning's career, their chief concern was for their children.[1] Indeed it was the only thing which sometimes deflected Canning from his political pre-occupations. The poor health of his eldest son determined Canning's acceptance of the Lisbon Embassy. In 1818, when his daughter was ill, Bagot wrote to Binning, 'I am very sorry to hear what you tell me of Canning's girl. I trust in God she has got well again. If anything should happen to the girl it would kill Canning upon the spot.'[2] When his eldest son died in April 1820 Canning was prostrated with grief and this sorrow played a considerable part in his temporary desire to leave active politics and in his willingness to accept the Indian Governor-Generalship. Canning was in every way a contented husband and an adoring father.

In the early years of his married life this image offended gossip-seekers; it is not surprising, therefore, that signs after 1801 of a growing friendship between him and Lady Bessborough[3] should have evoked some spicy rumours.[4] The Prince of Wales was aware of these and, at least according to Lady Bessborough, he even believed that, next of course to Granville,[5] Canning was closest to

[1] There were three sons: George Charles, who died in 1820, William Pitt, who was drowned at Madeira in 1828, Charles John, who became Earl Canning and Governor-General of India; and one daughter, Harriet, who married the 1st Marquess of Clanricarde. Their daughter, Elizabeth, married the 4th Earl of Harewood. The 6th Earl was the late husband of H.R.H. The Princess Royal.

[2] BAG, vol. 2, p. 77.

[3] Henrietta, Countess of Bessborough (1761–1821), daughter of John, 1st Earl of Spencer and younger sister of Georgiana, Duchess of Devonshire. Married 1780 Viscount Duncannon, who succeeded his father in 1793 as 3rd Earl of Bessborough. There were four children, including a daughter Caroline who married William Lamb (Melbourne) and whose misfortunes dominated the latter years of her mother's life.

[4] See Ethel Colburn Mayne, *A Regency Chapter* (1934), p. 167.

[5] Lady Bessborough first met Granville (Lord Granville Leveson Gower, later 1st Earl Granville) at Naples in 1794. He was then twenty-one and twelve years her junior. It was the beginning of a romance which survived until 1809 when he

her own heart. This he seemed to confirm several years later when, susceptible as ever to the charms of a grandmother, he apparently laid sudden and clumsy siege to Lady Bessborough with a grand declaration of his own passion.[1] In token of good faith he offered to break with Mrs. Fitzherbert and Lady Hertford; as a further inducement he promised that 'Mr. Canning should be Prime Minister'. To this theme he constantly reverted and 'whenever he mentioned him it was in the tenderest accent and attempting some liberty'. Embarrassed as she was, Lady Bessborough confessed that she could hardly refrain from laughing aloud at 'the comicality of having the Pope[2] so coupled and made use of'. Her own interest in Canning had originally stemmed from her feelings for Granville,[3] his close friend since Christ Church days, and from her political devotion to Fox. With motives partly personal and partly political she deliberately tried to cultivate his acquaintance. At first she found him completely unresponsive but, after he resigned in 1801 with Pitt, the situation began to change. Canning's energies were then directed against Addington and his hopes were concentrated on a possible junction between Pitt and Fox. In these circumstances he could enjoy Lady Bessborough's company, and a friendship with very obvious political undertones for a while flourished. In 1806 there was an estrangement, initiated by Canning and no doubt caused by the disconcerting

---

married her niece Harriet (daughter of Georgiana, Duchess of Devonshire) and of a friendship which continued until her death in 1821. Devoted to her sister Georgiana and to her children, among her own many admirers she seems to have been seriously involved only with Granville. Her constant and voluminous letters to him almost constitute an autobiography in which her romantic attachment, always tempered and eventually replaced by a kind of maternal solicitude, is clearly revealed.

[1] This episode is described by Lady Bessborough in a letter to Granville probably dated late December 1809. See *The Private Correspondence of Granville Leveson Gower, 1781–1821*, vol. 2, p. 349.

[2] Lady Bessborough's nickname for Canning.

[3] In August 1798 she wrote to Granville: 'You are unjust to me about Mr. Canning. I am not prejudiced against him: it is he against me. But whatever I might be, are you not sure, my dear G. that I must be inclined to think well of and to like a person who loves you?' *The Private Correspondence of Granville Leveson Gower, 1781–1821*, vol. 1, p. 217.

political realignment which followed Pitt's death. The rift lasted for over a year, but thereafter friendly, though never very close, relations were resumed. Lady Bessborough hinted that the trouble was really due to Canning's desire to conceal from her what she imagined to be a budding romance between him and Lady Hester Stanhope.[1] Lady Hester, Pitt's niece, had been one of Canning's confidants at the time of his own courtship and their long-standing friendship was based firmly on mutual veneration of Pitt. But Lady Bessborough was a dedicated romantic and she could not easily accept the obvious explanation of Canning's particular attentions, after Pitt's death, to Lady Hester. Where the romantic attitudes of his age were concerned there seems little doubt that Canning was always an outsider.

Satisfied in his marriage and in the company of his more intimate friends he increasingly avoided society. 'He is very domestic; his wife is ugly and jealous, and he never lives in London; so that it is difficult to see him,'[2] spitefully commented Countess Lieven in October 1820. She herself, however, eventually succeeded in breaking down the barriers and, after a period of bitter enmity, they became political allies and intimate friends. After Canning's return to the Foreign Office in 1822 it was some time before they met. On 9th January 1823 she wrote to Metternich that her friend Lady Granville seemed very anxious to put her 'on good terms with Mr. Canning'. 'We are dining with him,' she added, 'tomorrow. He has detained the Granvilles in town specially to be present on this great occasion. It will be the first time we have met, he and I, since he became a great man. Lady Granville is extraordinarily arch about it — it is just as if she wanted to confer him on me as a lover. I shan't take him.'[3] On 11th January she reported: 'The dinner with Mr. Canning yesterday went off with a great deal of assiduity on his part, especially towards me. I thought he had a pleasing manner and rather more assurance. . . . Indeed

---

[1] Lady Bessborough made this insinuation in a letter of 28th August 1807 to Granville. *The Private Correspondence of Granville Leveson Gower, 1781–1821,* vol. 2, pp. 276, 277. 'He is there not only all day, but almost all night' was one of her comments on Canning's visits to Lady Hester.

[2] 3rd October 1820. L., p. 61.

[3] Ibid., p. 180.

I believe he can be managed.'[1] When the Lievens in turn gave a dinner for Canning, Countess Lieven had already decided that he could not be managed and that he ought to be removed. '. . . it was a very stiff dinner,' she confessed to Metternich. 'Mr. Canning hardly opened his mouth. The Duke was whispering in my ear the whole time, saying all the ill he could think of about my other neighbour (C). My husband was very angry with me for not talking enough to the latter, but I don't see the necessity of going to any great trouble. We hardly know one another, and I have a feeling that our enforced relations will not last long.'[2] But Canning was not easily dislodged and his successful resistance obviously piqued Countess Lieven. On the 28th June 1824 she wrote to Metternich of a dinner given by the Duke for the King at which Canning had been present: 'the King never stopped making jokes about him (C) to me. He remarked very rightly, that Canning is too gushing, that he hates me, and overwhelms me with attentions. The natural result of embarrassing someone is to be perfectly at ease myself . . . so our relations are very amusing. All the time that he is hating me and feeling embarrassed, he tries to be witty and makes clever remarks. But he is one of those men who always kill any conversation. You have continually to begin again; and I get bored.'[3] On the 20th July she again wrote, this time of a reception at the Marchioness of Hertford: 'Canning, who hardly ever goes out into society, put in an appearance. He came up to me with his usual alacrity and then stood rooted to the ground at my side, looking wretchedly awkward, as he always does . . . the truth is that there is a sort of attraction about people one hates. However, he amuses me much more than I amuse him.'[4] On 11th October the Lievens were Canning's guests and she described the occasion on the 12th to Metternich: 'Yesterday we went to a big dinner-party at the Cannings. It must be very entertaining to see us together — he attentive to excess, I polite but cold; both ready, on every possible occasion, to say the most biting things to one another. We always talk like people who are afraid both of forgetting something, and even breathing its name.

[1] L., p. 181.   [2] 31st January 1823. Ibid., p. 189.
[3] Ibid., p. 261.   [4] Ibid., p. 263.

A hint from one suggests endless meanings to the other. Probably we are always quite innocent, but it would be impossible to look more guilty. In short, it is war, both in small and great things, waged without truce or respite.'[1]

After the complete failure of all intrigues and Canning's winning of the King's favour,[2] Countess Lieven, whose relations with Metternich were beginning to cool, began for personal and political reasons to change her own attitude towards Canning. On 26th March 1826 she informed Metternich: 'He (C) has become much more friendly with me since my husband left. He never pays calls, but he has come to see me several times; and the day before yesterday I had a private talk with him lasting over two hours. I suspect he was making a reconnaissance. He wanted to test my judgement and the capacity of my poor mind. He talked about everything, including you. There is no change in that respect. . . . He is quite as clever as they say. I fancy he is a man one might catch, but could never hold.'[3] Two days later she complacently declared: 'Mr. Canning came to see me again yesterday: this time we had an hour's *tête à tête*, because I was so ill that I could not stand any more. His visits excite curiosity in diplomatic circles. . . . Meanwhile we are getting to know one another. The first quarter of an hour is rather difficult; Mr. Canning speaks halting French; afterwards it goes swimmingly; for his way of expressing himself is highly individual. The word is always suited to the idea, no matter how unusual it is; and it is all so much to the point, so clear-cut, that it is a pleasure to listen to. . . . He has an odd habit, perhaps only when he is with me. When I am speaking he shuts his eyes as if he were asleep. I used to make you yawn; I make him fall asleep. I am lucky with Ministers.'[4] On 16th April 1826 she boasted: 'Mr. Canning asked me to dinner yesterday at his house, among all his intimate friends, as if I were one of them.'[5] On the 26th she added: 'His Sunday visits — for he never fails to give me a two hour *tête à tête* on that day — are quite an occasion for me. In the middle of a serious discussion a comic idea crosses his mind, and he bursts out laughing. I do not think he cherishes

[1] L., p. 275.   [2] See p. 128 below.   [3] L., p. 299.
[4] Ibid., p. 300.   [5] Ibid., p. 301.

hatred; for he has a strong sense of his own superiority. This conviction has taken root in him, and gives him a confidence which allows his wit full play. But how quickly it moves; how it gallops!'[1] 'Such intrigues,' she wrote 'such spying! They still cannot make out what my friendship with Canning can mean. They find every reason except the right one. We get on well together because our minds are well-assorted. In the midst of company his eyes meet mine. I know that look well. It means "Did you see the joke?" For he notices everything; small things as well as great. He seizes on the ridiculous so promptly and so amusingly that everyone is afraid of him. He is biting and sarcastic. He keeps one on tenterhooks. As he does not attract me I enjoy the fun. How you would have laughed at Windsor! I have not been so amused for a long time.'[2] As Countess Lieven well knew, there was little in this situation to make Metternich want to laugh. Canning's policies had succeeded and Countess Lieven was for political reasons delighted to have established a friendly relationship. Canning, for his part, was conducting delicate negotiations with the Tsar and in these Countess Lieven had a useful part to play.[3] Though mutual convenience drew them together, there is no doubt that they enjoyed one another's company. Countess Lieven could not resist a rising star and Canning had rarely before enjoyed talking to a clever woman. No sentiment, however, was attached to this sudden and political friendship. After his marriage, Countess Lieven was one of the very few women, outside his family circle, to whom Canning paid more than perfunctory attention.

It is perhaps because Canning was so conventional in his domesticity, so moderate in his appetites, so narrow in his interests, that he lived his public life with such intensity.

In Canning's character ambition was the dominant trait. Ever since his Eton days politics were his ultimate and cherished goal. When he found the road to Westminster open, he immediately began to dream of the highest office. All his energies were concentrated on the struggle to reach the top and he was constantly on the look-out for short cuts. He suffered anguish when any

[1] L., p. 302.   [2] 14th June 1826. Ibid., p. 308.   [3] See pp. 242–4 below.

contemporary seemed to have stolen a march on him. This impatience made him hot-tempered. He even contrived to quarrel with his friend and patron Pitt when advancement seemed too slow. After Pitt's death he played a lone hand and eventually overplayed it, with disastrous results to the career he so sedulously cherished. Many disappointments and humiliations were suffered before he acquired a certain patience and some mastery over his quick temper. In his last years little save gout and rheumatism could make him irritable and his emotions were under rigorous control. But, apart from occasional moods of despondency, his will to power survived. Its expression became less crude; he did not exult so obviously in the struggle; he learned to manoeuvre with dexterity, rather than with passionate exuberance; his indiscretions became calculated; when power was achieved his aim was to conserve and consolidate; his personal fortunes had, and with some justice, become more closely associated in his own mind with the welfare of England; gratification of personal desire had blended with the will to impose a policy; ambition was identified with a national trust. Though thus moderated, the fiery combative and competitive spirt of Canning's youth was in no way quenched. This was never so clear as in the last few months of his life, when he conducted a major campaign against heavy odds for the Premiership. In spite of desperate ill-health and a certain reluctance at the start he responded with relish to the spur. Indeed it might be argued that only such a spur could have enabled him to throw off the grave physical disabilities under which he had been suffering. Six days after he became Prime Minister he was reported 'amazingly well' and 'in the very highest of spirits'.[1] In spite of the shaky foundations upon which his Administration was based and the violent attacks to which he was personally subjected, he proved a confident and indeed a jaunty Prime Minister. Undoubtedly Canning revelled in his last triumph and in his brief tenure of the office upon which his heart had always been set.

No one was more conscious of his own ambitious nature than Canning himself. The knowledge made him extremely sensitive. From the beginning of his career he bitterly resented imputations

[1] Tierney to Bagot. 16th April 1827. BAG, vol. 2, p. 388.

that he was self-seeking; they were too close to the truth to be comfortable. Canning, therefore, consciously or subconsciously, constructed an elaborate defence-mechanism. He determined to create the reputation of being a man of inflexible principle and the least slur on his motives loosed floods of self-justification. He constantly reiterated his unwillingness to sacrifice principle to place, or loyalties to convenience. At times it seemed as if he were more anxious to convince others of his own integrity than concerned with the realities of the situation. On several occasions he became enmeshed in traps of his own contriving and was unable, with consistency, to accept compromises which otherwise would have been politically desirable and personally acceptable. Canning's complicated machinations to establish a blameless character (and perhaps to silence his own doubts) were inevitably misconstrued. They served to increase rather than diminish his reputation for intrigue. Professions were treated as manoeuvres and the integrity, which he clumsily sought to safeguard, was brought further into question. With time Canning's sensitivity on the score of his own reputation diminished and instead of insisting that he was a man of principle he came to hold solid convictions which spoke more easily for themselves, while experience made him less prone to make sacrifices on an altar of spurious virtue.

Though Canning was sensitive about his motives in seeking power he never lacked any confidence in his own abilities. This confidence supported his ambition and magnified his pretensions. It was not misplaced. Canning was endowed with a remarkable mind. The mechanism was superb and functioned like a high precision instrument. Its normal operation was an exhibition of virtuosity. As Greville noted in an often-quoted passage of his diary: '. . . Such was the clearness of his head that he could address himself almost at the same time to different subjects with perfect precision and without the least embarrassment. He wrote very fast but not fast enough for his mind, composing much quicker than he could commit his ideas to paper. He could not bear to dictate, because nobody could write fast enough for him; but on one occasion, when he had gout in his hand and could not write, he stood by the fire and dictated at the same time a despatch on

Greek affairs to George Bentinck, and one on South American affairs to Howard de Walden, each writing as fast as he could while he turned from one to the other without hesitation or embarrassment.'[1]

The impact of Canning's bristling intelligence was felt by all who came in contact with him. 'He is quite as clever as they say,'[2] was Countess Lieven's eventual judgement. This 'cleverness' was a source of weakness as well as of strength. Many found Canning a bit too clever for their taste. His Cabinet colleagues were frequently bewildered. His subtleties were suspect and the ingenuity of his mind suggested an intention to deceive rather than to elucidate. 'Poor Canning's greatest defect,' wrote Croker, 'was the jealous ingenuity of his mind. He like an over-cautious general was always thinking more of what might be on his flanks or in his rear than in front. His acuteness discovered so many tortuous by-roads on the map of human life, that he believed they were much more travelled than the broad highway. He preferred an ingenious device for doing anything to the ordinary processes. In lifting a coal scuttle to mind his fire (as I have just been doing), he would have preferred a screw or a pulley to his own arms. He could hardly have tea without a stratagem. I said of him that his *mind's eye* squinted; but this was altogether a mode of his *mind*, of the busy polyscoptic (may I coin such a word) activity of his intellect, for his heart and spirit were open, generous and sincere.'[3]

When Canning returned to the Foreign Office, Planta,[4] who had not yet learned to appreciate his new chief, complained that '. . . Mr. Canning was perpetually doing and undoing, writing volumes without understanding his subject, and scarcely ever sending a messenger without dispatching another after him in a few hours to bring him back that the notes might be corrected and altered.'[5] This restless perfectionism, which only those who knew Canning well could comprehend, was at times irksome even to old and trusted friends. Liverpool complained that Canning worked

[1] 9th August 1827. GRE, vol. 1, p. 183.
[2] 20th March 1826. L., p. 298.
[3] Croker to Brougham. 14th March 1839. CRO, vol. 2, p. 352.
[4] See p. 31 above.
[5] 30th January 1822, Mrs. A., vol. 1, p. 209.

with a 'twenty horse power'[1] and in late December 1826 he confessed to Arbuthnot that 'it was more than he could bear to be in office with Mr. Canning'. 'I am,' he said to Arbuthnot, 'on the best possible terms with Mr. Canning. We are cordial and friendly to the greatest degree, but you must be aware that being in office with Mr. Canning is totally different to what it was with poor Londonderry. Then everything was calm and tranquil, and nothing to worry me about trifles; but I have not strength and nerves to bear Mr. Canning's perpetual notes. He sends me a dozen of a day; every trifle, a remark from one of his Secys, a pamphlet, a paragraph in a newspaper, is cause for his firing off a note; and I live in continual dread every time the door opens that it is to bring a note from Mr. Canning, till I am driven half-distracted. Some people whose nerves are less irritable might not mind it, but I cannot bear it.'[2] Canning's omniscient authoritarian exactitude was equally apparent in his dealings with his own subordinates. Erskine was recalled from Washington with a reproof which made Foreign Office history. Sir Charles Stuart suffered under the lash. Lord Strangford could not forgive the manner in which he was upbraided. '. . . I *have* had a jobation! but such a jobation! No, nothing ever equalled it since the celebrated despatch to the Hon. David Erskine — my comfort is that people don't turn fools all at once — and that Mr. C. will find it hard to make folks believe that I am *quite* such a noodle as *he* makes me out to be.'[3] And later he wrote to Bagot, 'Happy man that you are! to be out of all this mess! to swig your curaçao in peace, and to be able to open your despatches without the fear of their actually exploding in your face.'[4] But even close friends like Bagot were not immune from Canning's criticisms, although the tone was more friendly; 'I was sorry,' conceded Canning, 'to have to snub or snouch you, in your old age (the old age of your Embassy) for disobedience to your instructions.'[5] Granville was frequently subjected to similar

---

[1] 31st July 1831. GRE, vol. 2, p. 174.

[2] 15th December 1826. Mrs. A., vol. 2, p. 65. This complaint was also known to Greville — see GRE, vol. 2, p. 174.

[3] Strangford to Bagot, 19th January 1826. BAG, vol. 2, p. 326.

[4] Ibid., 4th February 1826. BAG, vol. 2, p. 329.

[5] Canning to Bagot. 29th July 1824. BAG, vol. 2, p. 265.

treatment. 'It would be worth while,' was one of Canning's characteristic homilies, 'to make it an invariable rule to read over your despatches before you sign them. Some blunders in writing cure themselves by their obviousness; but this is not the case with the one in question. . . .'[1] Canning set himself such high standards and possessed so orderly and rapid a mind that he could not easily either understand or condone weaknesses in others. He developed a certain belief in his own infallibility and something like contempt for the opinions of others. This encouraged authoritarian tendencies, and because he so frequently found it difficult to explain to others what he was seeking to do he sometimes felt himself absolved from the necessity of explaining at all.

If Canning sometimes seemed too fussy in his thought, too elaborate in his stratagems, too critical in his chiding and too overbearing in his manner, there was no doubt of his ability to master specific problems. While foreign affairs was his own chosen field, he delighted to show that he could also pronounce with authority on questions like finance or Corn Law reform. His approach, like Peel's, was that of the professional expert on the Benthamite model: exhaustive study, reflection, conclusion. The best examples of his intellect in action can be found in his Foreign Office dispatches, which constitute a fitting memorial to his particular type of genius.

Canning's critical and analytical mind revelled in the intellectual exercise provided by wrestling with specific problems. He was seldom concerned with ultimate causes. There were set boundaries to his understanding. He could not, or would not, cross the threshold of his own known world. In that sense he was not a profound or an original thinker. He accepted Burke as the manual of his politics. Huskisson became his 'man of business', and via Huskisson he subscribed without question to interpretations of the economic doctrines of Adam Smith and to the monetary theories of Ricardo. He never suffered from any religious doubts. Those who considered that the times were out of joint could expect scant sympathy from Canning. He tended to dismiss as abstractions and obscurities whatever he could not readily

[1] Canning to Granville. 23rd November 1824. C.G.C., vol. 1, p. 206.

appreciate. The great struggle of ideas which the French Revolution had engendered represented to Canning no more than a conflict of bigotries. Those who, like the Lake poets, saw visions and dreamed dreams were to Canning no better than visionaries and dreamers. He does not seem to have realised that his own acceptance of the divine ordination of so many concepts, which he had not subjected to critical scrutiny, was no less obscurantist than the heart-searchings which he glibly despised. Canning's intellect was excellently adapted to the transaction of current business; he lacked the prophet's mantle.

His natural ability was supported by a prodigious capacity for work. At the outset of his political career Canning declared that 'the happiness of constant occupation is infinite' and he plunged into the perusal of State Papers with the abandon of a lover into the arms of his mistress. This passionate industry was devoted to every topic upon which he wrote or spoke. Even when worn down by sickness and weary of struggling he continued to work with remorseless persistence. The urge to labour, far from flagging, had become a habit. On his deathbed he was still composing imaginary dispatches. About a year after his return to the Foreign Office he had written to Bagot, 'I am just setting out for, I hope, 3 weeks holiday the first since September 16th 1822. I want them exceedingly for I am worn out with work and anxiety.'[1] But to Canning a holiday meant freedom to attend to business without interruption. As he explained when on a vist to Charles Ellis at Seaford: '. . . My office follows me here, and I think I have worked harder in this little low room of Charles with the sea murmuring (or as today raging) in my ears, than I have almost ever done, for the same space together, in Downing Street.'[2] Lord Dudley confirmed the picture with a few words written after Canning's death. 'His habits of industry must appear quite incredible to those who did not know him. I met him once at a country house where he went for what he was pleased to call his holidays. He had his secretaries about him soon after eight, had despatches ready before breakfast, then wrote all day till six. At tea-time he

---

[1] Canning to Bagot. 20th August 1823. BAG, vol. 2, p. 199.
[2] Ibid. 21st November 1825. BAG, vol. 2, p. 296.

established himself in a corner of the drawing-room to write his private letters; and this every day, only now and then with the exception of a ride and then during that he talked eagerly and fully on public affairs.'[1] To an old friend begging for an interview Canning once replied expressing regret that he could not oblige, and adding: 'Letters I can read, because I can borrow an hour from my rest at night, or early in the morning to do so. But I could no more have appointed a time for seeing you today than I could expect to take my ride before my dinner, or to dine at all.'[2] Such assertions are the prerogatives of office-holders; in few cases can they have been made with as much justification.

In addition to personally conducting the main business of the Foreign Office, Canning sought to master every subject upon which he might choose or be required to speak. He had quickly gained a great reputation as an orator and his career seemed to depend, to a considerable extent, on the influence which he was able to exercise, both in the Commons and on public platforms, by his speeches. To their preparation he devoted intensive study; rehearsing not only the spoken words but the gestures. In the performance itself Canning took an obvious relish. He claimed that during his maiden speech he had experienced 'a pleasure, almost sensual pleasure, hitherto unequalled' and he added with satisfaction, 'I had complete possession of all that I meant to say, and of myself and I saw my way clear before me'.[3] Canning's oratory remained a source of delight to himself. His audiences, both in the Commons and without, in an age unsated by public entertainment, were appreciative. Though individual victims of his blistering eloquence were resentful, his enemies did not hesitate to recognise his talents. Even Mrs. Arbuthnot confessed to enjoying his brilliant speeches. As an entertainer Canning ranked very high. But his listeners all too frequently were more impressed by the brilliance of his mind than convinced of the justice of his case. Perhaps he was too elaborate in his epithets, too steeped in classical tradition, too polished in his style, itself already a little out of

---

[1] Lord Dudley's Letters to Ivy, p. 327. BAG, vol. 2, p. 227.
[2] Canning to Mr. Pattison. 2nd March 1826. C.G.C., vol. 2, p. 183.
[3] *Canning's Journal.* D.M., p. 56.

tune with the times. The brilliance conveyed an impression that
he was not completely sincere. 'An actor,' commented Brougham,
'stood before us — a first rate one no doubt — but still an actor.
One never forgot that it was a representation we were witnessing
not a real scene.'[1] Brougham, even though their old rivalry eventually blossomed from mutual respect to active political co-operation, may perhaps be suspect as a witness; but there were many
others who, while admiring the performance, shared his reservations. Just as Canning was thought to be a bit too clever, so did he
seem to speak too well. If he had been less fluent he would no
doubt have been more trusted. But actor though he may have
been, he could not act dumb. Even if he might endeavour to
modify his style and his gestures to suit his audiences, he could
not hide his love of words or his delight in public speaking. This
pleasure existed quite apart from the political vocation to which
his oratory was theoretically subordinated.

Canning's delight in the composition and delivery of speeches
was akin to his love of conversation and to his relish in the exercise of his own wit. All forms of humour appealed to Canning.
Laughter was the only common denominator. Seriously as he
took life, he loved to make fun of everyone and everything. He
savoured the planning and execution of elaborate practical jokes;
he appreciated sheer nonsense, he did not despise puns; he produced quantities of satiric verse, some excellent; he made quips of
every kind, from the most brilliant and subtle to the most simple
and crude; he delighted in mocking and teasing his friends; he
frequently paid the same compliment to his enemies and to his
political opponents; he could be ponderously playful or coarsely
unkind; he could display dazzling wit or schoolboy silliness; the
ebullience was irrepressible.

Canning's love of laughter was a source of joy to the inner circle
of his friends. They provided an appreciative and indispensable
audience. Minor quarrels and occasional political differences were
often dissolved by accustomed banter. But Canning was too apt
to assume that all his friends and colleagues, and indeed his

---

[1] From Brougham's *Historical Sketches of Statesmen who lived in the Time of
George III*. G.C. & T., p. 18.

political opponents, could be treated in the same way as boon companions. Jenkinson frequently took offence at Canning's mockery and gibes. Ministerial colleagues were prone to resent the nicknames which Canning chose for them and the jokes which he made at their expense. Political opponents usually assumed deliberate malice. When Canning prepared to attack Addington's Ministry he wrote on 10th February 1802 to Sneyd: 'We shall worry the doctor like a pole cat, and all in good humour, at least on *OUR* part.'[1] Among manifestations of this good humour were the lines:

> *If blocks can the nation deliver*
> *Two places are safe from the French*
> *The first is the mouth of the river*
> *The second the Treasury bench.*

Addington and his colleagues failed to appreciate the good humour and never forgot the injury.[2] The wounds which Canning light-heartedly inflicted often went far deeper than he supposed and bred resentments which he himself found difficult to comprehend.

It was ever a relief to turn back to his chosen companions. There he could be certain of appreciation, understanding and admiration. To this kind of flattery Canning was particularly susceptible. He did not enjoy criticism or questioning of his judgement. Even his closest friends found him overbearing at times. But on the whole their automatic loyalty, and of course the constant approbation of his wife, provided the kind of balm he most required. But it was a dangerous indulgence and helped to increase the authoritarian tendencies of his nature. If Canning had ever been able to achieve absolute power, there are grounds for believing that he would have ruled with the aid of a coterie of favourites.

This fondness for retreating to the comfort of an inner circle

---

[1] BAG, vol. 1, p. 188.

[2] In spite of this, and of much further provocation on Canning's part, Addington himself did eventually allow his bitterness against Canning to mellow. See p. 100 below n. and p. 101.

was emphasised by his own diffidence in society. Though he loved public speaking he had a rather shrill voice and was embarrassed to speak in fashionable society. Indeed he generally remained silent. Furthermore he shared few of the tastes of the privileged class. In a Parliament of landowners he was something of an outsider. Almost totally lacking in acquisitive instincts, he was out of sympathy with the majority of those for whom material possessions meant so much. This difference bred mistrust and he in turn affected to despise the aristocracy. An impression of aloofness was created which gave offence to many. With increasing ill-health and increasing demands upon his time, he gradually abandoned all social functions which were not essential to official duties. He came to grudge every moment which had to be spared from his work; only with his family and most intimate friends could he find any kind of relaxation.

His health, particularly in the last five years of his life, ceased to stand up to the severe strains put upon it. His first serious illness seems to have occurred early in 1794, shortly after he had made his maiden speech. Over-excitement and irregular meals probably contributed to this collapse. At any rate, he decided to take his doctor's advice and to eat a solid meal before attending the House. He was also careful to avoid too vigorous compliance with the drinking habits of the age. Otherwise he gave little heed to his health. With the passing years, though prone to chills and an early sufferer from gout, his constitution stood up well to the demands which he made upon it. In September 1818, however, he suffered a very serious attack of gout and Bagot wrote to Binning: 'I think Canning has too much gout a good deal — I must write him a letter about it, and tell him not to eat cold ham between the courses, and sit writing for ten hours together and do a world of things of that kind which I know to be his practice.'[1] Before Christmas of that year Canning was again ill. In the winter of 1821 and of 1822 he suffered from bad bouts of gout and general ill-health. In the summer of 1823 he complained of being worn out in mind and body. Christmas found him bed-ridden, and in January 1824 he had a lingering attack of gout. In November of

[1] BAG, vol. 2, p. 86.

the same year he wrote, 'My rheumatism has called a little gout to its aid; and I am between both uncomfortably unwell.'[1] In March 1825 he suffered from a feverish chill and gout. 'You will have seen,' he wrote to Granville, 'that cold and fever did not save me from gout and that gout did not prevent me speaking on the Catholic question . . . the aggravation of illness which the exertion occasioned is gone off.'[2] But in April Canning was once more in pain, at times unable to write his name, and on the 26th sending a message to Liverpool that he was 'bound literally hand and foot'.[3] In August 1826 he was laid up with a chill and 'bile'; in December he was confined to bed, recovered for Christmas, but was soon after in bed again for a further three weeks. His health remained precarious and he died on 8th August[4] after a short sharp spell of illness. Thus, for the last nine years of his life, Canning was frequently ill and frequently in pain. From such pain little relief was to be found in early nineteenth-century England. Laudanum provided, at a cost, some solace. Otherwise the popular bleedings and blisterings, with occasional dispensations of mercury and bark, whatever their remedial value, were hardly soothing in their effects. On 23rd February 1827 Planta wrote to Stratford Canning of his cousin: 'He has been bled and cupped and cupped again and dosed with calomel — put into vapour baths and drenched with bark in its strongest form.'[5]

So if Canning was irritable in his latter years there can be little cause for surprise. The wonder is that in the face of deteriorating health he should have been able with such relative patience and calm to fight the most strenuous battles of his political life and to maintain such an extraordinary pressure of work.

'A truce,' he once said to Marcellus, 'to politics today . . . I am weary of them, let us read some Vergil. In my little domain like

---

[1] C.G.C., vol. 1, p. 205.

[2] G.C. and T., p. 428.

[3] C.G.C., vol. 1, p. 268.

[4] At the Duke of Devonshire's house at Chiswick, where he was invited for a rest and where he had been since the 20th of July; there were gloomy forebodings at the time because Fox had died in the same house and so Canning's host deliberately assigned him to a different room.

[5] F.C.M., no. 30, p. 19.

the old man of Galesius — '*Cui parva relicti iugera ruris erant*' —
I was looking over the Georgics. I was here — can anything be
more touching than these verses? —

> *Hic motus animorum, atque haec certamina tanta*
> *Pulveris exigui iactu compresci quiescent.* . . .

It must all end then in this little dust. What have I gained by so
many battles, many enemies, a thousand calumnies? . . . I can
attempt nothing of that which an inward and solemn voice seems
to dictate . . . I am like a bird which, instead of soaring to the
cliffs and the precipices, flies over the fens and skims the ground
. . . How often have I not been tempted to fly from society and
from power, to the literature which was the food of my boyhood,
the only refuge which is impenetrable to the delusions of fate.
Literature is a consolation, a hope, a place of rest for me. . . . Yet
still that desire of fame, which cannot at my age be called ambition,
drives me back to public affairs . . . human fame — mockery!!!
the ancients made her a goddess — a woman to be more seductive,
and dressed her in the attractions of patriotism. At this moment,
when I should like to dream of Vergil, I must go to encounter
Brougham in the Commons.'[1]

Such moods were rare, and desire for fame had in fact merged
into belief in his own indispensability for the welfare of England.
Upon his exertions, he was convinced, depended the continued
success of British foreign policy, the achievement of Catholic
Emancipation, the prevention of Parliamentary Reform and the
modification of the Corn Laws. In this light, the struggle for
power, instinctively undertaken and painfully pursued, became a
justifiable pattern of duty.

[1] Marcellus: *Politique de la Restauration* pp. 15–17, TEMP, p. 235. Vicomte
de Marcellus was the French Chargé d'Affaires.

THE POLITICIAN

(i) Struggle for Power

Canning's struggle for power was fought against a political background which, in spite of a ferment of new ideas and a rapidly changing economy, remained superficially stable. It was the King's responsibility to provide the country with a Government. No Government could survive for long without majorities in both Houses of Parliament. Most members of the House of Commons depended for their seats on the favour of the King or of landowning peers. Other interests certainly were represented, but neither the nabobs, nor the merchants, nor the new captains of industry, nor the independent country gentlemen could even collectively compare in authority with the firmly entrenched landed interest. If the great landowners had chosen to maintain a common front it is doubtful whether any Government could have survived against their wishes. Apart from the strength which he drew from the divisions of the aristocracy the power of the King depended on two main factors. He was by necessity and tradition the cornerstone of the Constitution; he also controlled vast patronage. Even though the extent of royal patronage declined during these years, the resources at the disposal of the King, or of his Prime Minister, remained, if properly husbanded, formidable.

Cabinets usually included, apart from some dedicated politicians, a number of great magnates and their relatives or representatives. The Duke of Buckingham, for instance, considered that he had a prescriptive right to at least one place in any Cabinet for himself, or for a nominee, so long as his dependents in Parliament supported the Administration. Although this particular claim was somewhat exceptional, a portion of honours and rewards for private disposal was regarded as the natural consequence of Government membership and the accepted price for Parliamentary support. No Administration could be formed without a series of private bargains between the Prime Minister and some of the leading landowners. No Government could remain in power without constant renewal of these bargains. For this reason no Prime Minister could continue in office if royal support was more than temporarily withheld.

The terms Whig and Tory confused contemporaries as they continue to confuse historians. In spite of party loyalties there were no real political parties in the late eighteenth and early nineteenth centuries. There were political groups held together more or less closely and for long or short terms by identity of interest, by personalities, by common enmity or by principle. All Governments were coalition Governments and at times this was the despair of the King. Ministries and the majorities on which they depended were like billiard balls. Very adroit management was required to keep them together. The apparent stability of Liverpool's long Administration is most deceptive. The point could not have been more clearly illustrated than by the crisis which followed his resignation. Certain combinations sometimes worked but their success did not depend on a party system. No political leader was in any sense the real leader of a party. Even Pitt, when out of office, could only command the loyalty of some fifty supporters. Canning's personal following was never greater than twenty. It is doubtful whether Liverpool had any personal followers at all. He owed his long tenure of office as much to divisions within his own Cabinet as to divisions among the great landed magnates. Because he was not the leader of a party he proved a Prime Minister under whom the most diverse elements could conveniently serve and prosper.

One of Liverpool's main preoccupations was the dwindling resources of royal patronage. It was quite insufficient, alone, to maintain majorities. One of the main preoccupations of the more intelligent members of the so-called Whig Opposition was whether principles should be sacrificed to personal loyalties and prejudice. Canning's Ministry of 1827 was formed on the assumption that royal patronage, though diminished, was still extensive and that measures, with some Whigs,[1] were more important than

---

[1] Brougham was the leader of this group. See p. 151, below.

men. The unreality of party divisions was manifest in the confusion which followed this experiment. But for Canning's death this complete new grouping might have held together.

In spite of some decline in the power of royal patronage and in spite of the growing influence of new interests and new opinions not directly represented in the House, England in 1827 was still a close oligarchy tempered by a monarchy. Divisions among the landed aristocracy, which at times threatened to bring all government to a standstill, enhanced the real value of royal patronage. Its use enabled Governments such as Pitt's and Liverpool's to survive. But it may be questioned whether the system could have continued to provide any kind of government but for the impact of the French Revolutionary and Napoleonic wars. Issues of principle, such as Catholic Emancipation, which might have provoked the emergence of opposed parties even within an unreformed House of Commons, became blurred in the midst of pressing national danger. There was a predisposition in favour of the *status quo* and an instinct that it must be made to work. This instinct survived the peace and was of great value to Liverpool; it inhibited opposition and held together the various groups and forces upon which his Government depended. Between 1822 and 1827 a spate of reforming legislation was carried out under the protective shadow of an outworn régime; these changes paved the way for further change and brought into relief the weaknesses of the system under which they had been achieved. Canning thought that Catholic Emancipation and Corn Law reform could be carried by dexterous manipulation within the old framework; Wellington was to view the carrying on of the King's Government as a series of rearguard actions; Grey, firmly but not very enthusiastically, was prepared to sponsor a measure of Parliamentary Reform. In the event there was no dramatic or conscious change in the balance of power. The old system gradually withered away and rival political parties emerged to fill the gap. But for many years they represented a necessary fiction rather than a political reality.[1]

[1] Even as late as 1869 Balfour, when contemplating a political career, confessed in his autobiography that the divisions between the two main political parties

When Canning was planning to enter politics the French Revolution already dominated the British political scene. In the spring of 1792, influenced perhaps by Mrs. Crewe and the Duchess of Portland, he became a convert to Burke's view of the French Revolution. In the light of this conversion he wrote a letter to Pitt explaining his attitude and offering his services to the Government. Pitt, who had shown previous interest in the young Whig prodigy, replied by giving him an appointment at Downing Street on Wednesday 15th August. This was their first meeting. Pitt promised to find a Parliamentary seat for Canning. It was understood that whoever the proprietor of the seat might be, Canning would owe his place solely to Pitt's favour; Canning, on his part, undertook to vacate the seat if his politics should at any time differ from those of the proprietor.

With this bargain the first and decisive step in Canning's political career had been taken. He had sworn allegiance to Pitt and he was to enter Parliament as a Government supporter. In the following months he gradually prepared Sheridan for this change of heart and Sheridan, in turn, warned Fox. In the spring of 1793 Mrs. Crewe volunteered to use her influence to get Canning into Parliament via the Portland interest.[1] Canning rejected the offer, declining to come 'in any man's train' and insisting: 'If I join Pitt I will go by myself'.[2]

Shortly afterwards his patience was rewarded and, thanks to Pitt alone, Canning became M.P. for the Borough of Newtown in the Isle of Wight. He did not in fact take his seat in the House until January 1794, but in November 1793 he was invited by Pitt to a political dinner where after a quarter of an hour he was able to declare: 'I was completely at my ease, as I could have been at Wanstead or at Ashbourne.'[3] Pitt followed this invitation by including Canning a week later in a Cabinet dinner; the Prime

---

then seemed to be blurred and that family ties were mainly responsible for directing him into the Conservative camp.

[1] The Portland Whigs, influenced by Burke, now supported the Government.
[2] FEST, p. 28.
[3] *Canning's Journal.* D.M., p. 47.

Minister further demonstrated interest in his new *protégé* by asking him to come and talk privately before the session opened. By 22nd February 1794 Canning could write: 'He and I, that is Pitt and I, are upon very comfortable terms. I go to him when I like, and ask questions and get notions and take advice, and he does not seem to be bored.'[1] Thus, rapidly, Canning became a favourite with the Prime Minister.

Assured of Pitt's favour, Canning calculated that a display of eloquence would prove the quickest road to advancement. His maiden speech was the first hurdle and he devoted such care to its preparation, and was so elated by the result (although it was in no way a sensational success), that he collapsed with a fever and was ill for about three weeks shortly afterwards. When he recovered his chief object was to be heard again in the House but his attempts were constantly frustrated and, apart from a few brief interventions, he was reluctantly compelled to silence. Once, when false hopes had been raised, he complained: 'The debate ended and Jenkinson and I went home together to supper at his house, grumbling against longwinded speakers, who prevented young folks from delivering their sentiments.'[2] On another occasion, when no Opposition speakers save Fox were forthcoming, he lamented that 'it was very unfair in opposition not to provoke us'.[3] In July, Parliament was prorogued; Canning felt that he had had far too few chances to show his mettle. Yet, when there was a Government reshuffle in the summer in order to admit the Portland Whigs, he seems to have been disappointed that no offer of office was made to him and he brooded with affected resignation: 'I have no reason to believe, from anything that I have ever heard that such a move could have reached to me when I know there are persons, who have been in Parliament who yet have nothing, and for whom something must in justice first have been done.'[4]

In January 1795 he was invited by Pitt, as an obvious mark of favour, to second the address. He took particular pains to make a good impression and endeavoured to avoid the 'too rapid a

[1] To Sneyd. BAG, vol. 1, p. 47.　　[2] *Canning's Journal*. D.M., p. 70.
[3] Ibid., p. 70.　　[4] Ibid., p. 75.

pronunciation' and 'too violent action'[1] for which he had been criticised. After this opportunity Canning once again found his efforts to speak frustrated. Following one particular disappointment he grumbled: 'I never went down more fully determined to speak than on this occasion. And it was not my fault that I did not.'[2] When his chance in that debate finally came, it was after four hours of Fox, two of Pitt and in reply to Sheridan. Not surprisingly he was listened to unwillingly and he mourned that 'the spirit of debating seems quite at an end for the session'.[3] His depression was increased by a comment, passed on to him by Boringdon, that his manner with Pitt was too familiar. This criticism moved Canning to a lengthy and very characteristic analysis. 'The complaint,' he wrote, 'was that my manner with Pitt in the House of Commons is too familiar — But whereas other persons, Country gentlemen and others, some of great consequence, and who have known and supported Mr. Pitt for years — treat him with the utmost respect and distance, and if they venture to address him at all, do it in a manner, the most humble and deferent. I, it seems, stand in no awe whatsoever — but talk to him without reserve or hesitation at all times and laugh and make jokes — and *once* was seen, when I wanted to speak to him, and he was looking another way, to put my hand on his shoulder. How can you conceive a more silly thing to trouble people's heads than this? I really scarcely know what part of my conduct it may be that gives so much offence — and as for the one flagrant fact of putting the hand upon the shoulder, it may have happened for ought I know, not once, but twenty times, as it is the most natural way of calling anybody's attention, who is sitting near you, and to whom you must not cry out by name — as that would interrupt the debate. I know indeed that I have, with people whom I like, old or young, great or small, something of a *caressing* manner (I think I must call it so, for I do not recollect any other word to express it) and so have a great many other people — a great many have it *not* — and with *that*

<hr>

[1] *Canning's Journal.* D.M., p. 79.
[2] Ibid., p. 81.
[3] Ibid., p. 86.

class it is not right to make use of it. Recollect among your acquaintance any ten or twenty persons — and you will find that there are some who you never meet without shaking hands, perhaps, or some other trifling salutation, if you meet them even ten times a day. You will find others, whom you like perhaps in all respects equally well, — but with whom you never think of exchanging any sort of *corporal* civility — even if you have not seen them for a week. Do you understand me? If you do, you will comprehend that one mistake of these good folks who are out of humour with me, is that they consider Mr. Pitt, naturally enough, as one of the latter class, the *non-shakers* — whereas he is in fact a very hearty, *salutation-giving*, *shake hands* sort of person — and one therefore whom I feel it is natural to take by the arm, or *to touch upon the shoulder even* (which is the great offence) as I do with Leveson or Frere or anybody that I most like, and towards whom I act most familiarly. But if it be wrong it must be altered.'[1]

As the session drew to its close Canning's impatience to achieve office could no longer be curbed. In March 1795 he had recorded in his journal: 'People would have it for this month past . . . that I was to be a Lord of the Admiralty — . . . all in good time. An office to be sure is a good thing, in many respects . . . but I am in no such violent hurry . . . and I think I have no doubts as to it being done, as soon as circumstances put it in Pitt's power to do it.'[2] But now, after another session in which he had had so little opportunity to shine in debate and with his friend Jenkinson already a member of the Board of Control, Canning felt that Pitt's memory required a little jogging. Accordingly he requested and obtained an interview, the substance of which he recorded at great length in his own journal.[3] From this account Canning's importunity and Pitt's patient solicitude are clearly evident. Canning complained bitterly of the lack of opportunities for speaking in the House, almost as if he resented the circumstances of the war and its Parliamentary repercussions

---

[1] *Canning's Journal.* D.M., p. 90.
[2] Ibid., p. 101.
[3] Ibid., pp. 101–10.

as a personal injury. Pitt commiserated. 'I certainly would not deny,' Canning somewhat unnecessarily proclaimed, 'that official employment was an object of my ambition.' He pointed out that, having no private fortune, office was a prerequisite for a political career. He added that he did not wish to face a third session on the same footing and that he 'did not like (after a certain reputation once gained), to be still considered as a young man, candidate for a place, and endeavouring to speak his way into it.' He then referred to the question of whether or not he should be called to the Bar. Pitt responded sympathetically and enquired what kind of office Canning had in mind; Canning replied that he wished some day to be Secretary for Ireland but in the meanwhile proposed a vacant Under-Secretaryship in Portland's Home Office department. Pitt pointed out that there were difficulties, but promised to investigate the matter, and in any case to search for an alternative if these difficulties proved insurmountable. A week later Canning pressed Pitt for a definite answer and was told that the Home Office Under-Secretaryship was not available but that 'he would do his best to find or make some arrangements that should answer my wishes'.[1] Dissatisfied with this reply, Canning made further but abortive investigations via the Duke of Portland's other Under-Secretary, Mr. King. He then left London and, on his way to Ashbourne, stayed at Belmont with the Malmesburys.[2] To Lord Malmesbury he poured out all his troubles and received much-needed comfort and encouragement; during his stay at Belmont confirmation was received that Pitt had been quite sincere in his reply that no opening was available at the Home Office.

In spite of Canning's doubts and fears, however, Pitt was able to redeem his promise by the transfer of Aust, one of the Under-Secretaries at the Foreign Office. This negotiation took a little while and it was not until after the session had commenced on 5th January 1796 that Canning formally took office. 'Pitt,' Canning wrote to Sneyd, 'has behaved about this business as handsomely as he has hitherto in every transaction that we have had together.'[3]

[1] *Canning's Journal*. D.M., p. 111.
[2] See p. 34 above.
[3] 27th October 1795. BAG, vol. 1, p. 51.

For the moment, even though enviously aware that Pitt had been Prime Minister at twenty-four, Canning was satisfied. On 17th December 1795 he wrote to Sneyd of his pleasure that his labours were now about to begin, and confessed that 'this state of delay had been very trying'.[1] In January 1796 he moved into a new house, 'a very pretty, small, snug, comfortable house',[2] and was soon engrossed in the work of his new office. On 16th January he wrote to Granville that 'the winds and waves had conspired to keep back all mails and messengers of the continent until I came into office; and they have come pouring in on me this week in such quantities, as the oldest clerk in the office does not remember ever to have witnessed before'.[3] With plenty to keep him busy, Canning was at last in his element and George Ellis reported to Sneyd: 'Canning has been working shockingly, but looks, when I saw him last in high health and beauty . . . you never saw such boots and leather breeches. Jenky after practising so long at reviews on a live horse, is not at all to be compared with him.'[4] In addition to the vast volume of official business which fell to Canning, he also found himself involved in a highly flattering, but dangerous intrigue. Peace negotiations were in progress, pursued with sincerity by Pitt and by the British Plenipotentiary Lord Malmesbury, but without conviction by Lord Grenville, the Foreign Secretary. Secret communications passed via Canning, and without the knowledge of his chief, between Malmesbury and Pitt. The Cabinet was divided and on many matters kept deliberately in the dark. In this complex situation Canning was the repository of confidences from all sides. His vanity was of course gratified, but the strain was considerable and his relations with Lord Grenville, at first excellent because, as he boasted, of his capacity for taking exceedingly to unpleasant men, gradually deteriorated. An open breach was prevented by the breakdown of the negotiations themselves. Routine work now alone occupied Canning and as a

[1] BAG, vol. 1, p. 53.
[2] Canning to Sneyd. 10th January 1796. BAG, vol. 1, p. 58.
[3] G & D, 29/8 Granville MSS. D.M., p. 159.
[4] BAG, vol. 1, p. 62.

new outlet for his energies he turned to the publication of *The Anti-Jacobin*. The first number of this periodical appeared on 20th November 1797 and, though the contributors were anonymous, their identity was soon established. Canning supported this attempt to answer Opposition taunts in kind with mischievous enthusiasm. Allied to a group of chosen intimates, working and meeting in secret, he gleefully transformed the jokes and jottings of private talk and personal correspondence into satire and parody. In the busy excitement of this patriotic pamphleteering adventure he did not count the cost to himself of offence so often gratuitously given or appreciate that his own reputation might, on balance, suffer damage in the process.

Preoccupation with *The Anti-Jacobin* and the increasing boredom of routine Foreign Office work under a difficult chief made Canning anxious for a change. He therefore welcomed his appointment in March 1799 as a Commissioner of the Board of Control. He described his new office as 'one of less emolument but more ease and dignity' and rejoiced that he would 'go frisking and flourishing about, so happy in new liberty, after three years of such slavery, as never was slaved'.[1]

Joy at his new-found liberty did not last long and Canning was soon restlessly anxious for advancement. On 28th November 1799 he wrote a long letter about his political prospects to Boringdon. In it the usual invidious comparisons were made. 'I might mention,' he argued, 'without too much arrogance, Lord Castlereagh, now two years Minister of Ireland; the Speaker, soon after thirty, placed in a chair which was supposed, of all things, to require *years* to fill it; Lord Grenville, *before* that age Speaker and a Secretary of State; it would, I say, be a little hard that, amidst all these instances of early achievement, *one* person should be selected as a victim to ancient prejudice; should be required to go through all the forms, to keep all his terms regularly, and to advance only step by step, till he should arive at the objects of ambition in a green old age; and I should feel a little impatient if I were to be that person.'[2]

---

[1] Canning to Bessy Canning. 22nd February 1799. *Western Letters.* D.M., p. 191.
[2] G.C. & T., pp. 60–1.

The death of Mackenzie, Lord Privy Seal of Scotland, provided Pitt with an opportunity for a minor Ministerial reshuffle and, in spite of the angry importunities of the Grenville family group, Canning was rewarded with the office of Joint Paymaster-General and on 28th May 1800 admitted to the Privy Council. He had progressed a further step towards the Cabinet.

But a shattering blow was in store. In February 1801 Pitt, who had wrestled unsuccessfully with the King's conscience over Catholic Emancipation, resigned the Premiership and at the same time urged his friends and colleagues to remain in office under the new Prime Minister, Addington. Canning regarded himself as Pitt's chosen disciple and he conceived that loyalty demanded his own resignation. As he put it to Sneyd on 14th February 1801: 'Pitt resigns, no matter for what reason and I feel it right to follow him out of office. Most other people feel it right to stay in, and form the new Administration. *He* is of *their* opinion — which is rather hard upon me you will say, and so it is perhaps. But I am of my own, and that is enough . . . I never liked anything less. . . .'[1] On principle, therefore, Canning resigned and the sacrifice was all the more galling because Pitt seemed by no means favourably impressed by this display of excessive and indeed embarrassing loyalty. During the interval between Pitt's resignation and the formal handing over of the seals to Addington on 14th March, Canning made efforts to persuade Pitt to withdraw his resignation and, together with some of his friends, sought to achieve the same result by hints to Addington. Pitt, although one of the ostensible reasons for his resignation had apparently disappeared,[2] remained adamant and Addington, far from being moved by Canning's hints, was merely confirmed in his mistrust of their author. These suspicions had been aroused by a spate of rumours, regarding expressions of opinion on the part of Canning and his friends, highly unflattering to the character and ability of the Premier designate. Granville denied the

---

[1] BAG, vol. 1, p. 180.

[2] Pitt's Irish policy had been blocked by the King's conscience but he had now promised not to raise the Catholic Question again during the King's lifetime.

truth of these rumours in a letter[1] to his mother but admitted that in private conversations the 'doctor' had been the subject of some mockery. Pitt, anxious that his *protégé* should not quarrel with the new Government, was at pains to promote a reconciliation between Canning and Addington. This, with some difficulty, was achieved. Canning, however, remained restless and disappointed; in this unhappy frame of mind he conceived that he had a grievance against Pitt and he wrote a letter complaining of ingratitude and unfairness. Pitt replied reasonably and patiently as to a spoiled but cherished child.[2] Canning was not mollified and on 12th July 1801 he wrote to Frere, dramatically claiming that he considered his 'intercourse with Pitt as closed for ever'.[3] The quarrel was one-sided and Pitt, realising that Canning's distress stemmed from frustrated ambition, generously sought to promote his *protégé's* return to the Ministry. Canning later confessed that he had 'actually got so far as to bring himself to believe that he could not bear being out of office much longer'.[4] Addington was prepared to co-operate and terms, via Pitt, were discussed.[5] Canning's pretensions however proved too great for any accommodation. Pitt's interest nevertheless served, as no doubt he had intended, to restore Canning's confidence in his own patron.

Canning found consolation for his latest disappointment when the terms of the Peace Preliminaries were submitted to Parliament. With these, he claimed, he could not but have disagreed and, therefore, would have found any Government office insupportable. In Hawkesbury's position, he argued, he would have cut off his right hand rather than sign. The whole of his own past conduct now seemed to be justified. 'I must act as I think right,' he wrote to Boringdon. 'My road must be through *character* to power; that I may take this road and miss the end, is very

[1] 20th February 1801. See *The Private Correspondence of Granville Leveson Gower, 1782–1821*, vol. 1, pp. 298–9.

[2] See Earl Stanhope: *Life of the Hon. William Pitt*, vol. 3, p. 316.

[3] FEST, p. 47.

[4] Canning to Frere. 30th September. FEST, p. 58.

[5] See Canning to Pitt. 28th August 1801. J. H. Rose: *Pitt and Napoleon*, p. 326. (A footnote suggests that the date of this letter should read 1804. But internal evidence indicates that the original date is perfectly correct.)

possible; nay, that by acting as I think right, I may not, as surely as I expect it, get even to my second stage — character — is very possible also; but *that* I cannot help; I will try no other course; and I am sanguine enough to believe that, after all, this course though not perhaps the quickest, is the surest.'[1] So Canning, morally justified in his own eyes, was prepared to be patient. He considered whether he would ever be able to serve under Addington and he came to the conclusion that if, knowing his principles, Addington were to offer at some future date responsible office, the answer might be yes. In no circumstances would he ever again be prepared to consider anything less than responsible office.

In the meanwhile Pitt's support of the Peace Preliminaries produced a case of conscience for Canning; he owed his seat to Pitt and therefore felt obliged to vote, in spite of his own convictions, for the Government. This crisis was resolved by a determination to resign his seat and seek for an independent constituency. On this occasion divergence of opinion was not accompanied by any ill feeling. Canning, however, was determined to be free to oppose the Government. On 7th November he explained his attitude in a letter to Frere: 'I need not say to you that the idea of the possibility of being entirely separated from P. — of taking part on a different side from him in the House of Commons is very painful to me. But surely the situation in which he places me is cruelly unfair. Determined, he assures me, never again to take a leading part in public life himself, and devoting himself to the support of a man, of whom I know he must, and does think as I do, that he is utterly unfit to fill the station in which he is placed — has he a right (indeed he does not pretend to it) or am I, in the most refined construction of what I owe to him, bound — to consider my allegiance as bound up in his, and necessarily transferable with it? . . . I will not become factious if I can help it — I really have no inclination to it — and I do believe I shall be able to guard myself against any seductions, either of ill company, or of tempting opportunity: but I believe too, at least I very much hope, that a temperate and mitigated Opposition in Parliament, in which one should judge and act

[1] 29th October 1801. G.C. & T., p. 67.

fairly upon *measures* as they arose, contending, however, uniformly all the while and upon every occasion that the *Man* was utterly the fool he is, that it is mischief and madness to trust the Country in his hands — might do a great deal of good, and presents a highly respectable line of Conduct, not to say a very amusing one — for the opposition to a fool *quaetenus* fool, would be a new, and hitherto unexhausted ground.'[1]

In the New Year, accordingly, Canning opened a campaign against Addington both within and outside Parliament. Once again, as with *The Anti-Jacobin*, he found a congenial outlet for his energies and for his wit. The Prime Minister and his colleagues provided easy targets and Canning in his enthusiasm was frequently merciless.

While attacking the Ministry on the one hand, Canning strained every nerve to make public contrast of Pitt's talents on the other. On 28th May 1802 he organised a dinner in Pitt's honour at which his own verses, entitled '*The Pilot that weathered the storm*', were read; in the House he lost no opportunity of eulogising his former leader. These attentions on the part of his self-chosen champion, however gratifying, were as embarrassing to Pitt as the anti-Government campaign itself. Time and again he urged discretion and moderation on Canning; time and again Canning begged that Achilles should emerge from his tent. In the face of Pitt's obstinacy Canning decided that he must be served in spite of himself and that the campaign must continue, with the manoeuvres as far as possible concealed from Pitt. Thus in November he planned a petition which was to have been addressed to both Addington and Pitt, pressing for the latter's return. By accident, however, Pitt got word of the plan and immediately stirred himself to prevent its execution. Canning was downcast but not desperate. 'I am quite aware,' he wrote, 'that we did not do half of what we might have done; but recall the *fetters* in which *we* act from the dread of misrepresentation to Mr. P.'[2] On 8th December 1802 Canning insisted in the House

---

[1] FEST, pp. 61–2.

[2] Canning to Rose. 6th December 1802. *The Diaries and Correspondence of the Rt. Hon. George Rose*, edited by L. V. Harcourt, vol. 1, p. 466.

F

that Pitt 'must endure the attachment of a people whom he has saved'.[1] In spite of previous differences of opinion Grenville and Canning now began to co-operate in bringing pressure to bear on their former leader, to the latter's further annoyance.

Events, however, at this juncture came to Canning's aid. Addington himself made an approach to Pitt but the approach was hedged with such humiliating conditions that Pitt took offence. Canning was jubilant; Pitt's return to office with the present Ministers as colleagues could, in the circumstances, offer little hope of advancement to Canning; Pitt's return after their defeat, on the other hand, held out glittering possibilities. Canning savoured Pitt's account of the negotiations and reported gleefully to his wife: 'P. out of delicacy would not tell me that my name had been mentioned. He would not like me to think that I had been any obstacle to his return — nor to take merit with me for his resolution not to return without me. But the knowledge of this circumstance has completely softened my heart towards him. . . . He cannot offer me anything that I will not take. Is that being good?'[2]

These hopes, however, proved premature and with the resumption of hostilities against France in May 1803 Pitt re-emphasised his support of the Ministry and reminded Canning that: 'We must make sacrifices in the case of war, and from you I must exact the sacrifice even of the best turned, and most pointed sentences against the Dr.'[3] He advised both Canning and Grenville to be magnanimous in their attitude to the Government and he insisted that their opposition had made them unpopular. He was, however, prepared to discuss the possibility of forming an alternative Government and he listened, albeit with disapproval, to Lord Grenville's plan for the exclusion of Hawkesbury. So firm were the bonds now established between Grenville and Canning, and so eager was Canning to convert Pitt to Grenville's views, that he even proffered justifications for the attempt to exclude Hawkesbury. Old friendship was obviously

[1] Therry, vol. 2, p. 63.
[2] Canning to his wife. D.M., p. 238.
[3] Ibid., p. 240.

at a discount. Canning's alliance with Grenville, notwithstanding the hostile attitude of the Grenville clan to his own promotion in 1800, was based on their joint contempt of Addington and their genuine doubt of his Administration's ability to wage war against Napoleon with sufficient vigour. In spite of their importunities they made little real headway with Pitt and on 23rd May Canning commented: 'Poor P! . . . he disapproves and despises as heartily as one can desire the incredible imbecility of the Addingtons — he hates the thoughts of defending them — but he has not *nerves* either to contemplate the possibility of acting against them himself, or to give his direct sanction to any opposition to them.'[1]

Once again Canning decided, without Pitt's approval, to make himself the interpreter of what he believed must be Pitt's real desires. After consultations with the group of followers, many of them personal friends, who now regarded Canning as their Parliamentary leader, he arranged for Patten, one of their number, to move a vote of censure against the Government. Thus, it was hoped, Pitt would be forced into open opposition. To Canning's disgust, however, Pitt insisted that he would vote with the Ministry. 'Shabby,' Canning complained, 'to vote against us, but speak for us — expressing his disapprobation of the conduct of the Government — but turning round on the point that it was not the time, nor Parliamentary censure the mode, for removing them.'[2]

In the event, on 3rd June, Pitt decided, rather than vote with the Opposition, to move the adjournment of the House. On this issue Canning and his followers, who were determined not to be deprived of a debate on the censure motion, voted with the Government. Pitt found himself in a minority of 54. After the debate which accordingly followed, Canning was only able to muster 34 votes against the Government. The paucity of Pitt's Parliamentary strength deeply grieved Canning but he took comfort from the reflection that the division on the adjournment had separated 'Pitt completely and for ever from Addington'.[3]

[1] Canning to his wife. 23rd May 1802. D.M., p. 247.
[2] Ibid. 30th May 1803. D.M., p. 249.
[3] Ibid. 4th June 1803. D.M., p. 251.

This was, of course, a false surmise. But it gave Canning some hope. 'Things are bad enough,' he commented on 9th June, '. . . but worse things than these have been mended before now.'[1]

When the House reassembled in October, Canning again fell victim to despondency and complained that 'Pitt is so much worse than ever as to his plans of action or rather inaction'.[2] He even suspected Pitt of having provided information for an article of a slighting nature against himself. He began to despair but then had what he described as a 'full and *most satisfactory* Conversation'[3] with Pitt. At last it seemed that the ex-Premier was prepared to join in open opposition. Furthermore, he seemed more disposed to listen sympathetically to the schemes which Grenville and Canning had been pressing for the formation of a great Ministry which would include Fox and would exclude the majority of the old gang.

But once again Canning was too sanguine in his hopes. Possibly his impression of the conversation had been little more than wishful thinking. When he went to visit Pitt at Walmer on 1st January 1804 he wrote fretfully: 'I wish I may have arrived to any good purpose but I doubt it. There has been a terrible relapse.'[4] He even reverted to the notion, reserved for his darkest hours, that he should abandon Parliamentary life. By 9th January he was a little more hopeful and detected in Pitt 'no shabby tenderness, except for Cast[lereagh] — and for him in a much less *whiny* way than heretofore.'[5] Canning's vehemence and lack of appreciation of the realities of the political situation must indeed have been a sore trial to Pitt, and Pitt's patience is surely some measure of the affection and esteem which he reserved for Canning.

Events, however, rather than Canning's promptings, once again served to bring Pitt's policy into line with his disciple's nagging zeal. After a temporary lull during the King's illness, Pitt spoke critically of the Government's conduct of the war

---

[1] Canning to his wife. 9th June 1803. D.M., p. 253.
[2] Ibid. 9th October 1803. D.M., p. 254.
[3] Ibid. 10th October 1803. D.M., p. 256.
[4] Ibid. D.M., p. 257.
[5] Ibid. 9th January 1804. D.M., p. 259.

and on 12th March actually voted with Fox; during the debate, although Canning would have liked to follow Addington and 'maul him',[1] he desisted lest this violence should deter Pitt from the road which he now at length seemed disposed to follow. This unaccustomed restraint suggested that Canning was learning a little the hard way. He could not, however, easily trust Pitt out of his sight and on 11th April 1804 pursued him to Walmer and once again subjected him to the usual pressure. 'He seems,' Canning wrote, 'in perfectly good heart indeed — but shudders a little at the brink, just as I suppose George does at the edge of the tub of cold water. He must *in*.'[2] After a debate on the 23rd the Government majority was down to 52 and Canning found Pitt's speech 'everything that one can wish — the most complete, general and unqualified condemnation of Ministers — and the plain declaration twice repeated, that "from them and under them no good could possibly be expected". Thus he has kept his word ... I did not speak — after Pitt there was nothing to say. And I did not like throwing myself away.'[3] On the 26th the majority for 'Mine Goose' was reduced to 37 and this time Canning spoke to 'good effect'. 'With Cast[lereagh] I was in perfect good humour and playfulness — but with the Doctor I am afraid not so ——'[4] Canning was able to reassure his wife that Pitt, far from being annoyed, had enjoyed the joke against Castlereagh.

The Government was now obviously crumbling and Canning's moment of triumph seemed at last to have arrived. But, during the crucial negotiations, Pitt, for obvious reasons, did not take Canning into his confidence and Canning, consequently, was in an anguish of excitement and fear. When Pitt cautioned Lady Harrowby 'against calling *any* people fools or beasts (as she sometimes does) for there is no knowing whom one may be obliged to have', Canning complained: 'I like this not. It looks Hawkish and Castleish.'[5] A brief conversation with Pitt, however, convinced him that the latter was still personally anxious

[1] Canning to his wife. 15th March 1804. D.M., p. 261.
[2] Ibid. 11th April 1804. D.M., p. 263. George was Canning's eldest son.
[3] Ibid. 23rd April 1804. D.M., p. 263.
[4] Ibid. D.M., p. 265.
[5] Ibid. D.M., p. 267.

to form a broad Government. But on 7th May Pitt saw the King
for three and a half hours and the results of this interview confirmed Canning's worst fears. The King refused to consider Fox,
to whom both Grenville and the Whigs regarded themselves as
pledged. 'So,' mourned Canning, 'we are to have shabby narrow
government after all. Alas! Alas! Alas!' Gone was his castle in
Spain. 'And under this government,' he asked his wife, 'would
dearest dear have me Treasurer of the Navy or Secretary at War?
I think she would not." Canning could not tolerate the thought of
accepting a subordinate office in a Ministry where the chief
figures, apart from the Prime Minister, were to be men such as
Camden, Hawkesbury and Castlereagh — when in fact, save for
a change at the top, the Government which he had been railing
against for the past years was to continue almost unchanged. It
was in fact Canning's first major political defeat and a shattering
blow to his ambition and to his pride.

He left London to take counsel with his wife. Perhaps she
exercised some influence upon him; perhaps he could no longer
bear to be excluded from office. At any rate he accepted the
Treasuryship of the Navy and wrote to his wife maintaining:
'I am quite, quite persuaded to have done well and wisely in
accepting it . . . I have really made *more* people *more* happy than
I believe I ever had it in my power to do by any one action in
my life before; and that so far from a slight or degradation, the
appointment will be considered by everybody as a complete
triumph to me, and will refute and bring to shame a crowd of
lies and calumnies that have been circulating with incredible
industry and have . . . had an effect upon Pitt's mind painful beyond what we in our anger with him would have thought of
believing.'[2] Having thus convinced himself of the wisdom of
accepting office in circumstances which a few days previously he
had regarded as intolerable, Canning also managed to make himself believe that the situation was not a flattering one for his
senior colleagues. 'Castlereagh,' he continued, 'does not stir —
and I do assure my own love his continuance where he is, is not

[1] Canning to his wife. D.M., p. 268.
[2] Ibid. 13th May 1804. D.M., p. 269.

considered as a mark of high consideration . . . Hawkesbury has been kicked from the Foreign to the Home Department with as little ceremony as (indeed less than) I used in making Brown under-Butler again after he had officiated as Butler. And he sinks in estimation accordingly. . . .'[1]

It was not a very happy fame of mind in which to re-enter Ministerial service.

Although, during these years, Canning had established himself as a formidable figure in Parliamentary debates and although he had created the nucleus of a small personal following in both Houses, he had also seriously jeopardised the career that he sought so sedulously to promote. But for Pitt's extraordinary patience and faith (and even Pitt was once reduced to complaining that 'nobody did his cause so much disservice as Lord Grenville in the House of Lords, except Mr. Canning in the House of Commons'[2]), Canning's conduct could have caused a fatal alienation. The enmity of Addington and his supporters had been so successfully courted that they could not be expected easily to forgive. Hawkesbury and Castlereagh could hardly relish the fact that Canning had such a poor opinion of their talents; though they forgave more easily they did not forget. The chief sufferer from Canning's violent and self-seeking opposition was Canning himself.

In office, but excluded from the Cabinet, Canning now began to see in this circumstance a cause for congratulation. 'Oh but the Cabinet,' he wrote, 'the poor Cabinet — stuffed — such people! I am afraid they are laughed at very much — I can plainly see that many of Pitt's most devoted are by no means satisfied with the arrangement. . . . I would not be the thirteenth as the thing now stands for any consideration and depend upon it, dearest dear, be assured of it — the thing is a good deal better for *me* as it is.'[3] Though a member of the new Government, Canning was in no way inclined to be its friend. On 23rd May

---

[1] Canning to his wife. 13th May 1804. D.M., p. 269.
[2] *The Diary and Correspondence of Charles Abbott, Lord Colchester* (1861), vol. 1, p. 423. D.M., p. 230.
[3] Canning to his wife. D.M., p. 272.

1804 he grumbled to his wife: '. . . to take my seat between whom I wonder? I think I shall hardly bring myself to do it — and if I can possibly avoid it I think I shall certainly take no part in debate. I hate the thoughts of the Treasury Bench (I said to P today) for except for yourself, who is there that I can sit near with comfort — or with whom exchange a word in the course of debate?'[1] Canning's only comfort was that Pitt was once again treating him with something of the old confidence. And yet Pitt was again destined to be sorely tried. Hawkesbury, who was sensitive to Canning's somewhat contemptuous attitude, took offence at a reference which the latter made to his removal from the Foreign Office and offered his resignation to Pitt. Canning volunteered explanations and his own resignation. The incident was patched up. But Hawkesbury let it be known that he had interceded with Pitt in Canning's favour. Canning now extracted from Hawkesbury a written denial that he had made any formal apology and kept the document because, as he later told Sneyd, he considered Hawkesbury 'a lying shuffling hound'.[2] The importance of this episode is that its real cause lay in Canning's envy of his old friend. Though he affected to despise the Cabinet he was in fact burning to be included. In November 1804 there seemed to be a chance. Lord Harrowby, the Foreign Minister, was reputed to be ill; a reshuffle seemed in prospect; there was talk of a temporary appointment; Canning hastened to Pitt and offered his temporary[3] services; Pitt showed interest; Canning was jubilant; but difficulties supervened and no action followed.

In December, to Canning's horror, Addington, now Viscount Sidmouth, re-entered the Ministry as Lord President of the Council; Harrowby now did resign, but in favour of Lord Mulgrave for whom a place had to be found. At first it seemed to Canning that there was no alternative but to offer his own resignation. He hesitated and eventually remained critical and uncomfortable in office.

[1] D.M., p. 272.
[2] Canning to Sneyd. 9th February 1805. BAG, vol. 1, p. 219.
[3] Canning to his wife. D.M., p. 278.

In April 1805 when his chief, Lord Melville, was attacked in the house for corruption and compelled to resign, Canning's speech in defence made a most favourable impression. '. . . there is,' wrote Lady Bessborough,[1] 'no one who has done well but the Pope. He in true manly honesty and courage stood forth alone, in defiance of Public Opinion, in defence of the friend he thought wronged; every other friend or dependent has left him to his fate.'[2] From this affair, which led to serious differences between Sidmouth, whose supporters rejoiced to settle old scores, with Melville, and Pitt, Canning emerged with credit. Opportunities were presented for urging Pitt to secure Sidmouth's dismissal and eventually, on 7th July, after Pitt had refused patronage to Nathaniel Bond and John Hiley Addington,[3] Sidmouth tendered his resignation. 'I am but just returned,' Canning wrote to his wife on the 9th, 'from Putney where I went on with Pitt last night after dining at Nepean's. He is in the best possible disposition and for the first time in these four years I think, we were as much at ease together as we used to be. And the Dr. is gone for ever. . . .'[4] Not only was the Cabinet now purged of Sidmouth, but Pitt began to discuss possibilities of an Irish Secretaryship with Canning; there were also hints of a reversion to the programme of a broad Ministry. But the summer wore on and no definite offer was made to Canning, while the King's continued opposition to Fox and the pretensions of Fox's followers made it obvious that no major Governmental change was likely.

Canning whipped himself up into a mood of despair and poured out his soul to Pitt during a private dinner on 24th October 1805.[5] Canning started by suggesting that he should go

[1] See p. 40 above n. 3.

[2] To Granville Leveson Gower. See *The Private Correspondence of Granville Leveson Gower, 1781–1821*, vol. 2, p. 82.

[3] Nathaniel Bond was a Winchester contemporary and John Hiley Addington was Sidmouth's brother. For this episode, and Sidmouth's consequent resignation, see *The Annals of the Addington Family*, by E. M. G. Belfield, p. 86.

[4] Canning to his wife. 9th July 1805. D.M., p. 285.

[5] He gave a full account of their conversation in a letter to his wife. Ibid., pp. 288–94.

to Ireland as Secretary until such time as a Government which he could really support had been formed. If there was no prospect of such a change then he would prefer to retire altogether. Pitt tried to interrupt but Canning insisted: 'No — first hear me quite out . . . from the beginning of the present government my life has been one continued series of mortifications: I pass over all but one — but that I must dwell upon . . . because it is one, the only one perhaps, in which I think you behaved personally ill to me. I mean in what passed between me and Hawkesbury and you and me respecting him.' Canning went on to argue that he had withdrawn his own resignation out of consideration for Pitt but that Pitt had let him down by allowing the impression to gain currency that Canning's fate had rested on Hawkesbury's decision. Was this fair? 'Ought you in return to sacrifice me to a liar and a coward — for such he is — I know him to be so — you, when you have occasion to try him home, will find so too. But do not mistake me. I do not mean to deprecate his talents or usefulness.' Intemperate recriminations continued and after soft answers Pitt eventually enquired whether Canning meant to insist that he could never 'consent to sit in a Cabinet with Hawkesbury'; Canning replied that he would not 'consent to being exhibited in a light of inferiority' and went on with his diatribe. Against Castlereagh, whom, he confessed, 'upon nearer intercourse I grow to like, as much as the difference of our natures admits, very cordially', he had no grievance save that Castlereagh held two offices which were usually Cabinet appointments. This finally gave Pitt his chance to intervene and he began to outline his own plans for Canning's admission to the Cabinet, possibly retaining his present office. 'It is Cabinet after all that makes the whole distinction,' Pitt pointed out. He had struck the right note. Canning's recital of griefs subsided and his resentment faded away. They met frequently during the next few weeks and reverted to the same agreeable topic. Canning considered that he had a promise of promotion in the New Year.

In December, Pitt had an attack of gout and Canning visited him at Bath and read over to him a poem which he had been composing on Ulm and Trafalgar. On 9th January 1806 Pitt returned to Town, but his health had not improved and it became gradually clear that he would not recover. On 23rd January he died. Grief overcame all other feelings and in the midst of mourning Canning for a while forgot the blow to his own fortunes.

From henceforth, in politics, Canning owned no master. As he later claimed, his political allegiance was buried in Pitt's grave. Leader of a small personal following, he also regarded himself, though others disputed the succession, as the residuary legatee of Pitt's tradition. In this mood of gloomy exaltation, he watched the formation the 'Ministry of All of the Talents'. Royal objections to Fox, who became Foreign Minister, were at last overcome. Grenville, with whom Canning had so long campaigned, was Prime Minister. The great Ministry of their dreams had been created. But how changed were the circumstances! Pitt was dead and in the new combination Sidmouth once again found a prominent place. Canning, with his personal supporters and most of the leading members of the late Ministry, were now in opposition. Although he had never yet held Cabinet office, Canning assumed that he was the natural leader of that Opposition; certainly he was one of its only effective speakers in the Commons and certainly he was prepared to oppose as a matter of course.[1]

When, in the summer, Fox fell seriously ill Grenville, seeking fresh strength for his Government, made tentative offers of Cabinet office to Canning. In his new and self-appointed role as leader of the Pittites, Canning objected, not on principle, but because he did not wish to join alone. Just before Fox's death, Grenville proposed a modest bargain. 'It is hardly necessary to say,' Canning wrote to Boringdon, 'that I could not accept, or report to those with whom I act such a proposal.'[2] Grenville raised the stakes but Canning was still not satisfied with a situation in which 'Lord Ellenborough, Windham, and the Doctor

[1] It has been suggested that Canning's opposition marked a significant constitutional development. But it seems more probable that his attitude on this and similar occasions was determined by his character and by ambitious calculations rather than by any political theory.

[2] 24th September 1806. G.C. & T., p. 103.

remaining as they are and every Foxite in the place, out of which every friend of Mr. Pitt has been turned to make way for them'.[1] After Fox's death Canning worked out his own terms for joining the Government. 'Five seats [in the Cabinet], one of them without office,' he conceded, 'I would have undertaken to propose.'[2] The places were to have been for Lord Chatham, Castlereagh, Canning himself, Westmorland or Liverpool and Eldon without office. What Canning was in fact contemplating was a new coalition. He explained to Boringdon that in no other circumstances could he feel sure of carrying enough weight where policy-making was concerned in the 'All Talents' Administration. Changes of such magnitude were not to Grenville's taste; as Canning commented: 'He would have been glad to win individuals but he had no desire to wed the party. I do not say that I blame him, but unluckily I cannot be won alone.'[3] The negotiations seemed to have established Canning's position; he had no great desire or expectation that they would succeed. The Government was divided and beset with difficulties. On the Catholic Question it was meeting growing royal resentment. Its collapse seemed a probability. In that event the King would turn to the Opposition and here Canning believed that he had now manoeuvred himself into a predominant position. Although Pitt was gone, Canning's own political prospects had never seemed brighter and ambition counselled patience. He, therefore, deliberately pitched his immediate claims too high, was gratified by their rejection and continued vigorously to oppose Grenville's Ministry.

For the first time in his political career Canning's calculations proved correct. In February 1807 the King felt himself strong enough to demand a pledge from Grenville on the Catholic Question; rather than conform he resigned and George III called upon the ailing Duke of Portland to succeed. The Duchess of Portland had been a patron of Canning's in his youth and the Duke's son was his brother-in-law by marriage. These circumstances, perhaps more than the place which Canning now believed he had created for himself, made him the immediate repository

---

[1] 24th September 1806. G.C. & T., p. 104.
[2] Ibid., p. 105.   [3] Ibid., p. 105.

of the Duke's closest confidence. On 15th March 1807 Canning reported to Boringdon: 'I was with the D. of P. last night for two or three hours; and am now confident that he *would* undertake the Government. I have endeavoured to impress upon him those considerations with regard to "the Doctor", which I think most likely to have weight with him, and which I really believe to be perfectly true — the little good, and the great harm, that a connexion with the Sidmouth party would do to us.'[1] On this occasion no disappointments were in store for Canning, although perhaps he was inclined to overrate his own influence in achieving the final result. On 25th March 1807 he wrote exultantly to Boringdon: 'As my fate was not decided till two-o-clock today, you may possibly not yet know that I am at the Foreign Office, and will, perhaps, be pleased to receive from myself the assurance that I am so.'[2]

In the new Ministry Canning's position seemed to be a splendid one. His own most bitter opponents were excluded from office. The Prime Minister, who was not expected to be more than a respectable figurehead, was well disposed in his favour. His erstwhile rivals, Hawkesbury and Castlereagh, were respectively Secretaries for Home Affairs and War and Colonies; at the Foreign Office he could be regarded as their senior in status. True, the leadership of the House and Chancellorship of the Exchequer had gone to Spencer Perceval, but Perceval was a Pittite whom Canning, in his own opinion, had patronised, of whom (save for their difference on the Catholic Question) he thoroughly approved and from whom he did not at this stage fear future competition.[3] The remaining members of the Cabinet were peers whose claims to any real authority he did not take too seriously. In his own eyes he was the leading member of the new Cabinet and he certainly held one of its most important and most absorbing offices. For the present this was good

[1] G.C. & T., p. 121.   [2] Ibid., p. 122.

[3] The only known difference between them was over the Catholic Question. Perceval was a firm 'Protestant' and had earned a reputation for soundness during the anti-Catholic agitation of 1806–7. On the other hand Canning, although still a believer in Catholic Emancipation, considered himself bound by Pitt's promise to George III and therefore precluded from any sponsorship of Catholic claims.

enough. As for the future, struggles might lie ahead, but at least he seemed to be in an excellent tactical position to meet them with success.

It was therefore with feelings of unclouded satisfaction that Canning flung himself into the exacting but highly delightful duties of his new office. For a while all was well, but his supreme confidence in his own abilities gradually made him critical of the shortcomings, real and imagined, of his colleagues. Intent upon the successful prosecution of the struggle against Napoleon, Canning viewed with growing disquiet Castlereagh's administration of the War Office. He deplored the lack of unified control in the direction of the war. Real leadership, with Portland only a Premier in name, was in abeyance. But nevertheless, to Portland Canning felt constrained to appeal. After the dubious results of Moore's campaign in Spain, which Canning defended in the House, he had convinced himself that it must become his business to obtain Castlereagh's transfer. Accordingly on 24th March 1809 Canning wrote to Portland tendering his resignation on the ground that he could no longer work with Castlereagh.[1] Portland consulted the King and it was agreed that Castlereagh should be transferred to some other office. In return for this promise Canning withdrew his resignation and also agreed that, in the light of the international situation, the transfer should be temporarily postponed. He, however, was led to believe that the arrangement would be communicated in the meanwhile to Castlereagh. This, in fact, unknown to Canning, was not done. Desultory efforts were, however, made by Portland to cope with the unfortunate problem and on 18th July 1809 Earl Bathurst wrote to him offering his own office as an alternative place for Castlereagh and 'as the means of making an arrangement which might induce Mr. Canning to continue in his Majesty's service or of strengthening his Majesty's government if his resignation could not be prevented'.[2] But Portland continued to delay; the Walcheren expedition was in preparation and the moment

---

[1] A copy was enclosed in a letter from Canning to Bagot of 25th March 1809. BAG, vol. 1, p. 295.

[2] BATH, p. 98.

seemed most inopportune for a change at the War Office. After the disastrous failure of that adventure, Canning once again brought renewed pressure to bear on Portland. At a meeting on 6th September Canning was horrified to learn, not only that Portland himself proposed ro resign on grounds of ill-health, but also that Castlereagh was still completely in the dark about the proposed transfer. Canning decided on the dramatic gesture; he tendered his own resignation on 7th September.

By this means he aspired to solve the two problems which now confronted him: the Castlereagh question and the Portland succession. He had hoped for more time to deal with the second (and bargaining with Perceval had been in progress) but in the circumstances he felt that both must be met at once. He started from the somewhat dubious premise that no Ministry could be constituted without his co-operation. On the basis of this assumption he calculated, either that he would be invited to form a new Ministry himself or that if Perceval accepted to move to the Lords, he would secure the lead in the Commons with Perceval or some other figurehead as Premier. In either event he would be in a position to insist on Castlereagh's removal from the War Office.

Canning's appreciation was mistaken on two main scores: he had not reckoned on the violence of Castlereagh's reactions and he had underestimated Perceval's strength.

As soon as Castlereagh discovered the ostensible reason for Canning's resignation, he resigned himself and challenged Canning to a duel. They fought on the 21st September 1809 on Putney Heath and Canning suffered a slight wound in the thigh. To most observers Castlereagh seemed the aggrieved party and sympathy was generally on his side. Canning's reputation was prejudiced at a moment when he had staked much upon it.

Even before the duel was fought, however, the odds had already turned against Canning. While proclaiming, as a tactical move, that Perceval was the obvious choice for Premier, Canning made clear his own unwillingness to serve under such leadership; he believed that Perceval would not have the strength to meet the challenge and that his own pretensions must triumph. Arbuthnot summed up the dilemma when he wrote to Huskisson on 12th September: 'The holding together of the present Administration seems impossible, for Canning, as you know, has pretensions which his colleagues will not agree to, and without him the business of Parliament could not be carried on.'[1] Even Arbuthnot, however, had underestimated Perceval. The latter, though disappointed, was not dismayed by Canning's attitude. His own opinions on the Catholic Question made him acceptable both to the King and to the majority of the existing Cabinet; he had not made so many enemies as Canning nor had he acquired such a reputation for intrigue; during the Government crisis his own position improved as that of Canning deteriorated.[2]

The King was besieged by advice from various quarters, including a Cabinet suggestion that he should have recourse to Grenville and Grey with Canning as Premier; but Grenville and Grey were reluctant to enter a Ministry knowing that they did not possess royal confidence and, to his relief, the King was faced with no real alternative but the existing Ministry. Consultations and manoeuvres continued but, in their later stages, Canning was somewhat incapacitated by his wound and was a victim of the unfavourable publicity which the duel had aroused. Perceval was invited to succeed Portland and, in spite of Canning's continued refusal to serve under him, he accepted the difficult task. Canning's gamble had failed; the Government, which he believed doomed by his withdrawal, managed to survive.

He was not unduly despondent. He convinced himself that he had had a struggle to get out of office and he wrote to Wilbraham: 'It used to be difficult to be in at all times, but I never knew that getting out again was a matter of so much difficulty before.'[3] He felt that Perceval's success was bound to be short-lived and his own triumphant return inevitable. He took comfort from the King's friendly interest in his wound and rejoiced that he had

[1] HUSK, p. 62.

[2] For further information about the crisis, its antecedents and consequences, which was not available to me at time of writing, see Denis Gray: *Spencer Perceval* (1963).

[3] 19th December 1804. BAG, vol. 1, p. 344.

'every reason to be satisfied with the unvarying kindness of the King'.[1] He did not anticipate any obstacles in that direction to his future prospects.

Colour to the confidence which Canning manifested was afforded by the trials and troubles of Perceval's Government. Lord Wellesley, who had succeeded Canning at the Foreign Office, was not an easy colleague. Governor-General of India from 1797 to 1805, he had returned embittered by the attacks which were the reward of all great Indian administrators, accustomed to command, capricious, restlessly ambitious and very conscious of his own undoubted talents. Similar in temperament to Canning they soon became, as they were to remain in spite of occasional misunderstandings, firm friends and political allies. Now, impatient with what he regarded as the feeble war effort, Wellesley constantly pressed for a strengthening of the Administration and, above all, for the inclusion of Canning; others to be approached were Sidmouth and Castlereagh. Negotiations proceeded slowly and on 10th April Canning confided to Bagot that, in his opinion, 'every effort of W[ellesley] unaccompanied by a tender of his resignation will be baffled and despised — baffled by P[erceval] and despised by the K[ing]'.[2] Wellesley was not yet prepared to threaten his own resignation but he did in June offer to surrender his office to Canning; the offer was acceptable to Canning provided that Wellesley himself remained in the Cabinet and that arrangements were made to suit various other supporters. Although Canning now seemed disposed to serve under Perceval, he hedged this willingness with so many reservations and stipulations that the negotiations eventually broke down. One of Canning's objections was that Wellesley had seemed to consent 'that the question of any proposition to me should depend for its

---

[1] 19th December 1809. To Wilbraham. BAG, vol. 1, p. 347.

On 13th October 1809 he had written to Huskisson: 'Perhaps it may not be uninteresting to you to learn how the King and I parted on Wednesday. Nothing could be kinder than his manner to me. Instead of avoiding (as I imagined he would) the subject of the duel altogether, ... he began immediately to enter into all the particulars of that event, the situation of the wound (which he made me point out to him on his own royal thigh).' HUSK, p. 69.

[2] BAG, vol. 1, p. 351.

G

decisions on an answer of Lord Castlereagh'.[1] These requirements, which Canning relayed in detail to his own friends,
suggest his real lack of enthusiasm for the whole project. To be
wanted was flattering and reassuring, but the more convinced of
his own indispensability he was, the less attractive became the
project of a negotiated settlement. Accordingly on 25th September
1810, in a letter to Perceval, Canning effectively closed the door
to any further bargaining by demanding unequivocal terms
which he knew Perceval was in no position to offer.[2]

It is difficult to resist the impression that Canning's conduct
was determined by a belief that the days of the present Government were in any case numbered and that his own ambition
would not be served by propping up a crumbling edifice. The
King's mind was again beginning to fail and by November he
had suffered a final relapse. The Government thus lost its chief
prop and a revolution in palace politics was confidently forecast.

In the New Year, when the Regency Bill with its temporary
restrictions on the powers of the Prince Regent was under discussion, Canning voted on 5th January with the Opposition
and succeeded, with his supporters, in putting the Government
in a minority: He boasted: 'I could have changed the majority
of 13 against the Ministers into one of 9 for them — with my own
forces only — and with those who went with me into a majority
of 20 *at the least*.'[3] After this display of independence, however,
he generally supported the Ministry and the main provisions of
their Bill were eventually carried. The Prince Regent made
tentative approaches to Grenville and Grey but their attitude was
so unsatisfactory that he was not encouraged to attempt any
decisive action. Wellesley remained dissatisfied with the conduct
of the war and with the Cabinet in which he served. He was in
high favour with the Prince Regent and there was frequent talk
of major changes. Canning's letters to Bagot suggest that he,
like so many others, was finding it particularly hard to gauge the
political barometer. At times he felt certain that the Prince

[1] Canning to Wellesley. 23rd September 1810. BAG, vol. 1, p. 358.
[2] See S. Walpole's *Life of Perceval*, vol. 2, p. 153.
[3] To Bagot. 5th January 1811. BAG, vol. 1, p. 366.

Regent would simply allow matters to drift; at others that Wellesley would, with the Prince's backing, become the architect of general Ministerial reconstruction. He was gratified to learn that the Prince Regent 'professes himself to be, and professing it I suppose *is*, very favourably disposed towards me'.[1] On 16th September he wrote to Bagot of intelligence that the Prince Regent had directed Wellesley 'to submit to him the plans of an administration of which he and I were to form the basis — that such a plan was submitted — and *not* approved'.[2] On 18th September he wrote warning Huskisson not to make any disparaging remarks about Wellesley because they might reach the Prince Regent's ears and Wellesley was speaking well of him to the Prince.[3]

With the restrictions on the Regent's powers due to be removed in February 1812, 1811 ended in an atmosphere of general uncertainty.

No drastic change followed this event, although the Regent did once more unsuccessfully endeavour to persuade the Whig lords to join a coalition Government. On the failure of these negotiations Wellesley, who had remained in office since January only at the Regent's special behest, definitively resigned. Opposition to the Ministry's inflexibility on the Catholic Question and to their general conduct of the war, which he had only suffered believing changes to be imminent, were his grounds for this gesture. Yet the Regent did not dismiss his Ministers and Perceval's Government struggled on. As a desperate hope Liverpool was commissioned to make a direct offer of Cabinet office to Canning. This he rejected in a friendly letter to Liverpool on the sole ground of his differing with the views of the Cabinet on the Catholic Question. Now that restrictions had been removed from the powers of the Regent, Canning regarded himself as at last absolved from the promise which Pitt had made to George III; he planned, therefore, to take an active part in the campaign, which Grattan was promoting, for Catholic Emancipation. The members of Perceval's Cabinet, whatever their personal views,

[1] Canning to Bagot. 29th August 1811. BAG, vol. 1, p. 373.
[2] Ibid., p. 376.   [3] HUSK, p. 75.

were still pledged among themselves to oppose any immediate consideration of Catholic disabilities. In the light of Wellesley's resignation it would not in any case have been easy for Canning, on this occasion, to accept the invitation without, as he pointed out, loss of public character. Castlereagh, however, though sharing Canning's opinions on the Catholic Question, was not so obviously committed in the matter nor in any such close relation to Wellesley; and he, together with Sidmouth, now entered the apparently tottering Administration.

With Perceval's murder on 11th May 1812 its fate seemed finally sealed. During the political crisis which followed Canning was faced with what proved to be the great moment of decision in his life and, in the light of what followed, he made his gravest miscalculation. But even though its effects were magnified by pure chance, that miscalculation was initially caused by his own over-confidence and self-centredness.

After Perceval's death attempts were made to reconstitute the existing Ministry with the inclusion of Wellesley and Canning. Both refused the overture, Wellesley on the conduct of the war question and Canning on the Catholic Question. After this failure a private member in the House moved an address on 21st May 1812 to the Regent begging him to form a strong and efficient Administration. The Regent then summoned Wellesley and entrusted him with the formation of a comprehensive Ministry. Wellesley immediately consulted Canning and it was agreed that Wellesley should approach the Whigs and Canning the Tories. In a letter to Wellesley Canning confirmed that the principles of the Administration were to be: 'First, that the whole question relating to the Roman Catholics shall be taken into early and serious consideration, with a sincere and anxious desire to bring it to a final and satisfactory settlement. Secondly, that the war in the Peninsula shall be prosecuted with the best means of the Country.'[1] Canning then expressed himself ready to co-operate with any persons who accepted Wellesley's proposals and agreed to set aside minor points of difference. He added: 'On the other hand should any personal objection be taken to acting with me (as

[1] HUSK, p. 77.

I know has been done on former occasions) I earnestly beg and insist, that no pretensions of mine may be suffered to stand in the way of an arrangement, otherwise agreeable to H.R.H. the Prince Regent, and calculated to afford the Country the advantage of an efficient and comprehensive Administration.'[1] The Whig lords, motivated by pride and prejudice, refused to serve under Wellesley on any terms; the leading members of the late Ministry, apart from other objections, could hardly be expected to join an Administration pledged to Catholic Emancipation. If the Prince Regent had commissioned Canning and not Wellesley to form a Ministry, and if the Catholic Question had been allowed to remain an open one, there is some ground for believing that the leading Tories might have been prepared to serve; in the circumstances they certainly were not. The Prince Regent, however, having chosen one unsuccessful nominee, was not disposed to take any further initiative. Accordingly he next turned to the members of the late Cabinet with a request that they should decide who ought to be invited to form a Ministry. Their choice fell upon Liverpool and operations were resumed where they had been left off after Perceval's death. Again Liverpool sought out Canning. Their youthful friendship had suffered many strains, but, though Canning tended to minimise Liverpool's abilities, Liverpool preserved the greatest respect for Canning's talents. Furthermore, Liverpool was endowed with sound and practical common sense. At such a crucial moment in England's destiny he did not wish her to be deprived of the best services available; nor did he wish to face a difficult House of Commons without the guaranteed support of Canning's blistering eloquence. Therefore he exerted himself and was able, thanks to Castlereagh's cooperation, to make what Canning described as 'the handsomest offer that was ever made to an individual'.[2] Castlereagh would vacate the Foreign Office in Canning's favour; Lord Wellesley would obtain the Irish Secretaryship; the Catholic Question would remain an open one; suitable places would be found for

---

[1] HUSK, p. 78.

[2] According to Stapleton these were Canning's own words to him. G.C. & T., p. 208.

Canning's supporters. There was only one fly in the ointment. The lead in the House of Commons was to remain with Castlereagh. Canning managed to convince himself that, while not requiring the lead for himself, he could not serve under Castlereagh. 'I do assure you . . .' he wrote on 18th July 1812 to Arbuthnot, '. . . that I am desirous of coming into the Regent's service, and that I should consider a re-union with Liverpool in office as an object the most desirable, publicly and privately. But the price to be paid on coming in would cost me a bitter pang — *not* from any personal feeling towards Castlereagh upon my honour, but from a sense of humiliation — hard to endure, and I think unnecessary to be proposed to me. I have not demanded the lead for myself. It is not my fault that such a thing as lead has been known or named in these discussions. I should be contented if it could be put in abeyance between C. and me — as it would be if continuing nominally with the Chancr. of the Ex. in a third hand — even in Van's. Why not? He can live in the House — write the letters — give the dinner, and read the speech — and C. and I could assist him in the House — doing the business of our respective Departments. As to the Department — I need not tell you that my offer to take the Chancr. of the Ex. was really what it purposed to be, an attempt to solve the difficulty. I need not tell you that the Foreign Office is the only one for which in point of taste and liking I have a decided preference — that as to office therefore I am perfectly contented. Could C. be prevailed upon to take the Home Department? . . . P.S. I must press Pole for Cabinet. . . .'[1] On the following day Canning wrote in a similar strain to Liverpool, adding: 'I am ready to act cordially with him (Castlereagh) on a footing of equality in the House of Commons, but it is the feeling not only of my friends, but of every man whom I have consulted, that neither my public character and reputation (the one means through which any man can be useful in high office) nor the interests of the Prince Regent's service well understood, will allow of my consenting to enter into the Government on the condition of acting under Lord Castlereagh in the House of Commons.'[2] Canning laid

[1] A., no. 5, p. 7. [2] HUSK, p. 82.

particular stress on the attitude of his friends, and their vehemence in his own cause was perhaps not without influence, but the impression remains that he held out on a quibble. Was the concern for his public character and reputation genuine? If so, it was, in this case, almost pathological. Did he not in his heart of hearts believe, as he had believed with Perceval, that Liverpool's Government would not last and that he would, eventually and by general acclamation, be called upon as the saviour of his country on his own terms? The suspicion lingers. A year later he showed, in a letter to Granville, how bitterly he had come to regret his decision. 'I am afraid,' he wrote, 'no possible combination of circumstance can place me again where I stood in July last year; and it is of no use to reflect where I might have been now had the tide of that time been taken at the flood.'[1]

In the event Liverpool for a while refused to regard Canning's conditions as final. And as late as 28th July 1812, when Liverpool did write a note to Arbuthnot telling him 'that all was over with Canning',[2] Arbuthnot frantically appealed to Huskisson: 'Do for God's sake come up the very instant you get my letter and knock me up at any hour of the night.'[3] Huskisson obeyed the summons, only to receive this reproof on 1st August from Canning: 'I had not the slightest expectation of your return to town, nor can I comprehend why Arbuthnot should have taken upon himself to send for you.'[4] Canning then went over the events of the past weeks and concluded that all was quite settled as far as not joining the Administration was concerned. Ten years were to pass before a similar opportunity again occurred.

Excluded from office by his own deliberate choice, Canning now remained in the House of Commons as an independent supporter of the Government and as leader of a small group (varying between 14 and 20) of personal adherents. He had little cause to differ, on matters of policy, with the Government and there was small scope for action. He did, however, succeed in

[1] Canning to Granville. *The Private Correspondence of Granville Leveson Gower, 1781–1821*, vol. 2, p. 470.

[2] Quoted by Arbuthnot in a letter to Huskisson. HUSK, p. 82.

[3] Ibid., p. 82.

[4] Ibid., p. 83.

capturing the limelight by his open sponsorship of Catholic claims and by carrying a motion in their favour by 253 votes to 106. The question had been declared an open one among Government supporters, but the Regent was now known to be veering towards his father's convictions; Canning, therefore, seemed on this occasion to be emphasising obstacles to his own ambition for the sake of a cause in which he believed.

In September 1812, at Liverpool's request, Parliament was dissolved. According to one of Canning's supporters, Liverpool thereby hoped to weaken Canning's position. Whether such a motive existed or not, the result was certainly achieved. The large majority which the Government now secured made the votes of the Canningites of little practical consequence. Though the Government might continue to fear Canning's eloquence and even to miss the support of his talents, their own grasp of power was henceforth secure.

At the dissolution Canning was for the second time, and chiefly on Mr. John Gladstone's initiative, invited to stand for the 'popular' constituency of Liverpool. Gladstone, father of the future Prime Minister, was a leading merchant of the 'Port of the Industrial Revolution'. Liverpool's expansion had been rapid. In 1770 no more than six thousand bales of cotton entered the Mersey, but by 1800 imports had reached a quarter of a million. Even more lucrative, though more transient, had proved the Slave Trade in which Liverpool successfully undercut London. According to Fay's calculations, 303,000 slaves were conveyed between 1783 and 1793 in Liverpool ships;[1] these same ships carried textiles and provisions to the Guinea Coast and to the West Indies; they then returned with cargoes of sugar, cotton and tobacco. Some of the leading ship-owners, such as Gladstone, also acquired sugar plantations in the West Indies. These new capitalists, resigned since 1806, but in some cases still resentful about the abolition of the Slave Trade, now had interests in slavery, in the freedom of the seas and in free trade. In political allegiance the powerful corporation was predominantly Tory, but Whigs were well represented on other important associations

[1] See C. R. Fay: *Great Britain from Adam Smith to the Present Day*, p. 156.

such as the American Chamber of Commerce, the West India
Association and the Shipowners Association.[1] Interest frequently
clashed with political affiliation, while civic pride often trans-
cended political division. Disapproval of the Orders-in-Council,
which Canning had initiated in 1807 as Foreign Secretary, was
almost universal; the ensuing disputes with America and the
adverse effects on the cotton trade touched all Liverpool merchants too closely for any significant divisions. On the question of
slavery there was less unanimity. Not all merchants were planta-
tion owners and principles were not always a prohibitive luxury.
While agreeing and disagreeing on a variety of national issues the
merchants of Liverpool, whether Whig or Tory, were allied in
civic pride; they wished to be represented in Parliament by a
politician of outstanding distinction.

It was natural that the Whigs should have turned to Brougham.[2]
His successful opposition to the Orders-in-Council had made
him a Liverpool hero. Even though news of their repeal, which
his eloquence and persistence seemed to have forced on the
Government, did not reach America in time to prevent a declaration of war, Brougham's prestige was at its height. As a leading
opponent of the Slave Trade and of slavery he was not equally
popular with all Whig merchants and he was regarded with varying degrees of disfavour by the Tories. Their choice, almost
inevitably, turned to the other, and more established, great orator
of the moment — Canning. True he had initiated and throughout supported modifications and reassertions of the Orders-in-
Council; true, also, he had supported abolition of the Slave
Trade; but at least he had shown no signs of raising awkward
questions about the status of existing slaves and, above all, he
was the leading Tory orator and the most distinguished member
of the party outside the Government ranks.

At first Canning was reluctant to respond to Gladstone's
overtures. 'I have been,' he confided to Huskisson, 'fighting off

---

[1] These Associations eventually combined to form the Liverpool Chamber of
Commerce. See C. R. Fay: *Huskisson and His Age*, p. 355.
[2] See C. W. New: *The Life of Henry Brougham to 1830*, chapter VI, for an
excellent account of Brougham and the Liverpool Election.

Liverpool, to which I have many objections (being secure of an unmolested seat elsewhere), and have distinctly stated that I will incur no expense whatever.'[1] Pressure was, however, maintained and adequate funds were, without much difficulty, guaranteed. Canning consented to stand.

There were two other Tory candidates and the Whigs put up Creevey as well as Brougham to contest the two seats. At one moment it seemed as if the moneyed men of Liverpool would have agreed among themselves to settle for Canning and Brougham, but Brougham, probably out of deference to Grey's uncompromising disapproval of Canning, rejected the bargain. Liverpool was thus privileged to enjoy a public clash between the two foremost orators of the day. The electorate consisted of some three thousand Freemen of the Borough, out of a total population of about a hundred thousand. Most of them were working men and their votes were obviously open to influence and pressure. The real struggle was between the great merchants of the town and ranged far above the heads of most of the voters. Because of the reputation and personality of the two principal figures, the election took on the character of rival publicity stunts. Polling lasted for eight days. Brougham made a hundred and sixty speeches;[2] Canning did not lag far behind. In the evenings both candidates visited the Clubs, were lavishly entertained by their supporters and again exercised their wit and eloquence. Stratford Canning, who was supporting his cousin, commented on the bitter speeches which were exchanged on the hustings, and on the violence of the mob in the streets.[3] On the other hand it was noted with surprise that Canning and Brougham scrupulously avoided personalities. Furthermore, although in clashes between rival mobs two men were killed and a few injured, this, by Liverpool standards, was regarded as a relatively peaceful contest.[4] At one stage during the proceedings the Tories reverted to

---

[1] Canning to Huskisson. 28th September 1812. HUSK, p. 87.
[2] See C. W. New: *The Life of Henry Brougham to 1830*, p. 74.
[3] Stratford Canning's account of the election is quoted in his biography by S. Lane Poole, vol. 1, pp. 185–6.
[4] See C. W. New: *The Life of Henry Brougham to 1830*, p. 75.

the proposal that each side should be satisfied with one seat and agree to the return of Brougham and Canning. 'We are fighting it out,'[1] was Brougham's reply. The Tories then rallied their forces and in the final count Canning and General Gascoyne emerged at the head of the poll. According to Brougham, money had proved the decisive factor. As he wrote on 17th October 1812 in his memoirs: 'We ran them amazingly hard. On Sunday last they would have compromised; on Monday they thought themselves quite beaten; but on Wednesday things looked up, though Gascoyne only passed me yesterday at one o'clock. The fact is they all renewed their subscriptions, and said if £50,000 were required they were resolved to do it. They gave twenty and thirty guineas a vote. Our friends have not spent £8000.'[2] Brougham believed that it was his opposition to slavery which has been mainly responsible for this Tory financial rally. But his rejection of the proposed Tory compromise, and the anxiety of John Gladstone and his supporters to prove who, if seriously challenged, controlled the politics of Liverpool, seem more likely to have determined any extra deployment of energy and funds.

From the contest Canning and Brougham emerged with increased mutual respect. Superficially they had much in common; both inspired awe rather than confidence among members of their own parties; both could claim, although in Canning's case the obstacles had been slight and were mainly to be recalled in 1827, to have risen from the ranks; but in making comparisons, it must be pointed out that Brougham was always passionate in the promotion of public causes, whereas Canning, equally vehement in debate and in print, was more concerned with the execution than the principles of policy, which he generally took for granted. Undoubtedly, however, they shared a similar flair for publicity. Brougham had noted Canning's capacity for capturing public imagination and Canning now learned from Brougham some-

[1] Brougham to Grey. 13th October 1812. *Memoirs*, vol. 2, p. 60, quoted C. W. New: *The Life of Henry Brougham to 1830*, p. 76.

[2] Brougham to Grey. 17th October 1812. *Memoirs*, vol. 2, p. 61, quoted C. W. New: *The Life of Henry Brougham to 1830*, p. 77.

thing of the value of extra-Parliamentary speech-making; here-after he was to make increasing use of this medium.

His experience at Liverpool also convinced Canning of the importance of direct contact with the new class of rising cap-italists. As a result of this contact he became more alive to com-mercial interests. Although he never fell under the sway of a Liverpool pressure group, his appreciation of the material interests involved in foreign policy was enlightened and broadened. The election and its consequences were of major significance in Canning's future career.

From the excitement of Liverpool Canning returned to West-minster, where the Government was more securely in the saddle and smugly profiting from Peninsular victories against the French. There was little scope for Canning's eloquence and his most memorable speech was congratulatory in support of the vote of thanks to Wellington for his victory at Vittoria. In the circumstances Canning began to fret about the political future of his own supporters and during the summer of 1813 he formally disbanded his small group so that individuals might be free to accept office if offered. Huskisson and Sturges Bourne shortly afterwards availed themselves of the opportunity. Before the end of the year Liverpool indicated to Canning that the first Cabinet office which happened to fall vacant would be offered to him.

While rejoicing in the success of the war Canning could but ruefully regard the shift of his own fortunes. Liverpool was strong enough to be magnanimous. Not even Canning could any longer delude himself that his presence in the Cabinet was in-dispensable. He was, however, prevented from brooding unduly over his own political fate by the ill health of his eldest son. This worry for a while obliterated other considerations and in the autumn of 1814 he was planning to settle his family in Portugal for the winter. At the same time the Government had received information that the Regent of Portugal[1] was preparing to return home from Brazil. It was proposed that Canning should be

---

[1] The Regent, who became King John VI on the death of his mother Maria I in 1816, had retired to Brazil in 1807 at Canning's instigation. See p. 196 below.

nominated as ambassador to Lisbon in order to welcome him on his return. The plan seems to have originated from Liverpool's genuine desire to be of help to Canning. After some hesitation he allowed himself to be persuaded that public duty could thus be combined with attention to family problems. Canning remained abroad until May 1816 and was, therefore, absent from Parliament during the whole period of the resettlement of Europe. When, early in 1816, the Prince Regent had still failed to return to Portugal,[1] questions were asked by the Opposition about Canning's appointment. On his reappearance in the House he answered the charge that it had been a 'job' in a masterly speech which satisfied his critics. But he himself, in retrospect, regarded his acceptance of the Embassy as a mistake and nine years later confided to his secretary: 'I consider my having accepted the Lisbon Embassy as a great political mistake; in all probability I should have had the most influential post in the Government in the House of Commons long before, had I not fallen into that error. I laboured hard to avoid accepting the appointment, but it was so urged upon me by the King's Government, that I thought I had not the moral right, as a public man, to refuse it. If, therefore, the thing were now, with past experience, to be done over again, I should act the same part, and conscious of right, I must brave the consequences.'[2] This judgement seems to have been something of an over-dramatisation. Canning had previously resisted many calls to duty because he had feared they might damage future prospects. At the time when the Embassy was proposed his prospects were far from bright and he himself was chiefly concerned with the health of his son. No opportunities in fact arose, or seemed likely to arise, during his absence. The first vacancy in the Cabinet came in February 1816 with the death of the Earl of Buckinghamshire, President of the Board of Control, and that vacancy, as Liverpool had previously promised, was immediately offered to Canning. It is therefore difficult to see in what way the Lisbon Embassy, as far as Canning's career was concerned, had proved itself a mistake. On the contrary, in some way his absence helped to dissipate prejudice against him, while

---

[1] He did not in fact return until 1821.   [2] G.C. & T., p. 210.

at the same time he himself gained valuable experience of the
Continent both in Portugal and in France.

That prejudice against Canning was still alive is well in-
stanced by the exchange of correspondence between Liverpool
and the Prince Regent which preceded his Cabinet appointment.
On 8th February 1816 Liverpool wrote: 'Lord Liverpool has
no means of judging whether Canning will accept it [the Board
of Control] or not but if the offer is made to him and he should
determine to decline it he will have no ground of complaint
against the Government and his friends will have no cause to be
dissatisfied.'[1] On the following day the Prince Regent replied:
'. . . I can make no objection to your proposal respecting Mr.
Canning, but in reference to your letter, wherein you state that
you have only made a partial communication of that intention to
your colleagues; I must therefore both hope and trust that you
are satisfied that his introduction to the Cabinet, however personally desirable, will not be productive of disunion, or any want
of harmony in a Government, with which I am so perfectly contented and with which I and the Country have so much reason to
be well satisfied.'[2]

On 13th February 1816 Liverpool wrote, with the full approbation of the Prince Regent and the concurrence of all his colleagues, offering the vacant office and on 8th March Canning
replied with his acceptance from Torres Vedras. Thus he entered
Liverpool's Cabinet, almost unobtrusively, with Castlereagh as
Foreign Secretary and Leader of the House, Sidmouth[3] at the
Home Office, Lord Eldon as Chancellor and no one of his own
followers in any important office. Though the situation might be
humiliating to his pride, it did provide a chance, possibly a last

[1] ASP, vol. 2, no. 633, p. 147.   [2] Ibid., no. 635, p. 148.
[3] For details of the reconciliation between Sidmouth and Canning which took
place in 1812 see Canning to Granville. 18th August 1812. *The Private Correspondence of Granville Leveson Gower, 1781–1821*, vol. 2, pp. 445–6.
Sidmouth apparently took advantage of a casual meeting to hold out his
hands to Canning and to express regret for the 'unpleasant personal relation'
which had so long prevailed between them. 'I need not tell you,' wrote Canning,
'that I took both the poor Doctor's hands and shook and squeezed them with
perfect cordiality. He really moved me; considering too, that it may be *at least*
a question whether he be not the party that has a right to complain.'

chance, of returning to active political service. Canning's ambition had not changed but he does seem on this occasion to have
realised that he could no longer afford to despise limited objectives and that any hesitation on his part would have quickly
ensured the withdrawal even of the modest offer which had been
made. The law of supply and demand was operating in his disfavour and experience had at length given him wisdom to judge
and act accordingly.

When Canning joined the Ministry its popularity was already
beginning to wane; sympathising with its difficulties and convinced of the necessity for repressive firmness, he proved a useful
and loyal colleague. With Castlereagh, and even with Sidmouth,
he managed to work in comfortable accord. The business of his
own office he conducted with quiet efficiency and even with tact.[1]
Though, as was later revealed, he never gained the full confidence
of Lord Hastings, the Governor-General, satisfactory relations
were superficially and practically maintained. In the Cabinet his
experience, and in the House his eloquence, were at the disposal
of the Government on a variety of matters outside his immediate
departmental sphere. He seemed to have become so tame that,
apart from flashes of the old fire, it was almost possible to forget
that he had ever been suspect as a man of genius. That he fretted
somewhat in his new role is undoubted, but on the whole he successfully concealed both mortification and impatience.

On 29th January 1820 George III died and, with the Prince
Regent's accession to the throne as George IV, the reactions of his
troublesome and estranged wife, Queen Caroline, soon developed
into a major political problem. She had, since 1814, been living
abroad, and on her return to London in June 1820 the Cabinet
eventually agreed to the King's demand for private vengeance by
Act of Parliament. Canning considered that this faced him with a
crisis of conscience. He had been one of the Queen's intimate
circle of friends in his own youth; gossip, now almost universally

[1] See C. H. Philips: *The East India Company 1784-1834*. In his chapter on
'Canning's East Indian Policy' he describes Canning as 'uniformly courteous'
to the Directors (p. 211), and quotes substantial evidence in support of this
opinion.

forgotten, had credited him with being her lover. Though this charge appears to have been unfounded, they had consistently remained on friendly terms and Caroline was godmother to Canning's eldest son.[1] Furthermore, in 1814 Canning was among those who counselled her departure from England and his influence was believed to have proved decisive. No matter what her faults, and Canning certainly was not blind to them, he felt, or professed to feel, himself in a particularly delicate position where any measures against her were concerned. As soon as the Cabinet's decision regarding the Queen was taken Canning requested an audience of the King and submitted his resignation, arguing that in the circumstances he could not render unreserved service but that, if ever a mediator were required, he might once again be useful. The interview was a friendly one[2] and George IV insisted that Canning should withdraw his resignation, absolving him of the duty of taking any part in Ministerial proceedings against the Queen. Canning accepted the situation. Liverpool, possibly suspecting that what Canning really needed was promotion, then offered him the Home Office in succession to the ageing Sidmouth. On 30th July 1820 Canning rejected the offer in a letter to Liverpool on the ground that 'Lord Sidmouth's office is just the one upon the daily details of which this unhappy question must operate with the most sensible and constant effect . . .'.[3]

Early in August 1820 Canning left England and was abroad during the long stormy sessions when the Bill of Pains and Penalties was under debate. In the middle of November Liverpool, despairing of success in the Commons, dropped the measure. The Queen, however, refused to be satisfied with this success and continued to press various claims. It seemed as if the quarrel would drag on indefinitely and Canning, returning to England in December again, and on the same grounds, submitted his resignation to the King. This time it was accepted. Canning's attitude,

---

[1] See pp. 34, 35 above.
[2] According to the version which Canning seems to have confided to Frere, the King did refer to former allegations about Canning and the Queen, but in a spirit of dismissal and understanding. See note, p. 35 above.
[3] G.C. & T., p. 295.

with which George IV had appeared to sympathise in the previous June, now provoked a violent reaction. Enraged by the
turn of events, the King interpreted Canning's resignation as a
hostile move and one which seemed to confirm suspicions of bad
faith already aroused when some of Canning's friends in the Lords
had voted against the Government; admittedly Canning had then
hurriedly disclaimed responsibility and made professions of regret; but doubts in the King's mind had lingered and these now
helped to colour his judgement. Furthermore, old gossip regarding
Canning's former relations with Queen Caroline was eventually
revived; royal memories of personal grievance, however ludi-
crous, were stirred.

What of Canning's motives? Was he merely manoeuvring for
a more important Cabinet office? His rejection of the Home Office
in July does not support the suggestion. Nor does the consistency
of his own reasons for resigning. Even if the King might have been
expected to be understanding in July, it was obvious that his feelings would be very different in December. The threat of resignation in these circumstances could hardly have been a mere
manoeuvre. The intention must have been sincere. Were there,
as has sometimes been alleged, differences within the Cabinet over
issues of foreign policy? If so Canning can scarcely have regarded them as of vital significance because, during the following
summer, he seemed perfectly disposed to rejoin the Ministry,
while Liverpool was patently anxious that he should return. As
far as foreign affairs were concerned Canning, on the contrary,
had good reason to be satisfied with current policy developments.
His precise contribution to the State Paper of 5th May 1820 must
be a matter for speculation, but there is no doubt that he fully endorsed the views therein expressed. In so far as new trends were
observable, these were entirely in line with Canning's assessment
of the situation. It is therefore reasonable to suppose that, far
from wishing to leave the Cabinet over issues of foreign affairs,
Canning would have been inclined to remain in order to give
further backing to policies of which he approved. Was Canning,
as he maintained, then genuinely, if hyper-sensitively, embarrassed
by his personal predicament? Possibly so. But it can also perhaps

H

be suggested that lassitude, as well as scruples of conscience, played a part in his final decision. Canning had been seriously depressed by the death of his eldest son in April; preoccupation with his own career was no longer an obsession; a rest from responsibility would not be unwelcome; in that sense perhaps the professed cause of his going may have been something of an excuse. At any rate, after his resignation he quickly retired to Paris and gave the impression in his letters of being much relieved to have escaped from the imbroglio of public affairs.

Though escape may have suited Canning, his loss was not acceptable to the Prime Minister. Ways and means of securing Canning's return were soon under discussion. On 17th March 1821 Mrs. Arbuthnot recorded that her husband 'had had a good deal of conversation with Lord Castlereagh upon the subject of the changes to be made in the Government in order to bring in Mr. Peel and Mr. Canning'.[1] During the following months Liverpool persisted in his design in spite of violent opposition to Canning from the King. In mid-June Lord Liverpool 'intimated to his colleagues that, if the King persists in his determination not to have Mr. Canning into the Cabinet, he will himself resign'.[2] This often repeated threat merited rather more serious consideration than usual because Liverpool's wife, of whom he had been most fond, had died on 12th June 1821 and the Prime Minister was in particularly low health and spirits. On 18th June Mrs. Arbuthnot found 'Londonderry[3] quite tired of all discussion about Mr. Canning and changes in the Cabinet'.[4] Canning himself had remained a more or less passive spectator of these manoeuvres, but on 21st June he appealed to Liverpool: 'I entreat you not to press me upon the King . . . I am not surprised at the King's objection, nor do I think it unreasonable if it arises from the only cause to which I can attribute it.'[5] On 23rd June Canning again wrote to Liver-

---

[1] Mrs. A., vol. 1, p. 82.

[2] 17th June. Ibid., vol. 1, p. 102.

[3] Castlereagh, on the death of his father in April, had become 2nd Marquess of Londonderry.

[4] Mrs. A., vol. 1, p. 102.

[5] C.G.C., vol. 1, p. 24.

pool stressing other difficulties, 'such as the way in which Huskisson is to be passed over', in the way of returning to office. 'I need not ask you,' he continued, 'whether it be possible that I should come into the Government at one door, while Huskisson was going out at the other. Is it not better that I should be out, through the King's objection on my own account, than through dissatisfaction at your arrangement on Huskisson's? and would not the withdrawal of my name from the arrangement enable you, by some new casting of it, to do justice to Huskisson at the same time you would gratify the King?'[1] But Liverpool was, in this respect, most unwilling to gratify the King and on 27th June he wrote to Bathurst categorically stating that he did not wish Canning to be excluded because of the King's objections and arguing that that would merely enhance Canning's growing popularity.[2] Liverpool added that he was quite prepared to make way for others to form a Ministry on the basis of Canning's exclusion. In reply Bathurst denied that he wished to exclude Canning but confessed to a feeling that the moment for his re-entry was perhaps not opportune and to a dislike of the idea of dictating to the King.[3]

In the meanwhile George IV remained 'most violent against Canning' and 'abused Lord Liverpool', saying that 'he allowed himself to be led by Canning, and that he did not consult the Duke as much as he should'.[4]

Eventually the harassed Prime Minister compromised, and agreed to postpone changes until the autumn. At the same time he made it clear to the King that, if royal objections to Canning persisted, he himself would then feel constrained to resign. The following reply was received on 1st July 1821: 'The King consents to the proposal of Lord Liverpool that the frame of the Government should at present remain without any alteration. The King however desires not to be misunderstood. The King is no proscriber of persons and the King entertains no private feeling

[1] C.G.C., vol. 1, p. 27.
[2] BATH, p. 499.
[3] Bathurst to Liverpool. 28th June 1821. BATH, p. 521.
[4] 27th June 1821. Mrs. A., vol. 1, p. 113.

but what is consistent with that principle of duty which will ever make him the guardian of his own honour.'[1]

There, uneasily, the matter rested until a new solution for Canning's future, the Indian Governor-Generalship, was proposed. According to his own account Canning was approached early in November by the Chairman of the Court of Directors of the East India Company with information that Lord Hastings had resigned and that the Court favoured Canning as successor. At the Chairman's request this knowledge was passed on by Canning to Liverpool. But there were antecedents of which Canning was then ignorant. On 20th November 1820 Hastings had written to Bloomfield:[2] 'Long ago, I was warned that I should not consider Mr. Canning as friendly to me. It was not that he was supposed to have any positive indisposition towards me, but that he wanted my situation for another. . . .'[3] On 22nd January 1821 Hastings again wrote to Bloomfield: '. . . I have a perpetual discomfort which ought not to be concealed from you. Many accounts from home have assured me that Mr. Canning was keenly solicitous to have my place, but that finding the dislodging me would not be easily reconcilable to the directors, he was working to pique me into resignation.'[4] And then, on 20th June 1821 (having just heard of Canning's resignation), Hastings informed Bloomfield: 'Lest you should imagine that his removal from the Board of Control might alter my disposition I hasten to say to you that my solicitude to be freed from my present post remains unabated. . . . Mr. Canning and his instrument Mr. Robinson have placed me on a footing with the Court which must render the relations between us uncomfortable for both parties. . . . I should not rejoice at being relieved by Mr. Canning, not so much because his attaining his object would not be a merited result of the game which he has played, as because it would not be an advantageous choice on public grounds. The natives are extraordinarily well informed respecting all the characters that appear on the political stage in England,

[1] ASP, vol. 2, 935, p. 441.

[2] Sir Benjamin Bloomfield. The King's Private Secretary until the office was abolished in March 1822.

[3] ASP, vol. 2, no. 862, p. 375.

[4] Ibid., 893, p. 405.

and they would hold him as not of a caste fitted to preside over this Empire. Such an impression you may think of light consequence in the balance against his talents. It would not be so. The patient acquiescence of the Native Princes under our sway is much influenced by their not being put to conscious shame through bowing to an undignified repository of the British power.'[1]

By this time Hastings' suspicions and his fears had already become the subject of rumour in England. 'It now appears,' had noted Mrs. Arbuthnot as early as 3rd May 1821, 'that Mr. Canning's *own object* is to be made Governor-General of India and that his extreme anxiety to get Lord Wellesley to Ireland arises from his wish to get rid of so formidable a competitor. . . . I should think Mr. Canning in every way an improper person for so high a situation. The Vice-King of India, possessed of almost absolute power over I know not how many million of subjects shd be a man of high rank in order to gratify the inordinate love of *grandeur* of the English residents, and a man of high honour and of strict and impartial justice to promote the comfort and happiness of the Hindoos. I wd not trust Mr. Canning in so responsible a situation; he who, in this country at least is always intriguing and having some dirty underplot.'[2] These misgivings were not shared by the King. Nor was he moved by the doubts of Lord Hastings. On the contrary, before any approach had been made by the Chairman of the Court of Directors, the King had determined that Canning would and should succeed to the Governor-Generalship. In the light of this assumption George IV reviewed his own attitude to the immediate problem of Canning's return to office and wrote on 12th October 1821 to Londonderry: 'I understand it to be your settled opinion that it would be very useful to the Government to send Mr. Canning back to a Cabinet situation: this is a circumstance of great difficulty to my wounded

[1] ASP, vol. 2, no. 930, p. 437. When Canning was shown this letter in late November he vehemently denied the charges contained in it and, while accepting the fact that it confirmed Hastings' intention to resign, argued that he himself could not come forward as a successor until he had had an opportunity of personally answering Hastings' charges (Canning to Liverpool. 28th November 1821. ASP, vol. 2, no. 968, p. 472).

[2] Mrs. A., vol. 1, p. 90.

feelings; nevertheless to prove to you how sincere all my intentions are towards the Government, I would endeavour to make up my mind to this harmful arrangement, if you would continue, upon further reflection, to desire it; provided he is so placed that I many not be exposed to personal communication; and also upon the direct understanding that whenever India is open, he may be removed to that Government.'[1]

When, early in November, the Governor-Generalship was offered to Canning, it seemed that the game, from the King's point of view, had been won. No sooner, however, had Canning informed Liverpool of the offer than it was learned in London that Hastings now had no wish to resign and would only return if recalled. 'Here,' as Canning subsequently put it, 'was an end of the vacancy which, however, had been announced to the King.'[2] Royal plans seemed to have miscarried. But the King, according to Canning, sought to solve the difficulty by urging that action should be taken on Hastings' original offer of resignation and that the latest version of his intentions should be ignored. The Court of Directors, however, decided that the form in which the original offer had been submitted was unconstitutional and that consequently it could not, in any case, be accepted. 'Here, therefore,' commented Canning, 'there is really and substantially (as there was before morally) an insurmountable impediment to a new nomination at present, and my reason and feeling receive the sanction of law.'[3]

While the matter was under discussion various proposed changes in the Government, including the Irish Lord-Lieutenancy for Wellesley and the Home Office for Peel, had taken place. 'It is,' as Canning wrote to Morley, 'no longer therefore in the King's power to fulfil (if he were disposed to do so) his eventual holding out of office in case of the failure of his attempt to open India. It will not escape you that the alternative of office, *or* India, has never been proposed to me. These are the facts. I make no comment and wish no comment made upon them. It is true that India was *my*

---

[1] ASP, vol. 2, no. 958, p. 466.
[2] Canning to Morley. 12th December 1821. G.C. & T., p. 325.
[3] Ibid., p. 326.

own preference; but it is hardly fair not to add that in that preference one main ingredient was to save to the Government (or to Liverpool at least) the struggle for my readmission. And *if* it is true that there was a great wish to have me in office at home, *rather than India*, it is hardly fair not to add that that wish was never so expressed to me as to enable me to act upon it.'[1] This circumstance Canning attributed, and assumed others would also attribute, to 'the unaltered resentment of the King'.

Thus the situation appeared to Canning. The impression gained by Croker was somewhat different and on 20th December 1821 he wrote: 'Canning has been shuffling about India, yes, no — no, yes. The King will *not* have him at home. Canning hopes this disgust is, like all the King's dislikes, placable and temporary, and he therefore accepted India when it was *not* vacant, as a kind of rope to *hold on to* the Administration by, but unluckily old Moira [Hastings] has had a double rupture, and is perhaps already on his way home; this would clinch Canning for Indian exile, and he is now therefore punctilious about accepting poor Moira's place, before he knows that it is vacant — so folks talk; and there is, I believe, some truth in their talk. I am sorry to be obliged to confess that all Canning's conduct gives a handle to this sort of imputation. His genius is a bright flame, but it is

> *Brillant comme le feu que les villageois font*
> *Pendant l'obscure nuit, sur le sommet d'un mont.*

He is liable to every gust of wind and every change of weather; and it flickers, and it blazes, now climbing the heavens, now stifled in its own smoke, and of no use but to raise the wonder of distant spectators, and to warm the narrow circle that immediately surrounds it. If he does not take care the Canning bonfire will soon burn itself out.'[2]

While speculation, much of it unkind, was thus rife, Liverpool betrayed his own disquiet by avowing frankly to Bathurst on 23rd December 1821: 'I must say that I hold the keeping of the situation of Governor-General open for Canning as of vital importance.

[1] Canning to Morley. 12th December 1821. G.C. & T., p. 326.
[2] Croker to Vesey Fitzgerald. CRO, vol. 1, p. 218.

We shall find great inconvenience in his being here for any length of time out of office, and yet his return to office now is rendered nearly impracticable, even if the King's objections could be overruled.'[1] Liverpool had been outmanoeuvred, but his immediate worries were dispelled when confirmation was received of Hastings' departure from India and definitive resolve to resign. The Governor-Generalship was then again offered to Canning and, when his remaining scruples (the imputations made against him by Hastings) had been overcome, the offer was accepted.

The complicated and painful process which preceded Canning's appointment poses two questions. Did he, as Hastings alleged, plot his own campaign for the succession? Or, as other hostile witnesses maintained, was he merely engaged in a manoeuvre and eventually caught in his own trap? In answer to the first question, it seems that Canning was genuinely attracted by the prospect of India, both as a means of escaping from an awkward situation at home and in order to compensate for previous depredation of his wife's private fortune; on the other hand, there is no evidence that he viewed the prospect with sufficient relish to devote any energy or ingenuity towards its achievement. In answer to the second question, Canning's frame of mind at the time suggests that he had lost heart for manoeuvre and that he was for once prepared to let matters drift. Certainly he expressed relief when the decision was finally made and, after Castlereagh's suicide, when issues were once again in the balance, he wrote: 'I wish I were well on board the Jupiter. Nothing that can be proposed to me will make me glad to stay, though such a proposal may be made as would make the refusal to stay impossible.'[2] And after he had accepted such a proposal and was back at the Foreign Office he wrote on 5th November 1822 to Bagot in reply to a letter of congratulations: 'Your letter of the 12th October has given me one of the few sensations of real pleasure which I derive from my return to the Foreign Office. By far the greatest number of considerations public and private are against acceptance, and to the last day I hoped that the proposal made to me might be one that I

---

[1] BATH, p. 527.
[2] To Morley. 26th August 1822. G.C. & T., p. 362.

could refuse . . . the die being cast, I must make the best of that lot which has fallen to me, and place public duty against private liking and convenience. But ten years have made a world of difference, and prepared a very different sort of world to bustle in than I should have found in 1812. For fame, it is a squeezed orange, but for public good there is something to do, and I will try — but it must be cautiously — to do it. You know my politics well enough to know what I mean when I say that for Europe, I shall be desirous now and then to read England. . . . You *may* congratulate my wife, though not me, on our change of destination; for to her and my daughter the voyage and the climate of India are real escapes, in imagination at least, if not in reality.'[1] In a similar vein on 30th September Canning had written to Chateaubriand: 'Me voici donc, bien contre mon gré, et pour la vie, aux galères, dont je me flattais d'avoir échapper bellement, pour n'y rentrer jamais. Plaignez-moi, mon cher Chateaubriand, car vraiment, je suis à plaindre; et d'autant plus que tout le monde se plaît à me croire au comble de mes voeux.'[2] Thus, when the prime object of Canning's ambition was achieved, he himself claimed to be a disenchanted and almost disinterested spectator. His protestations, allowing for some dramatic licence, seem to have been sincere. He was confident that he could be of service to his country; but power, for its own sake, had ceased to exercise a spell.

The events which led to Canning's triumphant return to the Cabinet were, as ever in his public life, fraught with drama. On 12th August 1822 Castlereagh committed suicide. The King was then in Scotland and Canning about to pay a farewell visit to his Liverpool constituents. The Prime Minister at once concluded that Canning's presence in the Cabinet was essential and that he must be persuaded to forgo his departure. Time was Liverpool's problem. He knew that there would be opposition in the Cabinet, chiefly from Lord Eldon, to Canning's return; royal objections also required to be overcome. Furthermore Liverpool was aware that Canning would accept nothing less than the Foreign Office and the lead in the Commons; so that it was not merely a question

[1] BAG, vol. 2, p. 137.   [2] C.G.C., vol. 1, p. 47.

of inclusion, but inclusion on specific terms. Negotiations were, therefore, likely to be protracted but, in spite of Liverpool's appeals, Canning insisted on proceeding north to say his farewells on the assumption that there would be no changes in plan. On 16th August 1822 Countess Lieven wrote to Metternich that although 'the Canning faction was in high hopes, he had only Liverpool on his side; against him the Chancellor and everyone else'.[1] A few days later, however, the Countess was shocked to hear Wellington say: 'We want to put Canning in.' To this she replied: 'In Heaven's name, dont have him; that man will cheat you! This is my private belief. Canning has the most brilliant talents but no stability in his principles. He is excessively ambitious; no sooner in the Ministry than he would want to create a party. To form one he would have to put in his supporters; bit by bit, the Ministry would be completely revolutionised; he might even make a compromise with the Whigs. In short it seems to me impossible to place the least confidence in that man. He would be, in fact, the next Prime Minister; and what power would he not then possess!'[2] On 17th August George IV wrote suspiciously from Scotland to his Prime Minister who replied that he begged 'to assure your Majesty that nothing shall be said or done by him, during your Majesty's absence which can preclude, upon your Majesty's return, the most free, full and unfettered consideration of the arrangements in your Majesty's Government which, in consequence of the late sad calamity, may appear to be the most advantageous for the publick service.'[3]

On 1st September 1822 the King returned from Scotland and was intensely displeased to learn that, in spite of reassurances, Liverpool had been proceeding with plans to bring in Canning. 'The King had hoped,' he complained, 'that Lord Liverpool would not have made any approach on this subject as the King, whilst in Scotland, had particularly [wished] that the arrangements regarding India might not be disturbed.'[4] Having thus relieved his feelings, the King sought to discover whether Liverpool's remaining in office was dependent on royal surrender over Canning;

---

[1] L., p. 158.

[2] 21st August 1822. L., p. 163.

[3] ASP, vol. 2, no. 1039, p. 534.

[4] Ibid., 1042, p. 535.

unable to obtain a definite reply, the King consulted Peel, Sidmouth, Eldon and finally, on 7th September, Wellington. The last interview seems to have been decisive and Mrs. Arbuthnot was probably correct when she noted that 'the King gave up his opposition in deference to the advice of the Duke'.[1] On 8th September the King told Lord Liverpool that he was 'aware that the brightest ornament of his crown is the power of extending grace and favour to a subject who may have incurred his displeasure' and 'therefore permits Lord Liverpool to propose Mr. Canning's readmission into the Government'.[2] On the following day the King confided to Lord Eldon that he had been called upon to make 'the greatest personal sacrifice that a sovereign ever made to a subject, or indeed, taking all *the circumstances*, that man ever made to man'.[3] In the meantime, on 8th September, Liverpool had hastened to make an offer to Canning. A slight delay supervened. Some doubt exists as to the exact nature of this offer but on 11th September, in an interview with Liverpool, 'the whole heritage' was definitely proposed. Canning still seems to have hesitated. According to Countess Lieven he grumbled that the King's letter was 'exactly the same as being given a ticket for Almacks and finding written on the back "*Admit the rogue*"', and on the 12th was not disposed to accept 'unless the King withdrew offensive expressions in his letter'.[4] These scruples, however, were overcome, and on the 13th he replied affirmatively to the offer made, expressing the hope, but not on the condition, that promotion could be found for Huskisson.[5]

Writing to Metternich on 10th September Countess Lieven had already accepted Canning's return as inevitable and, trying to look on the bright side, remarked, '. . . the Ministers know him

---

[1] 13th September 1822. Mrs. A., vol. 1, p. 186.

[2] Letter quoted Petrie. *Lord Liverpool*, p. 259.

[3] ASP, vol. 2, no. 1044, p. 538.

[4] 13th October 1822. L., p. 168.

[5] For Canning's concern about Huskisson see Arbuthnot to Bathurst. 12th September 1822. BATH, p. 532. On the question of Huskisson's possible admission to the Cabinet at this stage see Liverpool to Arbuthnot correspondence from 21st October 1822 to 30th December 1822. A., no. 32, pp. 35-7; and Huskisson to Canning. 25th October 1822. HUSK, pp. 147-50.

for an intriguer; but if they offer him an important position, they deprive his intriguing spirit of its object. . . . If he makes difficulties they will send him packing. . . . Canning's present position is unique. The Opposition hates him; those who want him do not like him. His personal following is a mere drop in the ocean; and with that exception there is not a soul in the United Kingdom who has the slightest respect for him. In spite of all these reasons for keeping him out public opinion demands him; and he will receive the most important post in the government.'[1] Enthusiasm among the public and in the Press[2] was accompanied by anger and suspicion among his numerous political and personal enemies. Viscount Lowther[3] wrote on 9th September to Sir William Knighton: 'Canning will now conceive the Ministry could not go on without him, and being called upon when preparing to go to India, will dictate his own measures to the Cabinet, and if a general quarrel arises with his colleagues, he will resign. His opposition in the Commons would be *fearful*; no Government could stand it. So the Cabinet must come into all his projects. In India his voice would not be heard and out of sight is out of mind. He has such sudden twists and quirks, I know not whether he is most to be dreaded as friend or foe. If he had gone to India, the course would have been less embarrassing, but I suppose we must yield to circumstances and take him.'[4] Lady Londonderry was indignant and her brother-in-law, the new Marquess,[5] resigned his Embassy in protest. Mrs. Arbuthnot sympathetically noted their distress but added: 'However, I suppose it could not be helped and that it is true what the Duke says, that could Lord Londonderry (who was always anxious about the readmission of Canning into the Cabinet) look out of his grave, he wd approve of the appointment.'[6] To the great majority of Government supporters

[1] L., p. 168.

[2] Not *The Times*, where, as has been seen, he was described as a 'hired advocate'. But generally, after his farewell speech at Liverpool, the Press had been urging his return to the Ministry as Castlereagh's successor.

[3] A Lord of the Treasury.

[4] ASP, vol. 2, no. 1043, p. 537.

[5] Lord Charles Stewart, 3rd Marquess of Londonderry. Ambassador at Vienna.

[6] 16th September 1822. Mrs. A., vol. 1, p. 191.

Canning's return was at best an unwelcome necessity: to Canning himself it was a somewhat uncongenial duty.

Since the burden had been pressed upon him, and once he had decided to undertake it, however, he did so with the conviction that this time he was in to stay and for the purpose of achieving certain definite objectives both at home and abroad. Personal considerations were laid aside; the job alone counted and all manoeuvres must be carried out on the assumption that he would remain at his post; this implied patience and wary walking. The change which can be noted in Canning was due less to the lessons drawn from experience than to his own altered outlook. Once the struggle had commenced, however, there were frequent signs that Canning, although he preserved his new prudence, began to find pleasure in the fight and exhilaration in victory.

(ii) *1822–27*

Having re-entered Liverpool's Cabinet, Canning was faced with the problem of imposing his own will upon it. His natural opponents were the ultra Tory peers, Eldon, Bathurst, Westmorland, Sidmouth, Maryborough and, in a class on his own, Wellington. From Peel, Harrowby, Vansittart and Wynn he could not rely on any certain sympathy. Only from Liverpool, Lord Melville and Robinson could he anticipate support. For his purpose, therefore, the Cabinet must either be outmanoeuvred, or refashioned, or both. Success, in spite of Liverpool's backing, would be hard to achieve if royal hostility persisted; the recovery of the King's favour consequently imposed itself on Canning. Thus, in the midst of the labours of his office and the duties of leadership in the Commons, Canning struggled to win over the King and to cajole, confuse, or eliminate his chief opponents in the Cabinet. As the ultra Tories drew so much of their strength from royal favour, the winning of the King was the crux of Canning's campaign.

George IV did not take his responsibilities lightly. Perhaps because of the frivolity of his private life he was always anxious, in his royal capacity, to behave as he imagined befitted a King. Frequently in physical pain, fuddled with laudanum, living in a confusion of sham dissipation, hopelessly bored with constant striving to avoid boredom, he desperately wanted to do the right thing in public affairs. But he had little confidence in his own judgement. He was forever seeking advice and then a sympathetic audience upon whom to unburden the new anxiety which the latest advice had provoked. In 1822 Lady Conyngham was the reigning favourite and Sir William Knighton the King's close companion and personal assistant. He had been the King's physician since 1810. On Bloomfield's retirement in March 1822 he took over the duties, but not the office, of Private Secretary, being appointed instead Keeper of the Privy Purse. Although the King was happy to gratify the whims of Lady Conyngham, she could offer little contribution to any serious political discussion. Knighton, on the other hand, was a man of some ability and intelligence; to him accordingly the King poured out his doubts and his difficulties, with reasonable assurance that the physician would find formulas of comfort. Apart from Knighton, whose influence was only beginning to become established, the King chiefly trusted Wellington and the ultra Tory peers. George IV had gradually slipped into the belief that it became a King to be an ultra Tory. He also had come to the conclusion that his own destiny and the concert of Europe were, somehow, intertwined. This illusion Countess Lieven, the mistress of Metternich and the wife of the Tsar's ambassador, was of course at pains to encourage. In order to maintain her influence the Countess was prepared to make many sacrifices. 'Heaven preserve you,' she once wrote to Metternich, 'from the knees of the King and the Duke of York especially in 25° of heat.'[1] In her efforts the Countess was supported by her husband, by Esterhazy the Austrian and by Polignac the French, Ambassadors. In spite of mutual jealousies they combined to lay siege to the opinions of the King. He was a susceptible subject. He took pride in his knowledge of Continental politics. As King of Hanover he received dispatches from his German Minister which gave him a sense of superiority and independence. These dispatches he was not obliged to show to his British Foreign Secretary and Castlereagh had, in his early years at the Foreign Office,

[1] 13th September 1824. L., p. 271.

suffered considerably from the King's propensity to withhold information and to form personal opinions based upon it. Gradually, however, Castlereagh had succeeded in winning the King's complete confidence though towards the end a quarrel between Lady Castlereagh and Lady Conyngham caused a temporary coolness. Fancying himself as an expert on foreign affairs, George IV was unlikely to have had any great respect for the capacities of his new Minister, even if he had not already been hopelessly prejudiced against him.

The King was convinced that duty required him to keep a watching brief over foreign affairs; he believed that he would be shirking his responsibilities if he failed to be suspicious of his new Foreign Secretary. In these dispositions the King, of course, received every encouragement from the representatives of Russia, France and Austria.

Canning rightly did not underestimate the importance of winning over the King and he was pleased, shortly after assuming office, to be able to offer a vacant Under-Secretaryship to Lady Conyngham's son, Lord Francis Conyngham.[1] The King seemed gratified and Canning's enemies took prompt alarm. Writing on 6th January 1823 to Metternich, Countess Lieven commented: 'She [Lady Conyngham] is not particularly well disposed towards Mr. Canning and laughed with me over his cleverness in giving the post . . . to her son adding: "I should have been a fool not to take advantage of it." She told me however, that since the appointment the King has been on good terms with Canning, though not yet extravagantly so.'[2] As Canning's policy was causing alarm both at St. Petersburg and in Vienna the King's attitude was, from the Countess's point of view, disquieting. She began to probe and on 7th January reported to Metternich: '. . . I wanted to get him to tell me what he thought of Canning. He replied cautiously "he is a clever man. He is trying to win me over and shows every readiness to follow me in politics as well as in personal affairs. I wanted him to give Francis the post of Under-Secretary

---

[1] The suggestion came from the King — Canning had already made three unsuccessful attempts to fill the post. See ASP, vol. 2, no. 1053, p. 547.

[2] L., p. 176.

of State and he did it. True it was to his own advantage; for it was the cleverest move he could make. For the rest, he is a plebeian, and has no manners; as for his brilliant repartees, I have never heard any. He dined here and said nothing but yes and no." '[1]

The King soon began to mistrust the direction in which Canning seemed to be moving in foreign affairs. Wellington, Westmorland and Harrowby were also uneasy and their doubts magnified the King's; anxiety turned to alarm thanks to the promptings of Countess Lieven and Count Esterhazy; Metternich began to hope that a change at the British Foreign Office might be secured by royal intervention and Canning rightly sensed 'a plot to change the politics of this government by changing *me*'.[2] But though George IV grumbled, he could not see his way to any immediate action; he confided his troubles to Countess Lieven: 'I do not like him [Canning] better than I did. I recognize his talent, and I believe we need him in the Commons; but he is no more capable of conducting foreign affairs than your baby. He doesn't know the first thing about his job: no tact, no judgement, no idea of decorum. But what is to be done? Can I change any Minister? No for I should only get someone worse. That is the fix I am in. The best is bad; but the worst would be hateful and there is nothing in between. Wellington backs me. He thinks as I do.'[3] The Duke of York was more sanguine and believed that Canning's overthrow could be secured by a revolt against him in the Cabinet. Countess Lieven, at first sceptical, also became optimistic. On 14th March 1823 she told Metternich: 'I have had some talks with the Duke of York. He tells me that the Ministers are joining forces and that, between now and the first of next month, they will perhaps have got rid of their colleague. I dont go so fast.'[4] On 16th April she wrote more hopefully: 'What a speech from Mr. Canning in the Commons, on the 14th! The Ministers cannot work with him any longer. The imbroglio begins to get

¹ L., p. 178.
² Canning to Granville. 11th March 1825. C.G.C., vol. 1, p. 258. In this letter Canning gave his recollections of the incident.
³ As recorded by Countess Lieven in a letter to Metternich of 5th March 1823. L., p. 197.
⁴ L., p. 198.

interesting.'[1] On 20th April she reported: '. . . yesterday I dined
with Canning at the Austrian Embassy. I was put between him and
Wellington; they did not speak a word to one another. Canning
asked me a thousand and one questions about the King. To him,
the King is as remote as the man in the moon.'[2]

The King in the meanwhile replied, via Count Münster, to
secret messages from Tsar Alexander, Emperor Francis and Louis
XVIII approving their views, but pointing out that he could not
at present force these on his English Minister. This intrigue was
obviously embarrassing to Canning in his conduct of foreign
affairs but he rightly judged that his own position in the Cabinet
was too weak to launch a frontal attack; on the contrary that
would have played into the hands of the plotters; so he confined
himself to somewhat evasive tactics in the Cabinet and powerful
oratorical justifications in Parliament; from the tenor of his
speeches on 14th and 30th April 1823 in the House the Press
scented a Court intrigue.[3] By this oblique method of reprisal
Canning had in fact uncovered the weakness of his royal adver-
sary's position: fear of increasing already distressing unpopularity.

But the King did not take the warning given and deliberately
humiliated Canning in the presence of the French representative,
M. de Marcellus, at a ball at Carlton House on 11th July. According to Marcellus, Canning remained imperturbable but murmured
after the King had concluded and moved away: 'Representative
government has still one advantage that His Majesty has forgotten.
Ministers have to endure without answering back the epigrams by
which a King seeks to avenge himself for his impotence.'[4] Countess
Lieven writing to Metternich about the same occasion described
Canning as 'extremely vexed' and quoted the King as saying:
'"there is nothing more contemptible and clumsy than half-
measures and half-tones. I hate them. *Dont you Mr. Canning?*"
Canning did not answer a word', she continued, 'and we all

[1] L., p. 207.   [2] Ibid., p. 209.
[3] An article in *The Times* postulated that the King must be mad if he wished
success to French armies in Spain.
[4] TEMP, p. 246.
I

dropped our eyes.'[1] Early in August the King received M. de
Polignac at Windsor and Canning was in attendance; after dinner
George IV again used the particular privilege of his position to
emphasise disapproval of his Foreign Minister.[2] Nevertheless no
further progress was made by the plotters and by the end of 1823
the King seemed less assiduous in his policy of pinpricks. It may
not have been without significance that Countess Lieven fell ill
and left England at the beginning of October to winter in Italy.
Furthermore, according to Mrs. Arbuthnot, Knighton, for personal reasons, exercised himself for a while in Canning's favour
with the King. After new differences in January 1824, Canning's
credit with the King again seemed to improve. On 26th March
1824 Mrs. Arbuthnot complained '. . . Mr. Canning is in great
favour just now, because he has persuaded the King that he has
offered the Mission to the United States to Mr. Fitzgerald from an
idea that it would be agreable to the Conyngham family to get
him out of the County of Clare, and because the King wanted a
house he has in Pall Mall.'[3] A few days later she noted: 'It is
scarcely credible, but Lady Conyngham has taken great umbrage
at my going every Thursday to Lady Hertford's[4] and because I
have gone several times to Lord Hertford's box at the Opera. She
plagues the King to death about it and is also angry because the
Duke of Wellington does the same, and she says she will have a
party of her own and become *Canning and Catholic*. The King was
very angry at her saying this, but for the sake of a quiet life he
sent Sir Wm to London to talk about it with Mr. A. . . .'[5]

Even if George IV might condone Lady Conyngham's whims
for the sake of a quiet life, his hatred and mistrust of Canning,
though in abeyance, was still strong and his rage exploded when
Canning, out of deliberate policy, attended Lord Mayor Waith-
mand's banquet at the Mansion House on Easter Monday. The
Lord Mayor had been one of Queen Caroline's prominent de-

[1] 11th July 1823. L., p. 223.
[2] See Countess Lieven to Metternich. 9th August 1823. L., p. 226.
[3] Mrs. A., vol. 1, p. 295.
[4] Lady Hertford was Lady Conyngham's predecessor as royal favourite.
[5] 3rd April 1824. Mrs. A., vol. 1, p. 297.

fenders and the episode revived the King's personal grievances against Canning. He proposed to write a violent letter of protest to Liverpool. Wellington fearing the collapse of the Ministry counselled some moderation. The King's anger was turned away from Liverpool but persisted against Canning of whom he spoke 'with the deepest abhorrence'; he 'allowed,' however, 'that it would not do to turn him out upon it', and consented to modify the tone of his protest.[1] In this crisis Canning kept his head and his temper. While agreeing 'to apologize for any displeasure caused to his Majesty', he produced a very lengthy and detailed justification of his own conduct which Liverpool endorsed and forwarded to the King.[2] Canning was on strong ground and he could afford to be both temperate and firm. The King inevitably remained aggrieved.

In this mood he was prepared to take advantage of Cabinet divisions over the Spanish Colonies Question and on 30th May 1824 Neumann reported to Metternich that the King had shown more energy of late, so that there was a chance of replacing Canning.[3] Metternich, apparently with the King's approval, agreed to provide Canning's colleagues with weapons against him and corresponded secretly with Wellington.[4]

When Countess Lieven returned to England in May she was depressed to find Canning 'on the pinnacle of success'[5] and persistent rumours that Lady Conyngham had his interests at heart. Knowing nothing of the latest intrigues, she approached the King with some diffidence at their first meeting but was reassured and delighted when he claimed to hate Canning as much as ever. As the Duke reported to Mrs. Arbuthnot: 'the King as usual abused Canning to her, saying: "think of that d—d fellow wanting me to have the King and Queen of the Sandwich Islands to dinner, as if I wd sit at table with such a pair of d—d cannibals!"'[6]

[1] 2nd May 1824. Mrs. A., vol. 1, p. 357.
[2] Liverpool to the King. 5th May 1824. ASP, vol. 3, no. 1162, p. 72.
[3] See TEMP, p. 246.
[4] See Canning to Granville. 11th March 1825. C.G.C., vol. 1, p. 258 and also TEMP, p. 246.
[5] 9th May 1824. L., p. 257.
[6] 6th June 1824. Mrs. A., vol. 1, p. 319.

With Liverpool in bad health, the Cabinet bitterly divided, and the King in an irritable and relatively energetic mood, there was a flutter in the anti-Canning camp. On 10th June 1824 Mrs. Arbuthnot noted: 'the King sent for the Duke today to talk to him about Ld Liverpool's state. Knighton saw him yesterday and says he cannot *live* long, even if he quits office. . . . The King told the Duke that Ld West[morland] had gone yesterday to talk to him about Ld L. The King said the Duke was the only person he looked to; Ld West[morland] said that was very proper, but wd Mr. Canning serve under him. The King said he did not care, for it wd be an excellent opportunity of getting rid of him.'[1] But the Cabinet crisis upon which the King relied did not materialise and on 23rd July Canning's desire to open commercial negotiations with Buenos Aires was carried in the Cabinet in spite of Wellington's bitter opposition. During the month that followed, Canning's will continued to prevail and no pretext for royal intervention was provided. Nevertheless, on 2nd September Countess Lieven boasted to Metternich: 'The cabal against Canning grows in strength. The doctor speaks openly against him. The King said to me yesterday: he is a scoundrel and I hate him more every day. . . .'[2]

The death of Louis XVIII of France on 16th September 1824 precipitated a clash. Canning was then on a visit to Lord Wellesley, the Lord-Lieutenant, in Ireland. In an interview with the King before leaving for Ireland, Canning had spoken of the possibility of conveying condolences in person should occasion arise. From Ireland Canning now reverted to this notion but eventually decided against it. He did, however, propose to visit Paris in the near future because he was anxious to discuss the Spanish Colonies Question with the new King and his chief Ministers. George IV, aware of Canning's intentions, consulted Wellington and together they decided to try and keep the Foreign Secretary away from Paris. Accordingly on 5th October Wellington wrote to Canning advising against the visit.[3] An acrimonious correspondence en-

---

[1] Mrs. A., vol. 1, p. 321.   [2] L., p. 269.
[3] See *Despatches, Correspondence and Memoranda of the Duke of Wellington* (*1819–32*), vol. 2, pp. 313, 314.

sued. Canning objected to what he regarded as a royal betrayal of confidence; his irritation was magnified because Lord Westmorland had been in Paris at Louis XVIII's death, had lingered there, had solicited an interview with Charles X and had discussed the Spanish Colonies Question with him. After learning the views of the new King, he had failed to make any report to the British Foreign Secretary and had, instead, reported directly to George IV. The King, perhaps deliberately, chose this moment to express disapproval of Canning's draft reply to a letter from the retiring Ambassador in Paris, Sir Charles Stuart. 'The King,' he wrote, 'cannot approve Mr. Canning's answer to Sir Charles Stuart's letter. There are two ways of doing everything and the King is always disposed to take the kindest.'[1] 'Indeed,' retorted Canning to Liverpool, 'after having persecuted me for two years to recall Sir Charles Stuart without waiting for the *apropos* of the new reign; after having again and again declared his intention not to give Stuart the peerage; after abusing him as a Jacobin and disparaging him as a good for nothing diplomatic agent, when, to save his Majesty from importunity I take upon myself the ungracious task of discouraging all Stuart's expectations, and being the only person who has any kindness and consideration for him, consent to bear the whole obloquy of his unbroken uncompensated removal — this is my reward. But they are mistaken if they think I will acquiesce in such treatment or let them play their game for popularity at my expense (I say "they" because I know he has advisers).'[2] Taking into account Wellington's interference at royal instigation with his own plans, Westmorland's conduct in Paris and the King's attitude over Stuart's recall, Canning was thoroughly roused. On 17th October 1824 he sent copies of his correspondence with Wellington to Liverpool, explained his griefs and protested: 'it is high time to look about one and to beware of what Burke calls "traps and mines".'[3] Though Canning abandoned his projected visit to Paris he felt himself in a sufficiently strong position to threaten, not resignation, but exposure.

[1] Canning to Liverpool. 10th October 1824. C.G.C., vol. 1, p. 169.
[2] Ibid., vol. 1, p. 169.
[3] G.C. & T., pp. 400–1.

The warning was not entirely lost either on the King or on Wellington and a sullen truce emerged. The Duke, in his turn, forwarded the correspondence with Canning to Mrs. Arbuthnot and said that he had closed it: 'first because I can say no more. Secondly because after having said everything, we shall get into a war of words and phrases in which he must have the best of it. Thirdly my opinion is that ending the discussion where it is, he wont go [to Paris]. If I were to continue it, he will.'[1]

Fortified by this encounter, Canning pressed forward in the Cabinet his plans for the recognition of the Spanish Colonies. The King's efforts to encourage opposition, though they continued to harass, met with declining success. By 15th December 1824 resistance in the Cabinet was finally overcome and the decisive Minute was sent to the King. Thus abandoned by his supporters in the Government the King was thrust upon his own resources. He dared not openly oppose and, in reply to the Minute, he expressed disapproval and acquiescence. As Canning put it, 'The King consents though he does not concur.'[2] On the strength of this consent Canning now began the process of translating the decision into action. The King first sought to persuade the Cabinet to consult the 'Allies' before any active step was taken. After the failure of this manoeuvre he complained according to Mrs. Arbuthnot 'most bitterly (to W) of Mr. Canning, and said that his foreign policy had shut him out from the Councils of Europe and reduced him to the level of a King of the Netherlands'.[3] In this mood he keyed himself up for a final effort; on 27th January 1825 he wrote to Liverpool criticising the Government's policy and desiring 'distinctly to know from his Cabinet, individually (*seriatim*) whether the great principles of policy established by his Government in the years 1814, 1815, and 1818, *are, or are not, to be abandoned*'.[4] This attempt to revive divisions in the Cabinet collapsed in the face of the refusal of its members to give individual opinions. After a stormy Cabinet meeting on 28th January when

---

[1] 21st October 1824. Mrs. A., vol. 1, p. 351.
[2] To Granville. C.G.C., vol. 1, p. 214.
[3] 27th January 1825. Mrs. A., vol. 1, p. 372.
[4] G.C. & T., p. 416.

Canning said that 'it was all an intrigue of the foreigners to get him out, and that he did not know whether he ought not to go down to the House of Commons with the letter in his pocket and move an address to the King to know who had advised him to write the letter'[1] the Cabinet agreed to send a joint, and almost admonitory, reply to the King. Wellington, now thoroughly alarmed, advised George IV to resign himself to the inevitable and warned him that refusal to do so would lead to exposure in Parliament and possibly a *coup d'état*. Sulkily the King abandoned the struggle but, as a parting shot, insisted that the Prime Minister convey royal displeasure[2] to the Foreign Secretary for a long self-justificatory note of 1st February 1825 in which Canning dwelt 'with calculated' lack of tact on the leakage of secrets to foreign powers.

The King's courage thus seems to have deserted him and on 9th February Mrs. Arbuthnot wrote: 'It is very clear that Carlton House, having nearly picked a quarrel with Mr. Canning, are taking fright and beginning to be afraid of the consequences. Knighton advised the Duke to amalgamate with Canning. This knowledge put Mr. Arbuthnot into a great rage and he said that they might as well try to amalgamate oil and vinegar as the Duke and Mr. Canning, that the Duke had always uniformly tried to keep matters smooth, and to induce the King to bear with Mr. Canning, and that it was quite infamous to use such language.'[3]

Though frightened, the King, encouraged by Countess Lieven, still hoped to embarass Canning by receiving Metternich, due to visit Paris in March, at Windsor. The invitation had been previously and secretly made. Canning regarded this plan as part of the original plot against himself and assumed that, with the failure of the plot, the visit would be abandoned. To Granville he wrote on 11th March 1825: 'If he talks of coming to England do not encourage him. But as Esterhazy is going to meet him at Paris, I trust that he has given up the notion of a visit to Windsor. He

[1] Mrs. A., vol. 1, p. 374.
[2] 'The King trusts that Lord Liverpool did not fail to explain to Mr. Canning the King's displeasure at Mr. Canning's note of the date of the first of February.' ASP, vol. 3, no. 1191, p. 100.
[3] Mrs. A., vol. 1, p. 375.

would have come to triumph; I would not advise him to come to intrigue.'[1] But Countess Lieven persisted in her hopes and discussed revised plans with Metternich. 'Wellington,' she wrote, 'came to tell me that he was going to write to you to suggest a new plan of travel, which is this: you would embark at Dieppe and come to Brighton, where I should be and Wellington too. Thence you would go to Windsor, and you could leave England without going to London, and consequently without seeing Mr. Canning. He thinks it an admirable plan, because it would please your friends and infuriate your enemy; and he is so delighted with his idea that he does not doubt for a moment you will jump at it. Alas you are too wise ever to jump at anything.'[2] Canning presumably was aware of the new scheme and on 4th April he instructed Granville to convey a clear warning to Metternich: 'I very much wish too, in the same supposition (that of his being about to recommence his intrigues) that he should know how well I am apprised of all the *good* which he intended to me. I should like him to understand, that a renewal of similar attempts may lead to some such public manifestation of my knowledge of what has passed, as may let the House of Commons and the public into the secret. I wonder whether he is aware that the private communication of foreign Ministers with the King of England is wholly at variance with the spirit, and practice too, of the British Constitution. That during his reign of half a century, George III (whom all parties now agree in taking as the model of an English King) never indulged himself in such communications, and that the custom introduced in the time of my predecessor survives only by sufferance, and would not stand the test of Parliamentary discussion. I should be sorry to do anything at all unpleasant to the King, but it is my duty to be present at every interview between his Majesty and a foreign Minister. Nothing would induce me to go to that extent; but short of *that*, being in the right, I would justly resent, and pretty effectually repress, such manoeuvres as Metternich has been encouraging.'[3]

[1] G.C. & T., p. 428.
[2] 25th March 1825. L., p. 286.
[3] G.C. & T., p. 433.

The situation was by now already clear to Metternich; he had declined the original invitation and he did not need much prompting to realise the futility of further manoeuvres. But the warning, as Canning no doubt had intended, was not lost upon the King.

Fears at Court were crystallised and Knighton counselled surrender. Having suggested the policy, he was entrusted with its execution. On 27th April 1825 he called on Canning, who was ill in bed, and remained with him for nearly three hours. Metternich was made the scapegoat and the King was described as never 'so tranquil and comfortable, as he appeared at the present moment'. Canning rejoined that it was his object 'to make His Majesty comfortable and happy by placing him at the head of Europe, instead of being reckoned fifth in a great confederacy'; he also pointed out that he had been 'aware that the King had been afraid that the steps taken with respect to Spanish America would involve us in a war. . . .' Knighton admitted that 'the King had certainly entertained that fear, but now was perfectly satisfied his fears had been unfounded'. Knighton also conceded that 'he [H.M.] had certainly been very loath to give up all his continental gossipings to which he had been accustomed too much and too long'. The doctor then put his own services entirely at Canning's disposal and hinted that he would not be averse to a Government office; various other topics were discussed and when Huskisson's name was mentioned Knighton embarked on a great panegyric. Canning's impression was that Knighton 'evidently had at heart . . . to set himself right with me as to the intrigues of the last summer'.[1] He was not prepared, however, to assume at once that Knighton's *démarche* necessarily meant the royal surrender which seemed to be implied.

But though Canning was cautious, the change in the King's attitude was soon beyond doubt. On 6th May 1825 the Duke, after seeing the King, reported to Mrs. Arbuthnot, 'that he was very civil . . . but still it was different', and confirmed that the King was 'by means of Knighton, in direct communication with Mr. Canning'.[2] After the intermediary had done his work,

[1] This account of the meeting is a summary of Canning's Memorandum dated 27th April 1825. G.C. & T., pp. 437–43.
[2] Mrs. A., vol. 1, p. 393.

confidential relations were directly established between the two principals. In October the King professed himself ready to receive the Ministers of the new States early in November and Canning, in a letter to Granville, admitted: 'I am afraid that the King offers me more than I shall be able to take. For I have only one Minister, that of Columbia here, but I expect a Buenos Ayrean by the next packet.'[1] On 31st October 1825 Canning, in a further letter to Granville, complacently confided: 'the King, I hope (indeed I have reason to believe) begins to feel that I have *not*, as he was taught to apprehend lost to him his status among the powers of the Continent; but only changed it from the tail of Europe to the head.'[2] On 21st November 1825 Canning again wrote in high spirits to Granville: '. . . the King's reception of Signor Hurtado, the Columbian Envoy Extraordinary and Minister Plenipotentiary, has been all that I could desire. . . . And so behold! the New World established, and, if we do not throw it away,ours. '[3] The King had by now given tangible proof of confidence by showing to Canning his Hanoverian correspondence. Public expression of the altered situation was given on 20th December when, at a farewell audience for Esterhazy, the King paid a series of compliments to Canning (and to Esterhazy) at Metternich's expense.[4] The revolution in palace politics was complete.

While fear was no doubt the cause of the original Knighton mission to Canning in April, the King's own feelings seem subsequently to have undergone a genuine change. This change was clearly due to the success of Canning's policy. By approving Canning the King found himself applauded. The popularity which had eluded him for so many years was beginning, thanks to Canning, to return. The bitterness of surrender was quite forgotten as the King enjoyed his share in Canning's triumph. Canning, for his part, was pleased to play the courtier and lost no opportunity of gratifying and flattering the King; once his own projects were not being hampered, Canning's constitutional respect for the

[1] 11th October 1825. G.C. & T., p. 445.
[2] G.C. & T., p. 445.
[3] Ibid., p. 447.
[4] See Canning's Memorandum on Esterhazy's leave taking. G.C. & T., p. 448.

monarchy made the task a congenial one. Exchange of compliments soon became an established practice. While Canning obliged by appointing Lord Ponsonby to Buenos Aires, the King replied by offering a peerage for any of Canning's family or anyone he should choose to name.[1] Lord Ponsonby was an old admirer of Lady Conyngham. The King wished to keep him out of England. 'You will see,' Canning wrote to Bagot, 'that I refer Lord Ponsonby to you for instructions which I could not give. Among other things it is very difficult for *me* to say "Be as little in England as possible before your departure." But I wish it said or at least wish the thing to be so. There are *Pourquois* for it, *qui se n'expliquent pas.*'[2] On 13th February 1826 Mrs. Arbuthnot noted: 'Canning has also undertaken to get Lord Mount Charles made a Lord of the Treasury; the consequence of all this is, that Sir Wm says he loves Mr. Canning; and the King and Lady Conyngham cannot make enough of him. . . .'[3] Solidarity was manifest and Mrs. Arbuthnot's world reversed. On 22nd June 1826 she recorded: 'Mr. Canning has completely succeeded in gaining the King's favour . . . the Duke returned from Windsor fully satisfied that his reign was altogether at an end . . . they were all very much amused with Mme. de Lieven's courting Mr. Canning. She quite pursued him round the room to the great amusement of the whole party. Mr. Canning was there two days with his son, *a boy from Eton*! and Lord Clanricarde. The King asked for a holiday for the Eton boys in honour of Master Canning!'[4] Mrs. Arbuthnot's indignation was further aroused by news of a royal levee late in November. 'Everybody,' she wrote, 'was greatly disgusted by his (H.M.) paying particular attention to Lord Clanricarde.[5] I understand Lord. C. went into the Drawing Room looking pale and frightened, no creatures spoke to him, but the King took him by

---

[1] See ASP, vol. 3, no. 1234, p. 143. Charles Ellis, Canning's friend, was created Baron Seaford.

[2] 2nd December 1825. BAG, vol. 2, p. 305.

[3] Mrs. A., vol. 2, p. 12. Lord Mount Charles (subsequently 2nd Marquess of Conyngham) was Lady Conyngham's second son.

[4] Ibid., p. 31.

[5] Canning's son-in-law. He had recently been involved in an apparently discreditable gambling incident.

the hand and spoke most cordially to him, and in short received
him more graciously than anyone. . . . He [Wellington] thinks the
King entirely devoted to Mr. Canning. . . .'[1] So, by degrees, Canning became a royal favourite. He began to show the King selected items of Foreign Office correspondence. This and the confidential discussions which ensued were much appreciated. Canning exercised his wit and the King was amused. As leader of
the House of Commons he kept the King informed of proceedings
in brief and entertaining notes. In Canning the King discovered a
refuge from boredom. Public affairs, as presented to the King by
Canning, were never tedious or troublesome. He was not wearied
or upset. Instead he was entertained, and yet, at the same time
made to feel that he was accomplishing his royal duties. In return
for providing such satisfaction Canning ultimately gained the
King's complete confidence. At his death George IV noted: 'one
of the many agreeable qualities Mr. Canning possessed as the King's
First Minister was — that Mr. Canning never kept anything back
from the King. There were no minor secrets.'[2]

So, by patience and only in extremities by threats, Canning
defeated the King's intrigues; having accepted royal surrender he
then successfully courted and kept royal favour. But the initial
struggle against the King could not have been won unless Canning
had been able to dominate the Cabinet. Opposition in the
Cabinet, however, while it had been sustained by royal favour,
also survived its loss. That opposition stemmed partly from principle and partly from personal prejudice against Canning. His
foreign policy seemed in some respects revolutionary and was
disapproved, on principle, by the ultra Tories; its ramifications
were complicated and frequently beyond the capacity of colleagues to comprehend. Lack of understanding bred suspicions
which were magnified by the Foreign Secretary's methods. He
seemed to take unnecessary risks, to delight in publicity, to court
popularity and to take sinister pride in springing surprises. Though
he could usually win an argument he often left his opponents with
a feeling that they had been tricked. Wellington once described

[1] 28th November 1826. Mrs. A., vol. 2, p. 59.
[2] ASP, vol. 3, no. 1400 , p. 291.

both Canning and Liverpool as tricksters to Mrs. Arbuthnot and on another occasion he told her: 'I assure you when I am with these two gentlemen, I feel like a man who, going into a crowd, thinks it prudent to button up his pockets. I button myself up and take the utmost care what I say, because I know that they are always upon the watch to twist one's expressions into some sense at variance with the true one. If an unguarded word is uttered they note it down to quote against one the next week or the next month.'[1] While Canning's foreign policy was the first cause of concern to the 'Ultras', they also regarded his views on the Catholic Question as a permanent and dangerous threat to the existing order. His support of Huskisson's economic policies was another reason for disquiet. Only on the question of Parliamentary Reform could Canning be regarded as sound and, even here, anxious Tories sometimes feared that he might stoop to a bargain with the Whigs.

Differences in the Cabinet soon emerged after Canning's return. On 3rd May 1823 Countess Lieven described the situation with insight, if not with precison.[2] 'It is impossible,' she wrote, 'for this Government to work as one; their collaboration is fast reducing itself to a test of endurance. It is easier to believe that twelve of them will get rid of the thirteenth, than that the thirteenth will get rid of the other twelve; but when I reflect how clever the unlucky number is, and how singularly second-rate are his dozen colleagues I begin to be afraid that it wont be our friends who carry the day'.[3] Countess Lieven was wrong in thinking that Canning had no supporters. He could count, much to the annoyance of other colleagues, on the whole-hearted backing of the Prime Minister. 'It is incalculable,' later wrote Canning, 'what an impediment and perplexity *our* strict union (Liverpool's and mine) upon the great subjects of foreign policy is to the sighers after the continental school.'[4] This solidarity so infuriated Wellington that he complained to Countess Lieven: 'My Lord

---

[1] February 1824. Mrs. A., vol. 1, p. 284.
[2] There were only twelve Cabinet members.
[3] L., p. 212.
[4] To Granville. 17th January 1825. G.C. & T., p. 507.

Liverpool is neither more nor less than a common prostitute.'[1]
In addition to Liverpool, Canning could rely, after January 1823,
on Robinson as Chancellor of the Exchequer and Huskisson at the
Board of Trade. Melville, at the Admiralty, could be counted as a
friend while Wynn, at the Board of Control, was in no way committed to the 'Ultras'. Vansittart had been the victim of Canning's wit in the past, but was not a certain opponent. Peel, at the
Home Office, possessed sufficient intelligence and ability to rank
as an independent. Because they differed over the Catholic Question and because he did not fall under the spell of Canning's charm
he eventually became after Wellington, the favourite of the 'Ultras'; as Arbuthnot gleefully noted of him in a letter to Bathurst
on 29th August 1823: 'I observe he has great suspicions of Canning; and it annoys him not a little that Lord Liverpool should
be under such subjection to him.'[2] Similarly Mrs. Arbuthnot recorded a complaint of Peel's that whenever he spoke to Liverpool on any matter the Prime Minister replied, 'I'll speak to Canning about it.'[3] But these indications of jealousy and suspicion
were magnified by Canning's adversaries; Peel could not be
counted among them, save over the Catholic Question, in the
Cabinet. On the contrary he often gave Canning valuable support, notably over the recognition of the new South American
States.[4]

In order to consolidate his own position, Canning's first move
was to persuade Liverpool to reshuffle his Cabinet. In January
1823 Huskisson replaced Robinson at the Board of Trade and became a member of the Cabinet. Robinson succeeded Vansittart as
Chancellor of the Exchequer and Vansittart took Bragge-
Bathurst's place at the Duchy of Lancaster. The manoeuvre was
completed in October with the removal of Lord Maryborough.
Thus Canning gained one valuable friend, Huskisson, while two
certain enemies, Bragge-Bathurst and Maryborough, were elimi-
nated. After these changes, however, the composition of the

[1] 18th July 1823. L., p. 224.
[2] BATH, p. 543.
[3] 1st February 1824. Mrs. A., vol. 1, p. 285.
[4] See N. Gash: *Mr. Secretary Peel*, pp. 439, 440.

Cabinet remained unaltered during his Foreign Secretaryship. His most persistent opponents were the Duke of Wellington, Lord Bathurst, Lord Eldon and Lord Westmorland. The Marquess of Camden and Viscount Sidmouth tended to support the 'Ultra' line but, though in the Cabinet, held no departmental offices and were no longer very active members of the Government. While he maintained a certain aloofness Wellington was regarded by the anti-Canningites as their leader. In his capacity as the chosen and confidential adviser of the King, he provided the main link between the 'Cottage'[1] and the 'Ultras'. In January 1823 the Duke complained to Mrs. Arbuthnot that: 'Mr. Canning is upsetting all our Foreign policy and doing things in so hasty and unreflecting a manner as will get him into innumerable scrapes.'[2] By February Mrs. Arbuthnot noted: 'the Duke of Wellington, who was the most eager to have him, is now the most uneasy at all that is going on and says he had no conception what a man he was!'[3] In the face of growing opposition led by the Duke, Canning's main object was to impose his own conception of foreign policy on the Cabinet. His method varied between endeavours to convince by argument or to flatten by pressure. Argument involved endless discussion at Cabinet meetings and voluminous correspondence, particularly with the indefatigable Duke. Canning seems to have shown considerable patience in exposition but he was faced with the difficulty that the 'Ultra' peers, not only instinctively mistrusted, but often could not understand, the purport of his schemes. When persuasion failed Canning resorted to pressure. This pressure was of two kinds: private and public. Private pressure was brought to bear in the Cabinet mainly through Liverpool's good offices in threatening his own resignation. The 'Ultras' might have been glad enough to be rid of Canning; they could not face the prospect of losing Liverpool. On several occasions this threat proved decisive. Canning used public pressure

---

[1] The Royal Lodge at Windsor was known as the Cottage and the intimate circle, including the Lievens and Esterhazy, who enjoyed royal hospitality there were often referred to as the 'Cottage' or 'Cottage Coterie'.

[2] 12th January 1823. Mrs. A., vol. 1, p. 203.

[3] 7th February 1823. Ibid., p. 213.

by exploiting his own carefully cultivated popularity; he would parade policies at which the 'Ultras' baulked either in the House, or on public platforms or by the publication of dispatches and then, strong in popular approbation, would claim to his Cabinet colleagues that retreat was impossible. The system often worked but was obviously resented by its victims. Canning's greatest struggle was his attempt to secure Cabinet approval for the recognition of the independence of the Spanish Colonies. He used argument and both kinds of pressure. Eventually he did not overcome so much as gradually grind down opposition. During the meetings of 14th and 15th December 1824, when the decision was finally taken, Liverpool and Canning both threatened to resign and it was only after hours of discussion that the diehards, now reduced to Wellington, Bathurst, Westmorland and Eldon, capitulated. Subsequently Wellington complained to Countess Lieven that he had been 'overwhelmed', 'that he was the only champion of the good cause' and that 'the meetings of the ministers were nothing but a dialogue between himself and Canning with the others as audience'. He added that 'Canning was so furious with him that, a score of times, he was ready to take him by the throat'.[1] Writing on 17th December 1824 to Granville, Canning, too, testified to the violence of the occasion: 'You will learn from another source . . . what a campaign I have been going through. I am really quite knocked up with it: the Sot Privé[2] if he wished to avenge the alliance by giving me a bilious fever had nearly had his revenge. The fight has been hard, but it is won. The deed is done. The nail is driven. Spanish America is free; and if we do not mismanage our affairs she is English and *Novus saeculorum nascitur ordo*. You will see how nobly Liverpool fought with me on this occasion.'[3] In the crisis which subsequently developed as a result of the King's letter to Liverpool, Canning, as has been seen, threatened complete exposure of the 'Cottage' plot; Wellington possessed sufficient common-sense to realise the risks and therefore resigned himself and rallied his supporters to the maintenance

[1] 20th December 1824. L., p. 280.
[2] Lord Westmorland. A pun on the office of Privy Seal which he held.
[3] G.C. & T., p. 411.

of Cabinet solidarity. Canning's tactics had proved triumphantly successful.

Having mastered the Cabinet on this main issue, Canning proceeded, as has been seen, to conquer the King. The winning of royal favour was however not sufficient to dispel Cabinet opposition. The 'Ultras', though less disposed to cavil about foreign affairs, kept a jealous eye on home problems. But they met with little success in their attempts to stem the tide of economic and administrative reforms sponsored by Huskisson and Peel, and supported by Liverpool, Canning and Robinson. On the Catholic Question, however, Liverpool and Peel shared the views of the 'Ultras'. Here therefore there was some room for manoeuvre against Canning. In the spring of 1825 a crisis developed.[1] The third reading of Burdett's Catholic Emancipation Bill was carried in the Commons by 248 votes to 227. Peel tendered his resignation. Liverpool threatened to follow suit but confided to Arbuthnot that he was prepared to carry on if Peel could be induced to do likewise. Bathurst managed to persuade Peel to change his mind and in the meanwhile, Burdett's Bill was decisively rejected by the Lords. Canning now hinted that the Catholic Question could no longer be left in abeyance and insisted on raising the matter in the Cabinet. Bathurst was prepared to let Canning resign but Liverpool refused to countenance the suggestion. 'I cannot . . . ,' he wrote to Bathurst on 22nd May 1825, 'agree with you that it would be right for me to let Canning resign if the majority in the Cabinet should still be for keeping the matter *in abeyance*.'[2] This was the principle upon which the Cabinet had been formed and Liverpool saw no reason to move from a formula which had hitherto, from his point of view, proved so satisfactory. In the event Canning, having vindicated his right to raise the matter, signified that he was satisfied and prepared to abide by the old formula.

Apart from tactical threats of resignation, Liverpool frequently spoke with evident sincerity of his own wish to retire from the Premiership; and indeed his poor state of health made it

[1] For a full account of this crisis see N. Gash: *Mr. Secretary Peel*, pp. 413–20.
[2] BATH, p. 583.

K

seem unlikely that the choice would rest with him much longer. The problem of the succession, therefore, preoccupied the Cabinet. Canning's claims would obviously meet with opposition from the 'Ultras'. Though he sought, with some success, to avoid exacerbating the Catholic Question his motives were suspect and, mainly on account of this issue, his opponents in the Cabinet were able to retain vestiges of their former prestige and power. He was not in a position either to overcome their hostility or to suggest that the Ministry could dispense with their support. Thus though he could, while Liverpool remained Prime Minister, enjoy an ample measure of authority, he could not feel confident about succeeding to the Premiership. Indeed in November 1826 a move was made to secure his positive exclusion. The Duke of York from his sick-bed appealed both to the King and to Liverpool calling for Canning's dismissal.[1] This manoeuvre failed, not only because of the King and Liverpool's staunchness, but because the 'Ultras' themselves feared that the crisis which might follow would provoke the very calamity against which the Duke of York was seeking to guard; namely the triumph of Catholic Emancipation and of Canning. So long as Liverpool remained Prime Minister the *status quo*, which neither Canning nor his opponents were anxious to disturb, could be preserved. Without the guarantee which Liverpool's presence implied a trial of strength seemed inevitable. Though Canning had succeeded in imposing his will upon his Cabinet colleagues he had not, as with the King, been successful in dispersing all opposition.

(iii) *The Final Struggle*

On 16th February 1827 Liverpool succumbed to a stroke; his eventual recovery was soon known to be no more than a remote possibility. The much canvassed succession problem seemed at last to have been posed. At Brighton, where he was just beginning to recover from a serious illness, Canning immediately concluded that, if the policies to which he had devoted the past five years were to be maintained, he must continue to wield

[1] See Stapleton: *Political Life*, vol. 3, pp. 299–300.

effective power. With this object in view he resolutely applied himself to the critical struggle. On the morning of 18th February Canning received a visit from Peel and they easily reached agreement to advise the King that the Government should for the present continue on the assumption that Lord Liverpool would recover.[1] The King entirely acquiesced in the course of action proposed.[2] Neither Peel nor Canning wished to precipitate the inevitable crisis. Canning was particularly influenced by the fact that important debates on the Corn and the Catholic Questions were pending in the House and he did not wish these debates to be prejudiced by conflict over the Liverpool succession.

News of Liverpool's collapse, however, immediately gave rise to a flood of rumours. Bets were taken on Canning's chances of the Premiership. 'The Clubs,' Mrs. Arbuthnot noted, 'and the public (that is to say the newspapers) settle that Mr. Canning is to be Prime Minister.'[3] This popularity was gratifying, but in the circumstances, somewhat embarrassing, and Lord Howard de Walden wrote on 23rd February to Huskisson to explain that 'Mr. Canning is *most anxious* (although he has only just expressed his anxiety thro' my father) that no friend of his shd talk *of his wishes,* or *in a way* to imply that *he* had either considered or discussed *any* arrangement for carrying on the Govt. . . . He wishes (and the K. too) that it shd be considered that Ld L. *may* recover, and therefore until something is decided about his state — that things shd go on as they do now, that [the] K. shd take no step whatever for the present.'[4] 'It is evident,' commented Mrs. Arbuthnot, 'that the Canning faction wish to make him [Liverpool] out better than he is and keep things as they are for the present, to ward off for a time the choice of a new Premier.'[5]

On 1st March Canning successfully moved the resolutions subsequently embodied in the Corn Bill and on 5th and 6th March the Catholic Question was debated. Surprisingly the

---

[1] See G.C. & T., p. 581.
[2] See 20th February 1827. Mrs. A., vol. 2, p. 82.
[3] 22nd February 1827. Ibid., p. 83.
[4] F.C.M., no. 29, p. 19.
[5] 5th March 1827. Mrs. A., vol. 2, p. 85.

'Protestants' found themselves in a majority of 4 (276 — 272). The majority was so small, however, and might so easily be reversed that it did not suggest the time was yet ripe for an all 'Protestant' or an all 'Catholic' Administration. Canning's enemies argued that this situation was to his liking because it provided him with a good case for claiming to lead a mixed Cabinet. Mrs. Arbuthnot complained that it would be difficult for the Duke to refuse to serve in such a Government and she feared that 'all the mischief would be done by *driblets* and by such slight degrees that the Duke would never have a point at which he could take his stand'.[1] Canning himself interpreted the vote as meaning that the Catholic Question must remain an open one in any new Administration and that a temporary truce should be declared. He, therefore, saw no reason on that score why the existing Ministry should not be reconstructed under his own leadership.

In the meanwhile he was faced by a move on the part of individuals in the Whig Opposition which, on the one hand, increased his own strength and, on the other, threatened his prospects. This was a suggestion in the Press, inspired by Brougham, that a coalition should be formed with Canning at its head. The suggestion was violently rejected by a number of leading Whigs, including Lord Grey, and was seized upon by Canning's enemies among the ultra Tories as evidence that he had for long been plotting with the Whigs and that he was utterly unfit to lead the Tories. Though Canning's desperate endeavours to rally his Tory supporters and the obviously improvised nature of his eventual negotiations with the Whigs were to prove the falsity of this accusation, it seemed at the time plausible enough. At any rate a group of ultra Tory peers, led by the Duke of Rutland, easily allowed themselves to be convinced that the time had come for action. Wellington was their candidate for the Premiership. On 5th March the Duke of Rutland wrote to Mrs. Arbuthnot asking her to use her good offices with the Duke to persuade him to 'become the head and champion of the party which it is the fashion to say has received its death-blow by the

[1] 10th March 1827. Mrs. A., vol. 2, p. 87.

two inflictions which in two short months it has sustained'.[1]
Mrs. Arbuthnot found herself in an awkward position. She
knew that the Duke, although unwilling to serve under Canning,
was not prepared to be regarded at this stage as a candidate for
the succession. She feared, by raising the subject, to incur his
displeasure and yet she was nevertheless most anxious that he
should play the part for which he had been designated by the
'Ultras'. Her husband shared her views and was prepared, without consulting the Duke, to put the idea, via Knighton, into the
King's head. Accordingly Arbuthnot in a lengthy interview with
Knighton, argued that the new Premier must be a 'Protestant'
and that 'no one would do but the Duke'.[2] When the Duke
heard of this conversation his reactions were violent. 'I have
been,' confessed Mrs. Arbuthnot, 'in a state of a good deal of
annoyance this week in consequence of the Duke's fear that Mr.
Arbuthnot's conversation with Knighton may have the appearance of an intrigue, and give the King and Knighton reason to
believe that the Duke wishes for the post of Prime Minister, and
that Mr. A's conversation with Knighton was with his knowledge and for the purpose of forwarding that work. I never saw
the Duke so much vexed about anything in my life. . . .' The Duke
apparently declared 'that he would rather serve under Mr.
Canning than be supposed to quit from anything like personal
pique'. In order to set his mind at rest, Wellington 'went, however, to Knighton and told him that he considered himself quite
out of the question and since he did that he has been rather more
tranquil'.[3] In addition to the tentative manoeuvres of the Arbuth-
nots, Wellington was being directly approached by members of
the 'Ultra' group and urged to sanction the sending of a representative to the King to propose his candidature as Prime
Minister. The Duke rejected all these advances but the 'Ultras'
nevertheless decided to make their own views known to the
King. Among their allies was the 'Catholic' Duke of Buckingham,

---

[1] F.C.M., no. 41, p. 31. The 'two inflictions' were Liverpool's stroke and the
death of the Duke of York.
[2] 14th March 1827. Mrs. A., vol. 2, p. 90.
[3] 22nd March 1827. Ibid., p. 92.

who had as early as 21st February written to Wellington claiming that '. . . the Catholic question must and will be carried. Is it not better to take the measure into your own hands . . . Mr. Canning will not do. Everyone is proud of his talents, but no one trusts his principles.' Buckingham, who wanted a family share in the spoils of office, then offered his own support to Wellington in any Ministerial capacity and suggested 'If not, send me to India'.[1] Wellington replied with a well deserved snub.[2] 'The D. of Buckingham,' noted Mrs. Arbuthnot, 'is a dirty shabby fellow and I am glad the Duke would have nothing to do with him — but I still do not like that he should repulse them all so unceremoniously; it is however very honourable and honesty is the best policy.'[3]

The intrigues of the Tory peers reached their height when in the last days of March they began to importune the King to exclude Canning. George IV refused to show his hand. But Canning, with good reason, remained confident of royal support. The attitude of the Tory peers only served to irritate the King and to reduce the possibilities of securing a 'Protestant' Premier.

While the principal actors in the drama, Wellington, Peel and Canning, remained generally above the intrigues which were being pursued during the month of March, certain facts began to emerge. The King was determined not to join in any discriminatory move against Canning. Wellington and Peel knew that Canning would not serve under either of them. Canning had reasons to doubt whether Wellington or Peel would be prepared to serve under him; nor was there any certainty that either would accept a man of straw as Premier in a Canning controlled Cabinet. Canning's own popularity, if the Press could be regarded as a yardstick, was such that it would not be easy for any Ministry to be formed without his approval.[4]

[1] F.C.M., no. 15., p. 10.
[2] Ibid., no. 17, p. 12.
[3] 22nd March 1827. Mrs. A., vol. 2, p. 93.
[4] In the final stages of the struggle the Press was almost unanimous in support of Canning. 'The extraordinary thing,' as Temperley has commented, 'is that even the most liberal and popular journals vied in upholding the Royal Prero-

On 28th March the King, who had received a message from Lady Liverpool formally confirming her husband's wish to resign, took the first active steps in the quest for a new Prime Minister. He received Canning and Wellington separately at the Royal Lodge at Windsor in order to clarify his own position and to obtain their advice. The King explained that his conscience would not permit him to appoint a 'Catholic' Prime Minister, but that he would like to see Liverpool's Government reconstructed with a 'Protestant' peer in Liverpool's place as Premier. Wellington apparently expressed the opinion that the King must choose between Canning and Peel 'or some third person under whom both would consent to serve'.[1] Discussion then turned to Canning's complaints of a cabal of Tory peers against him. 'At the same time, however,' according to Mrs. Arbuthnot, 'the King set out facts which prove how justly he is detested by a party whose head he pretends to be, while in truth he is taking advantage of his position to undermine their interests. The Duke said something to the King about his desire to keep the Catholic question quiet, upon which the King said that he understood from Mr. Canning that the persons in the kingdom who were the most anxious to keep the question quiet for him were the *Opposition*, that he knew Lord Lansdowne was ready to come in on these terms, that Mr. Brougham, who knew he was personally disagreeable to the King, consented to remain without office. The King said Mr. Canning had had no personal communication with Lord Lansdowne, but knew these were his sentiments.' To this the Duke apparently replied: ' "And now, Sir, can your Majesty be surprised that the Tory Party detest Mr. Canning? Can you be surprised that they cabal against him as a measure of defence against a man who is himself engaged in such a cabal as this? And still more can yr Majesty be surprised that we, his colleagues, who are the victims of such a cabal, refuse to see him placed at our head? I will now tell Your Majesty what I

---

gative, and in praising the King for his firmness in refusing to be bound by the 'iron circle" of prejudice.' TEMP, p. 437.

[1] *Colchester Diary*, vol. 3, p. 501. (Conversation with Colchester, 15th May.) F.C.M., intro., p. xxxv.

have never told you before — I *knew* all this intrigue with the Opposition — I knew more than Your Majesty, for I knew that Lord Grey (who is also supposed to be displeasing to you) was to be thrown overboard and that the Catholic question was to be sacrificed in this effort to obtain place and power. And can Your Majesty now imagine that we can consider ourselves safe with Mr. Canning at our head?" The King had not one word to say to this but he spoke with great anger about the Tory Lords caballing and said he would not submit to such dictation. The Duke said they really had not, but that they felt a great anxiety upon the subject and that he had himself prevented their meeting or doing any thing improper or disrespectful by the King.'[1]

Thus enlightened by Wellington the King received Canning who advised that a purely 'Protestant' Ministry should be formed.[2] In giving this advice Canning can hardly have been sincere. A purely 'Protestant' Ministry would have been difficult to construct and would probably have resulted in civil war in Ireland. But Canning, in tendering such advice, presumably hoped simply to underline the impracticability of its acceptance. He judged, no doubt rightly, that George IV wished his conscience to be forced and that, provided the choice did not seem to stem directly from him, he would be very glad to have Canning as a 'Catholic' Prime Minister in a reconstructed Liverpool Administration. In making this assessment of the King's attitude Canning was perhaps assisted by the memory of a remark made at a previous interview. 'You are,' the King had said, 'the fittest man to be Minister and the man I should like to appoint; but what a clamour there would be throughout the country if I made a man with your opinion about the Catholics, Minister; I should never hear the last of it.'[3] Canning now made it clear, in further conversation with the King, that, if the Ministry were to be reconstructed, he could not be satisfied with anything less than

[1] This whole account is as recorded by Mrs. Arbuthnot on 30th March 1827. Mrs. A., vol. 2, pp. 97, 98.

[2] For Canning's account of this interview see G.C. & T., pp. 582–6.

[3] According to Canning's account to Lord Lansdowne of his first interview with the King after Lord Liverpool's seizure on 22nd February 1827. *Lansdowne's Memorandum*. 19th April 1827. F.C.M., no. 173, p. 120.

the Premiership or the substantive power of First Minister. George IV eventually suggested that the Cabinet should be advised that the office of First Lord of the Treasury was vacant and invited to propose a nominee from among Tory peers holding Lord Liverpool's opinions on general questions. Canning deprecated the idea but agreed to consult Peel about it.

Canning accordingly returned to London on 29th March in the evening and discussed the King's suggestion with Peel who agreed in disapproving. On the following day Peel was received at Windsor and pointed out to the King that his proposal was 'really throwing the apple of discord among them'.[1] The King agreed to abandon the project. The brief meeting between Canning and Peel had been a friendly one, but it left Canning somewhat in the dark as to Peel's eventual attitude. 'What his ultimate decisions may be — or might be' — he confided to Knighton — 'I cannot say. But it is impossible to do more than justice, by any expression of mine, to the frankness and generosity, and self-denial, of his declarations.'[2] Further discussions still left the situation uncertain although it became increasingly obvious that there was little hope of Peel remaining a Minister in an Administration of which Canning was the ostensible or the substantive head.[3] Wellington, in the meanwhile, was anxious to discuss the situation with Canning, but uneasy lest his own conversation with the King at Windsor had been relayed. On 2nd April Arbuthnot had a long conversation with Knighton: 'It appears,' recorded Mrs. Arbuthnot, 'that the King did tell Mr. Canning that the Duke was opposed to him; he told him, too, what the Duke said about the Opposition (one can hardly conceive how the King can be such a fool or so unfair) and he sent Mr. Canning away impressed with a belief that the Duke

---

[1] 1st April 1827. Mrs. A., vol. 2, p. 98.

[2] 29th March 1827. F.C.M., no. 61, p. 43.

[3] See *Henry Hobhouse's Diary*, 2nd April 1827. F.C.M., no. 60, p. 48. Hobhouse also claimed that Canning was annoyed that he had not been invited to form a Government and that this irritation was increased by proceedings in the House on 30th March, 'for when Tierney alluded to Canning's becoming Prime Minister there arose a vociferous cheer from the Opposition benches, which was very faintly returned from the Ministerial side of the House'.

was at the head of a cabal against him. Mr. Canning was naturally
most deeply offended. . . . Sir Wm told Mr. Arbuthnot he was
quite sure the King was drunk when he talked with Mr. Canning
. . . that he was also sensible that he had got himself into a scrape,
for when he (Sir Wm) left Windsor the King said to him "My
dear friend, I rely upon you to get me out of all this business and
to manage so as to prevent their quarrelling". 'Accordingly
'Knighton was very desirous that Mr. Arbuthnot shd go to Mr.
Canning and explain that the Duke had said nothing that could
be the least unfair or unjust to Mr. (C).' The advice was taken
and 'Mr. Canning received him very cordially . . . Mr. A assured
him that the Duke had never said anything to the King which
could justify Mr. C in being offended, and that he knew he had
been very much concerned by observing from Mr. Canning's
manner that he was dissatisfied with him. Mr. Canning immediately said he was perfectly satisfied, that it passed entirely from
his mind and that he hoped the Duke wd accept his excuses and
think no more about it. He then said how desirable it was that
he and the Duke shd talk the whole subject over together. . . .'[1]
An appointment for 1 o'clock on 3rd April at the Foreign Office
was made. They talked for three hours but according to Mrs.
Arbuthnot, 'only discussed the *principle* advisable for a new
Govt'.[2] Canning referred to the possibility of forming an entirely
'Protestant' Government and the Duke rejected the possibility
of forming either an all 'Protestant' or an all 'Catholic' Administration. In her account Mrs. Arbuthnot insists that no mention of who should be head of the Government was made, but
there is reason to suppose that Canning in fact sounded the Duke
on whether he would be willing to serve in a mixed Government
with Robinson, transferred to the Lords, as its head, and that the
Duke signified dissent. The discussion, however, seems to have
been a friendly one and Canning reported to Knighton: 'Everything that was in doubt between us has been cleared up satisfactorily, and we parted, as you would have wished, all being
left well.'[2] Canning probably still thought that the Duke might

[1] 3rd April 1827. Mrs. A., vol. 2, pp. 99, 100.
[2] 4th April 1827. Ibid., p. 102.

be induced to remain in a reconstructed Ministry while Wellington himself may yet have hoped that Canning's services could be retained under a 'Protestant' Premier.[1]

At Windsor the King was visited by the Duke of Rutland who attempted to press the case against Canning and endeavoured to hint that the Duke should succeed Liverpool. These efforts met with little response from the King who deftly turned the conversation to trivial topics.[2] On 5th April he returned to town from Windsor. At Wellington's suggestion Peel and Canning held a further meeting and later on Canning and Wellington again met. After these meetings Canning confided to Knighton: 'My belief is that he (the Duke) and perhaps Peel too, hoped the explanation between me and the Duke would end in my begging him to take the government. I mention this, because it is contrary to the belief which I had before stated to you, that the Duke never thought of himself for that post. Further light has changed that belief entirely.'[3]

Although Canning could not count on the support either of Peel or of Wellington, he had during the past few days concluded that the King would eventually give him the opportunity of forming a Ministry and that the time had come to consider what Tory forces he could rally, with the King's assistance, in the Commons. He consulted Croker who advised that nothing could be done 'without the help of the aristocracy' and enclosed a list of 96 Tory and 54 Whig members of the House of Commons returned 'by the influence of some of the Peers'.[4] 'Am I to understand then,' Canning replied, 'that you consider the King as completely in the hands of the Tory aristocracy as his father, or rather as George III was in the hands of the Whigs? If so George III reigned and Mr. Pitt (both father and son) administered the government in vain.

I have a better opinion of the real vigour of the Crown when

[1] G.C. & T., p. 588.
[2] See Rutland to Mrs. Arbuthnot. 4th April 1827. F.C.M., no. 71, p. 52. The King apparently spoke of a painting of Maria, the Oaks filly, 'which was in the room'.
[3] 5th April 1827. G.C. & T., p. 589.
[4] Croker to Canning. 3rd April 1827. CRO, vol. 1, p. 367.

it chooses to put forth its own strength and I am not without some reliance on the body of the people.

And whether in or out of office (an alternative infinitely more indifferent to me than you perhaps imagine, and with the inclination of my choice, if anything to the latter) I will not act (as I have never acted) as the tool of any confederacy, however powerful; nor will I submit to insult (without resenting it according to the best of my poor ability) from any member of such confederacy, be he who he may.'[1]

These fine phrases gave way to more careful consideration and on the following day Canning wrote: 'Your list is good for nothing without commentary. Add therefore, if you can, to these names, the *price* that Government pays for their support, in Army, Navy, Church and Law, Excise and Customs, etc. And then calculate what number of unconnected votes the same price distributed amongst others would buy in the market if the Crown were free?'[2] On 6th April Croker replied: 'I send you a memorandum which I think, will surprise you. The aristocracy, powerful as it is, does not enjoy a great share of political *office* in the House of Commons. So that, in fact, a Government has less to give them, than at first thoughts one would have supposed. Depend upon it, the aristocracy is the *unum necessarum*, or, at least, an *indispensable* ingredient, and that in order to conciliate and manage them the Union of the Duke, Peel and yourself is absolutely necessary. I know very well that many of these grandees are very unreasonable, and I believe that there has been too much indiscreet and even offensive talk (though I have not myself heard any) but indiscretion and offenses are, I suppose, inseparable from the excitement which a state of things like the present naturally produces. If you, Peel, and the Duke are once agreed, all the rest will soon subside into their accustomed channels and flow along without even a murmur, which God grant.' From his memorandum Croker concluded that 'of 116 members returned by the Tory aristocracy only 18 held political office and of those 18 no less than 12 are persons on whom the

---

[1] Canning to Croker. 3rd April 1827. CRO, vol. 1, p. 368.
[2] CRO, vol. 1, p. 370.

patrons confer that favour at the request of the Government'.[1]
In all, Croker reckoned that 203 seats in the Commons might be
regarded as being in the hands of the Tory aristocracy.

The conclusion seemed clear. Canning must make further
endeavours to gain the support of his present colleagues or he
would be obliged to turn to the Opposition. Wellington and
Peel, however, remained adamant in their refusal to serve in a
Ministry of which Canning was either the ostensible or the real
head. With the King's approval Canning suggested that Peel
might be transferred to the Lords, given the lead there and
moved from the Home to the Foreign Office. Peel, however, insisted that his views on the question of Catholic Emancipation
were too strong for him to serve in whatever capacity under a
'Catholic' leader. On 7th April Arbuthnot informed Peel that
Lord Melville, though a 'Catholic', was unwilling to serve under
Canning.[2] The remaining 'Protestants' were equally unwilling to
commit themselves in any way to Canning. On 9th April the
King, after Lord Eldon had confirmed that a 'Protestant'
Ministry led by Peel was out of the question, summoned Peel and
requested him to invite Canning to serve under Wellington's
Premiership. It was the King's last duty to his conscience and to
the 'Ultras'. Canning inevitably rejected the proposal and at 3.30
on 10th April was summoned by the King and commissioned to
prepare with as little delay as possible a plan for the reconstruction of the Administration. The King, probably deliberately, did
not specifically nominate him as Prime Minister but Canning,
not without some justice, assumed the intention.

Although he had few guarantees of support from his colleagues,
he can hardly have been prepared for the rout which followed his
endeavours to keep together Lord Liverpool's Administration.
There were 41 resignations, including those of half the
Cabinet. The excuses varied but the Tory rebellion against
Canning's leadership was clearly manifest. A few waverers
could not resist the lure of office. Lord Bexley, with whose
services Canning would cheerfully have dispensed,[3] was prevailed

---

[1] CRO, vol. 1, pp. 370–2. [2] See F.C.M., no. 74, p. 55.
[3] See Canning to Knighton. 12th April 1827. F.C.M., no. 98, p. 65.

upon, as he claimed by the duty he owed to the King, to withdraw his proffered resignation.[1] The Duke of Buckingham, loath to be left out of any combination, immediately solicited the Indian Governor-Generalship.[2] But the overwhelming trend was desertion of Canning. The Duke even carried his hostility to resigning his army Command. This, he claimed, was due to the peremptory reply which he had received from Canning on enquiring who was to be the head of the reconstructed Ministry which Canning had been invited to plan. The Duke's original enquiry may well have been genuine because Lord Westmorland also, on receiving Canning's first approaches, had felt a need for clarification on this point.[3] However, the Duke's reaction was not even defended by Mrs. Arbuthnot who later judged that he had been 'in a huff with Mr. Canning about a matter of personal dignity'.[4] There seems to be no doubt that, in spite of previous good resolutions, Wellington acted on this occasion out of purely personal pique and that, while he might have maintained his resignation from the Cabinet as a matter of principle, there was no valid excuse for his refusal to remain Commander-in-Chief.

On 12th April Canning returned to the King with news of a major Tory rebellion. According to Lord Harrowby the King received him in bed — crying out, 'Well if you are not frightened, I am not. *Non me aspere torreat*. After this usage, if you were to present me a list of names entirely "Catholic", I should accept it and say it was not your fault and that you had done everything in your power to avoid driving me to this extremity.'[5] This outburst was probably in reply to Canning's exhortation: 'Sir, your father broke the domination of the Whigs. I hope your Majesty will not endure that of the Tories.'[6]

But Canning had as yet concluded no definite bargain with

---

[1] See Bexley to Canning. 13th April 1827. F.C.M., no. 104, p. 70.

[2] See Buckingham to Canning. 12th April 1827. F.C.M., no. 93, p. 62.

[3] See Westmorland to Canning. 10th April 1827. No. 83, p. 58.

[4] 21st August 1827. Mrs. A., vol. 2, p. 138.

[5] *Viscount Sandon's Memorandum*. 12th April 1827. F.C.M., no. 101, p. 67.

[6] GRE, vol. 3, p. 88. The words were repeated to Greville by Melbourne who claimed to have heard them from Canning himself.

the Whigs and, pending negotiations, a Cabinet of some kind needed to be formed. Negotiations proved difficult and protracted. Canning relied mainly on place seekers and on his friends. The Earl of Harrowby and Wynn retained their former offices. Huskisson remained at the Board of Trade and combined this office with the Treasuryship of the Navy. Lord Bexley, as has been seen, withdrew his original resignation and returned to the Duchy of Lancaster. Sir John Copley[1] could not resist the lure of the Lord Chancellorship and gratefully succeeded Lord Eldon. Palmerston remained Secretary at War, but now, for the first time in a long career, entered the Cabinet.[2] Sturges Bourne, after much pleading on Canning's part, accepted the Home Office on the understanding that it was a temporary appointment. Viscount Dudley agreed, also temporarily, to take over the seals of the Foreign Office. Lord Granville, who had very unwillingly agreed to discharge the business of the Foreign Office while Canning was endeavouring to form his Ministry, positively refused, friendship notwithstanding, to accept that or any other Cabinet office. He returned, with relief, to his Paris Embassy. Lord Anglesey became Master of the Ordnance, acting as he claimed purely out of duty to the King. In succession to Lord Melville at the Admiralty, the Duke of Clarence was appointed Lord High Admiral, but without a seat in the Cabinet; this revival of an old title in favour of a royal prince was a successful stroke which had been inspired by Croker. The Duke of Portland, out of family loyalty and after an appeal by Mrs. Canning, agreed to become, for as brief a period as possible, Lord Privy Seal. Canning himself became Chancellor of the Exchequer. The previous holder of that office, Robinson, was transferred, in order that he might be leader, to the Upper House as Lord

[1] He became Baron Lyndhurst.

[2] Palmerston was first offered the Chancellorship of the Exchequer; this offer offer was promptly withdrawn when it became known to Canning that he had been involved in recent stock market speculations and that he was accused of 'carelessness' in the affairs of a company of which he was a director. The Governorship of Jamaica and afterwards, the Indian Governor-Generalship were proposed as alternatives. After he had declined these offers, Palmerston was confirmed in his old post, which he had held since 1809, but with the new dignity of Cabinet membership. See Pemberton: *Lord Palmerston*, pp. 25, 26.

Goderich and became Secretary for War and Colonies. By the end of April these provisional arrangements were complete and Canning was prepared to face the House.

As early as 15th April Goderich, with characteristic lack of nerve, communicated his doubts to Canning. The Prime Minister replied with some asperity: 'Planta[1] will have apprized you (by my desire) that it is utterly, physically impossible for me to find time, at present, to enter into written discussion upon hypothetical cases of difficulty. I can therefore only acknowledge your letter of this evening, and assure you that I do not in any degree share your apprehensions, and (while I do not assume to myself any right to control the feelings or direct the course of any other person) declare my own unalterable determination not to desert the King.'[2] Canning's confidence depended on the successful outcome of negotiations with the Whigs. Immediately after the avalanche of Tory resignations Canning made contact with Lord Carlisle, who on 14th April called on Lord Lansdowne 'to assure him of C[anning]'s wish not only to obtain his support and that of his friends, but that he should form a part of the Govt, that at present he did not know the materials that were in his possession for constructing a Government and therefore he could not make any distinct proposition'.[3] This first tentative move found the Whigs bitterly divided. The opponents of any compact with Canning, led by Lord Grey, were strengthened in their resolve by news of the appointment of Copley[4] as Chancellor and by rumours that Canning had pledged himself to the King to keep the Catholic Question in abeyance. Lord Londonderry had been busy circulating, to Grey among others, a minute of a conversation which he had had with the King implying that such a pledge had been given.[5] In fact Canning had insisted on

[1] Joseph Planta. Permanent Under-Secretary at the Foreign Office and one of Canning's warmest admirers. See p. 31 above.

[2] F.C.M., no. 126, p. 87.

[3] Carlisle to Holland. 14th April 1827. F.C.M., no. 119, p. 80.

[4] See Grey to Lansdowne. 16th April 1827. F.C.M., no. 141, p. 95, where he argued that Copley's appointment 'speaks a language too plain to be misunderstood' as far as the 'Protestant' character of the Government was concerned.

[5] See Grey to Ellenborough. 16th April 1827. F.C.M., no. 140, p. 95.

being 'as free as air' where the Catholic Question was concerned, but he had assured the King that he would use his influence to keep the matter in abeyance for the rest of the Parliamentary session. This was because, after the vote of 6th March,[1] Canning himself felt that some delay was now opportune; he also wished for time in order gradually to break down the King's resistance. Tactics, therefore, prompted the limited assurance which he had given the King. He was now faced with the problem of killing the suspicions which had been evoked among the Whigs without unduly alarming the King and his own remaining 'Protestant' colleagues. He was able without great difficulty to refute the validity of the implication behind the Londonderry minute and many waverers, including Lord Holland, were prepared to consider co-operation.[2] Grey's attitude however remained unchanged. In his wooing of the Whigs, Canning received greatest support from Brougham, who on 16th April, at the height of the Londonderry episode, insisted to Viscount Althorp: 'in one word disbelieve every word you hear. *All* the appointments *are provisional* — Copley's not at all certain — the communication to Lord Lansdowne quite frank and satisfactory — Lord Londonderry's story impossible — but it will be contradicted. If our friends had rather see Canning ruined than the Catholics emancipated and rather have an ultra Government formed than one nine-tenths liberal, in order to spite one man — good and well — they have now the opportunity. But I quit them with unspeakable disgust if such be their views — and give up politics as a mixture of lunacy and imposture.'[3] On the same day Brougham reported to Lansdowne: 'I have stemmed the tide here caused by the minute of Lord Londonderry.'[4] Brougham was assisted in his efforts by the attitude of many of the rank and file among the Whigs. As Tierney wrote to Bagot: 'in the meanwhile the delight of the majority of the libereaux knows no bounds. Joseph Hume swears that he will give no trouble, not no more, and that Mr. Canning is the finest fellow in the world. There are others who do not see matters in the same

---

[1] See p. 138 above.
[3] Ibid.
[2] F.C.M., no. 135, p. 93.
[4] Ibid., 143, p. 96.

L

light, and have yet to learn how matters are better than they were in Lord Liverpool's time, but they are looked upon as sour crabbed old men, or enthusiastic boys that are foolish enough to expect that statesmen should be models of honour and purity.'[1]

After much prompting Lansdowne found sufficient courage to respond to Canning's proposal for a meeting and accordingly on 19th April they conferred at Lord Carlisle's house.[2] Canning gave a frank summary of his own difficulties with the King and with his colleagues since 1822. He exposed Lord Londonderry's misapprehensions and gave a clear picture of the footing upon which he now stood with the King. Discussion then turned to the conditions upon which the Whigs might join the Government. Canning explained that the Catholic Question must remain an open one. He insisted that, as the composition of the Cabinet was, contrary to the King's original intention, to be predominantly 'Catholic', he felt bound by his own undertaking to seek for a more 'Protestant' complexion to the Irish Government and that he did consider himself pledged to the King on that point. He also stipulated that 'the question of Parliamentary Reform was not to be brought forward' and that the motion to repeal the Test Act 'was to be withdrawn or at least not pressed'. He made it known that Robinson had been promised a peerage with the lead in the Lords. After this statement of his own position and principles Canning offered places as follows:

House of Lords
  1. Lord Chamberlain
  2. Lord Privy Seal
  3. Secretary of State for Home Department

House of Commons
  4. One Cabinet Office
  5–6. 2 Privy Councillors' offices
  7. One Under-Secretary of State
  8. One Board Office

[1] 16th April 1827. BAG, vol. 2, p. 387.
[2] The following account of this meeting is based on *Lansdowne's Memorandum*. F.C.M., no. 173, p. 118.

Law

Attorney-General or Solicitor-General according to the arrangement that may be found practicable and to the person proposed.

On the following day heated discussion of Canning's offer took place among the Whigs. Some argued that Lansdowne should have been Prime Minister or at least that he should have obtained the lead in the Lords. Resentment was also felt that Canning was only inviting co-operation after he had failed to gain other support; the point was put that, in view of their Parliamentary strength, the Whigs should have been asked to assist in forming the Government rather than merely to join it. Eventually the terms, in the light of the sacrifices demanded, were judged unacceptable.

This decision of the party leaders was immediately questioned by Brougham and by Sir Robert Wilson who organised a protest, threatening secession from the Party, at Brook's Club. Their intervention proved decisive and the negotiations were resumed. Canning found himself able to propose a 'Catholic' Chief Secretary for Ireland, while Lansdowne agreed that the new Lord-Lieutenant should be a 'Protestant' provided he were moderate and not bigotted.[1] By 27th April a provisional agreement had been reached. The Duke of Devonshire and Scarlett were to take office immediately as Lord Chamberlain and Attorney-General. The entry of Whig leaders to the Cabinet would be delayed until arrangements for the Government of Ireland were completed. In the meanwhile Whig support for the Administration, as far as it could be pledged, was promised. '. . . So it appears,' commented Mrs. Arbuthnot, 'that they wd now come over as *single rats* but not in a body. It never can last!'[2]

The situation, from Canning's point of view, was indeed precarious. In the Lords, Grey and the 'Ultras' joined forces to pour scorn on the Administration. Thus, before any definitive arrangement had been made with the Whigs, Canning, with his

[1] See *Lansdowne Memorandum*. F.C.M., no. 217, p. 156.
[2] 26th April 1827. Mrs. A., vol. 2, p. 107.

uncomfortable and disparate caretaker Cabinet, was obliged to face Parliament. 'Mr. Canning, having tried all parties,' noted Mrs. Arbuthnot, 'has got a little click of his own personal followers . . . they are all saying they hold offices till others can be found. They are called the provisional government and the Warming Pans,'[1] and Countess Cowper remarked: '*the Morning Chronicle* says it is like people going to keep places for the first act of a play.'[2]

Their leader took his seat as First Lord of the Treasury on 1st May. In the Commons there was general confusion. On the Government benches sat Tories and the majority of the Whig Opposition, including the radicals Burdett and Alderman Waithman; the Opposition benches were filled by seceding Tories, by Tories who chose to sit there but nevertheless desired to support the Administration and by Joseph Hume and John Cam Hobhouse who, as radicals, felt uncomfortable on anything but Opposition benches. Peel, who claimed that his resignation stemmed from one single matter of principle, refused to lead the Opposition and it was left to Sir Thomas Lethbridge, an independent country gentleman, to assume the role of the Government's chief opponent. There were of course 'Protestants' on the Government benches and 'Catholics' on those of the Opposition. The relative strengths of Ministerial and Opposition parties was never tested because no division on purely party lines took place. Canning, throughout, remained confident of a large majority, believing that he could in a crisis rely on the backing of independent and uncommitted members. In the Lords the Ministry's situation was more precarious, particularly when Grey joined the ranks of Canning's Tory opponents. But though the baiting of Canning became a popular sport there was no powerfully concerted opposition. Debate in both Houses began with a re-enacting of the differences and disputes which had preceded the formation of the Ministry. In the Commons, Peel opened with a long justification of his own resignation. Brougham followed with an equally long explanation of why he had be-

[1] 1st May 1827. Mrs. A., vol. 2, p. 109.
[2] To Frederick Lamb. 1st May 1827. F.C.M., no. 283, p. 206.

come a Government supporter. Canning then, after paying tribute to Peel's attitude, embarked on an able justification of his own conduct. He devoted particular attention to the Catholic Question and was at pains to point out, on the one hand, that he hoped matters would be allowed temporarily to rest and, on the other, that the battle must eventually be resumed. In the circumstances his argument was both politic and statesmanlike. On 3rd May tempers in the House grew hotter. When Peel's brother-in-law asked whether Canning proposed to fill certain vacant offices the Minister replied 'pale with passion' and 'with the look of a demoniac' by the single monosyllable '*yes*'.[1] Various other awkward questions were put to Canning including his attitude to Parliamentary Reform. He replied uncompromisingly that he would oppose it, as well as the Repeal of the Test and Corporation Acts, to the end of his life. The reply, in the light of his dependence on the Whigs, was courageous. Reporting to the King on his troubled day in the Commons, Canning complained that 'Peel had certainly thrown away all the moderation in which he had professed and to a great degree preserved on the first night of the meeting'. He added that 'the standard of *Opposition* is now openly raised,' and commented 'better this than a continuance of hollow pretences of unreal neutrality'.[2] In the Lords, while Wellington and other former colleagues sought to justify their own conduct, Lord Londonderry and the Duke of Newcastle were more bitter and more personal. The attack against Canning culminated on 10th May with Lord Grey's violent denunciation of the Prime Minister's career. Canning was so infuriated that he almost wished to accept a peerage in order to be able to reply. The opposition which thus manifested itself in both Houses was more irritating than dangerous.

The chief weakness of Canning's position lay in the obviously temporary character of his Cabinet and in the absence of any definitive settlement with the Whigs. The Duke of Bedford maliciously described the situation in a letter of 5th May to Lord

[1] 5th May 1827. Mrs. A., vol. 2, p. 115; and see Canning to the King. 3rd May 1827. ASP, vol. 3, no. 1323, p. 226.
[2] ASP, vol. 3, no. 1323, p. 226.

Holland: 'How ridiculous are these provisional ministers, and what is the object of this hocus-pocus work and pantomimic machinery? For tho' Lansdowne says he and Canning have thought it for the best, he does not condescend to tell us why. The Duke of Portland Privy Seal — God help him! Sturges Bourne, who I remember a briefless barrister, brought forward by Mr. Pitt, with scarce any pretensions to a subordinate office, Secretary of State! and to crown all, Ld Dudley Foreign Secretary! We are told these appointments are only temporary. You may appoint one of your stable boys to be your cook, and when your friends come to dinner with you, tell them the appointment is only provisional, but I believe they would be as little satisfied with it, as the Foreign Courts and Ministers will be with the provisional appointment of Ld Dudley, with his unfitness for business and various wanderings and *distractions*. Really the whole thing looks like one of Canning's jokes.'[1]

In order to improve the situation, Canning on 9th May re-opened negotiations with the Whigs and Lansdowne agreed to enter the Cabinet at once without Portfolio. Carlisle took the office of First Commissioner of Woods and Forests and Tierney became Master of the Mint, both with seats in the Cabinet. Abercromby took office as Judge Advocate-General and Sir James Macdonald as a Commissioner of the India Board. Thus the situation remained until the end of the session when in early July Lansdowne was transferred to the Home Office. Sturges Bourne then gratefully retired to the Woods and Forests while the Earl of Carlisle replaced the Duke of Portland as Lord Privy Seal.

The tightening of the coalition improved Canning's Parliamentary position and, with a few awkward moments, his Ministry successfully weathered the session. The most awkward moment was when the Government's Corn Law Bill was defeated in the Lords by 78 votes to 74. Lansdowne reported the defeat to Canning as 'the result of a combined movement of all those who are, for various reasons, ill-disposed to the Government'.[2] But,

[1] F.C.M., no. 290, pp. 213, 214.
[2] 4th June 1827. Ibid., no. 322, p. 236.

in fact, many of the Lords had been opposed to the Bill in question before the formation of the Government. The Press which had almost universally acclaimed Canning's Premiership remained generally favourable to the Ministry. Among a relatively wide section of the public Canning was popular[1] and so, because of his reputed stand against the aristocracy, was George IV. As early as 18th April Canning had suggested to Knighton that the King should show himself at the theatre.[2] The experiment proved highly successful and the King received an ovation. This situation was most gratifying to His Majesty whose fear of unpopularity was almost pathological. Canning had every reason to hope that, if he could keep his own Ministry together, the Catholic Question could eventually be carried without more than formal protests from the King. The Ministry however was not easy to keep together. The Whigs complained that their share of office and patronage did not correspond to the Parliamentary support which they brought to the Ministry. The definitive arrangements concluded in July were achieved in an atmosphere of jealousy and suspicion. Arbuthnot reported to Peel that, according to Holmes and to Herries, 'the exactions of the Whigs and their attempts to encroach, drive Canning nearly out of his senses'.[3] There was agitation that Lord Holland should be brought into the Cabinet and resentment that Canning insisted on retaining Portland and Sturges Bourne. Abercromby in a letter to Carlisle listed Whig grievances and regretted that 'the appearance is bad both for Canning and Ld Lansdowne. It looks as though there was a jealousy which I hope does not exist — it seems as if the one was grasping and the other yielding.'[4] Whig resentment continued after the July arrangements had been

---

[1] The extent of this popularity is difficult to measure. Professor Temperley points out that during his last illness one hundred thousand bulletins were circulated daily throughout London, while his funeral, 'despite its private character, was attended in a storm of rain by an innumerable and silent multitude'. The demonstrations which are alleged to have attended the burial of Castlereagh certainly provide a marked contrast. See TEMP, p. 316.

[2] F.C.M., no. 158, p. 107.

[3] 6th July 1827. Ibid., no. 340, p. 253.

[4] Ibid., no. 338, pp. 249–50.

concluded. Even Brougham, the architect of the coalition, showed signs of discontent and was obviously chafing at his own agreed exclusion from office. Apart from the importunities of the Whigs, Canning had to contend with the touchiness of his few remaining 'Protestant' supporters.

During the month of July various observers including Huskisson and Arbuthnot, came to the conclusion that the fate of the Administration depended on Canning's health. He, alone, it was felt, could keep the uneasy coalition together. His influence with the King, his popularity in the country and his general prestige were serving to paper a multitude of obvious cracks. Without Canning, the Whig party could reunite and, reunited, might possibly absorb the Canningites, but certainly would not any longer be prepared merely to share in a measure of patronage and power.

Canning appreciated the difficulties of the situation but was completely confident of his own capacity to exploit hard won victory. 'Be it as it may,' wrote Lyttleton on 22nd June, 'Master Canning acts much more like Cock of the Walk than any Minister has done for a long time. It does me some good to see a chance of a manly, united Ministry, and Canning notwithstanding 1000 old scores against him has gained, will gain, even with such old anti-Canningians as you know me for, if he goes on and prospers.'[1] He did not spare himself in any direction. At the end of the Parliamentary session he introduced his first and only budget. He continued, though well satisfied with Lord Dudley, to supervise the work of the Foreign Office.[2] He found time to attend to the complaints of the Whigs and to manoeuvre so that, in negotiation, he still contrived to get the best of any bargains struck. He was obviously as determined to avoid Whig dictation as he had been to reject Tory tutelage. 'What power that man has,' had commented Countess Cowper on 24th April, 'all his plans succeed.'[3] And indeed it did seem as if, thanks to his own

---

[1] To Bagot. BAG, vol. 2, p. 363.

[2] On 11th May Dudley had written to Bagot: 'I shall be here only till the end of the session, and my predecessor will I hope also be my successor.' But in fact, though Canning continued to supervise, Dudley remained in office.

[3] To Frederick Lamb. F.C.M., no. 240, p. 178.

ability and exertions, Canning would be able, as he believed, to hold the Government together and to achieve his major policy objectives both at home and abroad. But, at the pinnacle of fame, popularity and power and after a week's serious illness, he died on 8th August 1827. He had assumed that the victory upon which his last energies were expended was a decisive one but he had also assumed that he would live to manage the controls. No one else could take over. The validity of his presumed political triumph remained perforce untested. In the long struggle, which ended so enigmatically, to grasp and to hold political power, Canning dissipated such energy that it is possible to wonder whether the means and the end did not become confused. The answer may be found by considering whether the record of his achievements and the influence of his ideas justifies his claim to rank as one of England's greatest statesmen.

THE STATESMAN

(i) *The Constitution, Catholics and Corn*

Metternich and Canning were haunted by the same fear that any basic change in the Constitutional *status quo* would bring ruin to the States they respectively loved and served. This fear was, in Canning's case, engendered by the example of the French Revolution and crystallised by the political philosophy of Edmund Burke. Initially, however, Canning, whose intellectual curiosity had been aroused, viewed the Revolution with fashionable sympathy. Looking back in December 1792 he explained his early reactions to Wilbraham:

'Holding it as I do, to be an eternal and immutable principle, that what a Nation *wills* decidedly and unanimously with respect to its own internal Government and Constitution — *that* it has a right to accomplish without hindrance or interruption from without — I have all along wished that France might succeed in giving to itself, what it has all along appeared to *will* with a decision and unanimity almost unexampled in the history of nations, the form of a pure Republick. And to this wish I have perhaps been the more warmly inclined, because this form of Government having been never yet tried in the ancient or modern world, and being that into which *our* Government, if ever it should change at all materially, would be most likely to resolve itself; I could not but think it in some measure a fortunate circumstance for *this* country, that there should be a nation in Europe under such circumstances, as to be likely and willing to put this great experiment to the proof and to ascertain, what without such proof can never be ascertained convincingly — how far a Constitution so modified can consist with the happiness of a great and polished people.'[1] 'But,' continued Canning, 'when having gained the opportunity for the peaceful establishment of

[1] 12th December 1792. BAG, vol. 1, pp. 36, 37.

their Constitution — the French forewent the use of that opportunity and turned their thoughts to conquest, and the propagation of their faith in a manner and to an extent wholly incompatible with the first principles on which they assumed a right to found their Constitution, and on which they ought to have founded it . . . I cannot any longer wish that the Powers of Europe should sit tamely with their hands before them without endeavouring to throw some stop in the way of an insolence and implacability of ambition which is no less dangerous to every other country, than it is irreconcilable with the duty, the policy and the repeated profession of France.'

Thus Canning came to fear 'French arms' and 'the wide diffusion of French Principles'. Believing that the British Constitution was in danger, he began to consider its merits and concluded: 'As to this Country — though I am not so enthusiastically attached to the beauties of its Constitution, and still less so determinedly blind to its defects, as to believe it unimprovable — yet I *do* think it by much the best practical Government that the world has ever seen — that of America perhaps excepted, and of that indeed it is not quite fair yet to form a decided opinion — I do think it almost impossible to begin improving now, without a risque of being hurried beyond all limits of prudence and happiness. . . .'

As time passed Canning became increasingly attached to the beauties of the Constitution and more blind to its defects. In the Prospectus of *The Anti-Jacobin* the editors declared . . . 'We avow ourselves to be *partial* to the *country in which we live* . . . we are *prejudiced* in favour of *her* Establishments, civil and religious. . . .' This partiality and these prejudices formed the basis of Canning's political creed. 'To an impartial observer,' Canning proclaimed in 1818 at Liverpool, '— I will not say to an inhabitant of this little fortress — to an impartial observer, in whatever part of the world, one should think that something of this sort would have occurred. Here is a fabric constructed upon some principles not common to others in its neighbourhood; principles which enable it to stand erect while everything is prostrate around it. In the construction of this fabric there must be some curious felicity, which the eye of the philosopher would be well employed in investigating, and which its neighbours may profit by adopting.'[1] 'Our lot,' he boasted in 1822, 'is happily cast in the temperate zone of freedom: the clime best suited to the development of the moral qualities of the human race; to the cultivation of their faculties, and to the security as well as the improvement of their virtues: a clime not exempt from variation of the elements, but variations which purify while they agitate the atmosphere that we breathe. Let us be sensible of the advantages which it is our happiness to enjoy. Let us guard with pious gratitude the flame of genuine liberty, that fire from heaven, of which our Constitution is the holy depository; and let us not, for the chance of rending it more intense and more radiant, impair its purity or hazard its extinction!'[2]

So, like Burke, Canning was to discover a virtue, almost divine, in the established order. He noted a struggle in other lands between the principles of monarchy and democracy but he concluded: 'God be praised that in the struggle we have not any part to take. God be praised that we have long ago arrived at all the blessings that are to be derived from that which can alone end such a struggle beneficially, a compromise and intermixture of those conflicting principles.'[3] The balance, however, achieved over many years and by so many fortuitous circumstances, was precarious. Any tampering threatened disaster. 'I fear,' he confessed at Liverpool in 1820, 'to touch that balance the disturbance of which must bring confusion to the nation.'[4]

The most serious threat, in Canning's view, was any attempt to alter the system of Parliamentary representation. While prepared to consider the remedy of any flagrant abuse in a specific case, he refused to countenance modifications based on any general principle. 'I have,' he argued, 'never stated it as a beauty of the Constitution that Old Sarum should have but as many voters as representatives. Let it have two thousand, with all my heart. I have never stated it as a beauty and perfection of the Constitution, that this or that great peer should be able to return persons

[1] Therry, vol. 6, p. 360.
[2] Ibid., vol. 4, p. 380.
[3] Ibid., vol. 6, p. 410.
[4] Ibid., p. 391.

of his choice as representatives of the people in Parliament. I have never said that detected corruption should not be punished. In God's name, disfranchise other corrupt boroughs as you disfranchised Grampound. But I have said, and I repeat, that I see no way of counteracting the influence of property, that I can imagine no process of computation of close boroughs — on the ground, not of practical punishment, but of speculative improvement, and on the principle that the House of Commons ought to speak the direct sense of the people — which does not lead, by inevitable inference, to a total alteration of the functions of the House of Commons.'[1] He argued that any major change in the franchise system would inevitably affect the position of the Monarchy and the House of Lords. Reformers who focused their attention on the House of Commons were, he maintained, being disingenuous. 'Gentlemen,' he explained to his Liverpool supporters in 1818, 'the whole fallacy lies in this: the reformers reason from false premises, and, therefore, are driving on their unhappy adherents to false and dangerous conclusions. The Constitution of this country is a monarchy, controlled by two assemblies; the one hereditary, and independent alike of the Crown and the people; the other elected by and for the people, but elected for the purpose of controlling and not of administering the Government. The error of the reformers, if error it can be called, is, that they argue as if the Constitution of this country was a broad and level democracy, inlaid (for ornament's sake) with a peerage, and topped (by sufferance) with a Crown.

If they say, that, for such a Constitution, that is, in effect for uncontrolled democracy, the present House of Commons is not sufficiently popular, they are right; but such a Constitution is not what we have or what we desire. . . . But they look far short of the ultimate effect of the doctrines of the present day, who do not see that their tendency is not to make a House of Commons such as, in theory, it has always been defined — a third branch of the legislature; but to absorb the legislative and executive powers into

[1] From a speech at a public dinner at Liverpool, 30th August 1822. Therry, vol. 6, p. 400.

one; to create an immediate delegation of the whole authority of the people — to which, practically, nothing could, and in reasoning, nothing ought to stand in opposition.'[1] This, in Canning's opinion, could only be described as a Republic and to Canning a Republic was 'nothing but one continual struggle for office in every department of the state'.[2] Power was fatally divorced from responsibility.

In 1822, when speaking against Lord John Russell's Reform Bill, he extolled the virtues underlining apparent abuses. 'For my part,' he argued, 'I value the system of Parliamentary representation, for that very want of uniformity which is complained of in this petition; for the variety of rights of election. I conceive that to establish one uniform right would inevitably be to exclude some important interests from the advantage of being represented in the House.'[3] And later in the same debate he concluded: 'While we dam up one source of influence, a dozen others will open; in proportion as the progress of civilization, the extension of commerce, and a hundred other circumstances, better understood than defined, contribute to shift and change, in their relative proportions, the prevailing interests of society. Whether the House of Commons, in its present shape, does not practically though silently accommodate itself to such changes, with a pliancy almost as faithful as the nicest artifice could contrive, is, in my opinion, I confess, a much more important consideration, than whether the component parts of the House might be arranged with neater symmetry, or distributed in more scientific proportions.'[4]

The strength of his convictions was never more apparent than during the last months of his life. Though compelled to make a compact with the Whigs, he insisted that he would stand as a bulwark against Parliamentary Reform. On being questioned in the House he made his position quite clear. 'I am asked what I mean to do on the subject of Parliamentary reform? Why I say — to oppose it — to oppose it to the end of my life in the House, as hitherto I have done.'[5] So, throughout his political career, Canning remained consistent in his defence of the Constitution as he

[1] Therry, vol. 6, pp. 362–4.   [2] Ibid., p. 323.   [3] Ibid., vol. 4, p. 343.
[4] Ibid., p. 373.   [5] Ibid., vol. 6, p. 242.

understood it. Perhaps because his opinions had been formed under the impression of a threat of revolutionary contagion from France, any sign of social unrest represented a danger signal. During the Napoleonic wars fears of revolution in England faded and were submerged in the struggle for national survival. After Napoleon's defeat, amid the social unrest which followed the peace, these fears were soon reawakened. Canning unhesitatingly identified discontent with disaffection. Repression was the remedy. When Canning returned to Government service in 1816, his diagnosis had been made and his attitude to the problems posed was predetermined. As Bagot noted, with satisfaction, in a letter to Binning: '. . . I see plainly that Jacobinism is raising its crest again in a way it has not done for years — and that is the Antagonist of Canning. It is in his battles with this monster that he is always great and always useful.'[1] And a few days later he wrote to Sneyd: '. . . The Jacobins are abroad again, I see it plainly, and this is one of the many reasons why I rejoice in Canning's return to the Govt. I long to see him flourish his Brougham stick again.'[2] 'For let us not be imposed upon,' Canning dutifully warned in February 1817, 'by the trite and futile argument that our would-be reformers and revolutionists are but few in number. This may be, and it will be a consolation when the attempt shall have been suppressed; but it is no security against its success if we omit to take vigorous measures for its suppression. Experience is all the other way. When was a revolution effected in any State but by an active and enterprising minority? Can it be forgotten how frequently, in the course of the French Revolution, the world has seen sanguinary minorities riding in blood over the necks of their prostrate countrymen. As little should we lay to our souls the flattering hope that the bare absurdity — the monstrousness of any doctrine is a sufficient security against the attempt to reduce it into practice.'[3] Far from diminishing, his apprehensions grew and on 24th August 1818 he categorically declared: 'The dangers in my conception are greater than in 1793; the means of resistance,

---

[1] 1st June 1816. BAG, vol. 2, p. 18.
[2] 12th June 1816. Ibid., p. 22.
[3] Therry, vol. 3, p. 449.

and the sense of the necessity of resistance, comparatively nothing.'[1]

During these years Canning, while at the Board of Control, became the Government's chief spokesman in the Commons in defence of repressive legislation. There is no doubt that he believed in the reality of the danger and in the efficacy of the remedy. 'Do I exaggerate,' he told his constituents in March 1820, 'when I say that there was not a man of property who did not tremble for the tranquility and security of his home? — that there was not a man of orderly and religious principles who did not fear that those principles were about to be cut from under the feet of succeeding generations? Was there any man who did not apprehend the Crown to be in danger? Was there any man, attached to the other branches of the Constitution, who did not contemplate with anxiety and dismay the rapid, and, apparently, irresistible diffusion of doctrines hostile to the very existence of Parliament as at present constituted, and calculated to excite, not hatred and contempt merely, but open and audacious force, especially against the House of Commons?'[2] Rigorous repression, according to Canning, alone had saved the day; Peterloo was fully justified.

Not until 1822 did Canning begin to feel that the danger of a revolutionary tide was in recession; only then did he favour a somewhat milder attitude on the part of the Government. But, though he considered that the battle against the mob had been won, he continued to deprecate any hint of the necessity for Parliamentary Reform. Instead of using his eloquence to justify repressive legislation he could, once again, concentrate on defending his conception of the Constitution against the arguments of Parliamentary protagonists of change.

Though Canning was blind to the causes of popular discontent and rigid in defence of the Constitutional *status quo*, he himself nevertheless emerged, in certain spheres, as an advocate of change. It was perhaps over Catholic Emancipation that he most obviously assumed the role of a reformer. His opinions on this question were, characteristically, derived from his assessment of the Irish problem itself and not from any general principles of human

[1] To Bagot. BAG, vol. 2, p. 82. [2] Therry, vol. 6, p. 370.

rights. This was shown by his persistent refusal to support the repeal of the Test and Corporation Acts. The argument which he used in 1827 to defend this attitude was also typical. The Acts, he claimed, were to all intents and purposes a dead letter. An attempt to repeal them might, he feared, by reviving old controversies, prejudice the case for Catholic Emancipation.

From the outset of his career, possibly because of his Irish origins, he took a particular interest in Irish affairs. As early as December 1792, and after he had become a convert to Burke's view of the French Revolution, he wrote: 'In Ireland the Catholics pursue their claims as yet with moderation and temper, but if something be not done for them in the ensuing Session of Parliament, the consequences will probably be either war or massacre.'[1] His attitude changed somewhat when England was at war with France. In this emergency he began to doubt whether the time was ripe for any major changes in Ireland. When in late 1794 Pitt recalled Lord Fitzwilliam, the Viceroy, because he seemed to be moving too fast towards meeting Catholic claims, Canning approved Pitt's action. 'It is very possible,' he wrote in April 1795, 'to think with Lord F. that the complete removal of all the remaining restrictions on the Irish Catholics would be a wise and proper measure. I am myself inclined to be of that opinion. But wise or unwise in itself there are a thousand reasons for wishing to avoid the discussion of it in times of ferment and danger.'[2] As the situation in Ireland deteriorated, however, Canning began to feel, with Pitt, that the security of England itself was dependent on the conciliation and pacification of Ireland. In the light of this conclusion he supported Pitt's plan for a Union of Parliaments. Speaking in January 1799 in defence of Government policy, he tried to probe to the root of the problem. 'The fault,' he said, 'is in the nature of things and in the present disposition of property, and division of the classes of society in that country. They want commerce, they want capital, they want a generally diffused spirit of industry and order; they want those classes of men, who connect the upper and lower orders of society, and who thereby blend together and

---

[1] To Wilbraham. 4th December 1792. BAG, vol. 1, p. 31.
[2] *Canning's Journal.* D.M., p. 99.

M

harmonise the whole. But it is not an Act of Parliament that would effect these great and beneficial objects; no, it is only by a connection with a country, which has capital, which has commerce, which has that middle class of men, of whom skill and enterprise, and sober orderly habits are the peculiar characteristics; it is by such a connection alone, diffusing the means of wealth, and the example and encouragement of industry throughout the sister kingdom; it is by such a connection that so great and beneficial a change must be effected.'[1] Irish disaffection threatened British security; disaffection was the product of discontent; discontent could be cured by prosperity; prosperity would follow the close connection of which an Act of Union would be a symbol; therefore Canning supported the measure and was prepared to advise that Irish objections, however strong, should be overruled in deference to the real interests, and therefore the real wishes, of all Irishmen. There were flaws in the argument. But it had been used before and was to recur in many forms and circumstances. In his first approaches to the Irish problem Canning was typically English.

He maintained his interest in Irish affairs during the period of negotiation and on 22nd February 1799 he wrote: 'I have been thinking of nothing else for these two months, and luckily (in that respect) the winds and waves have been so good as to keep all foreign mails from coming in — so that I have had plenty of time to think of it. And the result of my thought is that it must succeed and will succeed, and that our poor Country will be saved, in spite of the folly and fury of *some* of its *mistaken* patriots, and all its self-interested ones. *Next* year I hope we shall be one People.'[2] Canning greeted the fulfilment of his hopes with enthusiasm. He does not seem to have believed that the success of the measure depended on immediate gratification of Catholic claims.

During the controversy which developed between the King and Pitt, Canning showed little solicitude for Ireland; he chiefly regretted that Pitt should have found cause to resign; he was determined to demonstrate loyalty by following his patron out of

[1] Therry, vol. 1, p. 149.
[2] To Bessy Canning. *Western Letters*. D.M., p. 192.

office but, clearly, he was not impressed by the urgency of the Catholic Question in Ireland.[1]

Irish affairs in general, however, continued to command his attention; and in March 1804 he supported an Opposition motion calling for an enquiry into the conduct of the Irish Government relative to the insurrection of 23rd July. '. . . I voted,' he said, 'for the Union between this country and Ireland. I was then an English member of Parliament; since that Union I have sat here as an Irish member, and I will now ask how it is possible for this House, the great bulk of which consists of English members, to refuse to inquire into a matter so generally interesting to the Empire at large and so particularly interesting to Ireland.'[2]

Three months later Pitt resumed the Premiership and Canning re-entered Government service as Treasurer of the Navy. In his subsequent quest for promotion he proposed himself for the Irish Secretaryship. Previously in 1799 he had confessed to Boringdon a desire to be associated with the Government of Ireland. On both occasions personal ambition and anxiety to promote Ireland's welfare were closely intermingled.

Canning was reconciled to remaining Treasurer of the Navy when Pitt promised Cabinet membership; but, as has been seen, Pitt died before that promise could be redeemed.[3]

During the next few years Canning found little time to spare much thought for Ireland. The excitement of posturing as leader of the Opposition and his subsequent tenure of the Foreign Office kept him fully occupied. During the anti-Catholic agitation of 1806–7 in England he observed a passive attitude; when in 1807 and in 1810 the Catholic Question was raised in the House, he refused support for Emancipation out of loyalty, so he claimed, to Pitt's promise to George III. However, during the relative leisure which followed his resignation in September 1809, Canning's attention reverted to Ireland and he undertook some study of the recent past. In principle he had always approved Catholic Emancipation. Now, in the light of his latest investigations, he became convinced that it was an essential and immediate objective; indeed, perhaps too easily, he concluded that it would prove a

---

[1] See p. 68 above.　　[2] Therry, vol. 2, p. 117.　　[3] See p. 81 above.

universal panacea. However, it was not until the Regency Bill had been passed in 1812[1] that he considered himself absolved from Pitt's promise to George III and personally free to act on his own conclusions. Accordingly on 22nd June 1812 he moved a resolution in the House that, early in the next session, consideration should be given 'to the laws affecting His Majesty's Roman Catholic subjects with a view to such final and conciliatory adjustment as may be conducive to the peace and strength of the United Kingdom . . .'.[2] He claimed that his motion was based on three principles. 'First, without subjecting myself to the suspicion of adopting any of those wild theories of abstract rights — of rights of man, and rights of citizens — which have been afloat in the world for the last twenty years, I may assume, as a general rule, that citizens of the same State — subjects living under the same Government — are entitled, *prima facie*, to equal political rights and privileges . . . exceptions undoubtedly there are: but upon those who maintain the exceptions, lies the *onus probandi* — the showing that they are necessary and just.'[3]

As his second principle, Canning maintained that 'it is at all times desirable to create and to maintain the strictest union, the most perfect identity of interest and feeling among all the members of the same community'.[4] Finally he argued that where 'a great permanent cause of political discontent' exists 'it becomes the duty of the . . . state . . . to take a question of such a nature into its own consideration'.[5] 'Consider,' he urged, 'how much the progress of public opinion has mitigated the violence of religious dissensions. Surely these are favourable circumstances for enabling us to unite with concession to the Catholics the indispensable condition of security to the Protestant Church; and it will be hard, indeed, if, in proportion as the obstacles diminish on the side of those who are to grant, they shall rise up and multiply on the side of those who solicit concession.'[6]

Canning showed courage, and gave evidence of genuine con-

---

[1] As he explained in a speech in the House on 15th February 1825. See Therry, vol. 5, p. 364.

[2] Therry, vol. 3, p. 356. [3] Ibid., p. 295. [4] Ibid., p. 296.

[5] Ibid., p. 297. [6] Ibid, p. 345.

cern, in championing the Emancipation cause at this juncture in his own career. By doing so, incidentally, he forfeited his cherished hope of representing Oxford in Parliament.[1] He had, however, the satisfaction of gaining a majority of 129 in favour of his resolution in the House. But this success caused a powerful Protestant reaction which was reflected in the new Parliament. The Prince Regent was now known to have been converted to his father's opinions. The Prime Minister and most of the Cabinet were staunch 'Protestants'. In these circumstances it is not surprising that, though opinion in the Government was free, there was little enthusiasm for experiments.

In February 1813, following the resolution which Canning had successfully carried in the previous year, Grattan moved for a committee on the claims of Roman Catholics. Much controversy and debate ensued on the question of securities which should accompany Grattan's proposals. As his amended Relief Bill finally emerged it included, at Canning's instigation, a royal veto clause on the appointment of Catholic bishops and deans. On 24th May the Bill was defeated in a packed House by 251 votes to 247. Because it implied a formal recognition of the Roman Church, the veto clause, intended by Canning to propitiate Protestant opinion, on the contrary provoked a measure of Protestant disapproval.

Catholic mistrust was more obviously aroused. Before news of the failure of the Bill was known to them the Roman Catholic bishops in Ireland had formally declared against its ecclesiastical clauses. O'Connell lost no time in pouring successful scorn on Grattan's compromising proclivities. Catholic opinion in Ireland was seriously split.[2] One way and another, Emancipation prospects seemed to have been prejudiced by Canning's well intentioned and theoretically politic intervention. In the meanwhile his own political position was weakened and that of the Government, thanks to victories abroad, strengthened. Although he

[1] At least according to the opinion which he expressed in the House. See Therry, vol. 3, p. 345. See also N. Gash: *Mr. Secretary Peel*, p. 215, where other considerations are held to have proved decisive.

[2] For a good account of the consequences of Grattan's Bill and of its failure in Ireland see N. Gash: *Mr. Secretary Peel*, pp. 153–62.

reverted when possible to the topic of Ireland, he ceased to be able to exercise any powerful influence.

When he joined Liverpool's Ministry in 1816 he was primarily concerned, at home, with renewed fear of revolution. The moment seemed inopportune for promoting reforms of any kind. Though he remained in favour of Catholic Emancipation, though he valued his right, as a member of the Government, to hold his own opinions, he was satisfied generally to hold them in silence. He concurred with the Irish Coercion Acts which were designed to suppress the widespread agrarian discontent currently manifested in crime and disorder. His lips otherwise remained sealed until in May 1819, in reply to Mr. Tierney's allegations of disunity in the Cabinet, he cautiously commented: 'An Administration decidedly and uniformly hostile to them [Catholic claims], would be equally likely to excite a clamour and to engender an irritation, at variance with the best and most essential interests of the Empire. In this case, as well as in many others, that which at the time it occurred was a bitter disappointment, has providentially turned out to be a most happy circumstance. The question is (in my judgement) gradually making its way in public opinion; and to public opinion it ought to be allowed eventually and soberly to settle the question. Such are my sentiments with respect to that question, the only important question on which any difference of opinion exists in the Cabinet.'[1] Canning may indeed have genuinely come to believe that Emancipation must await gradually dissipating Protestant prejudice, but his reply was more calculated to reasure his colleagues than to cheer Irish Catholics.

In April 1821 Plunket carried an Emancipation Bill in the Commons, including the veto clause. Canning, now no longer in Government office, gave warm and eloquent support. The Bill was rejected by the Lords. Canning, however, felt that capital could still be made out of Plunket's achievement. Accordingly in April 1822, when opposing Lord John Russell's motion that the House should seriously consider Parliamentary Reform, he introduced a reference to Plunket's Bill and then cheerfully maintained: 'I have not the slightest doubt that the House has run be-

[1] Therry, vol. 4, p. 135.

fore the sense of the country, which is now, however, gradually coming up to us. I have no doubt that in all our early votes on this most important question, we had not the country with us; but I am equally confident that the period is rapidly advancing, when the country will be convinced that the House of Commons has acted as they ought to have done.'[1]

Canning was now personally prepared to bring a little gentle pressure to bear. He was no longer a member of the Government and he no longer regarded revolution as imminent. On 30th April he moved a Bill 'for the purpose of restoring to Roman Catholic peers, the exercise of the right to sit and vote in Parliament'. In answer to accusations on the one hand that this was 'an insidious attempt to obtain a partial decision on the whole of what is called the Catholic Question' and, on the other, that 'separation of one class of the Catholic community from the rest, must necessarily prejudice the whole', he argued: 'If any measure be a step to advance the general question, it cannot prejudice that question; if it be, on the other hand, an obstacle to the success of the general question, then surely it must be hailed with delight by those who wish that question to be lost.'[2] In spite of these sophistications Canning carried the House by five votes. His Bill was of course designed as a preliminary step towards complete Emancipation. Continual opposition could be expected from the Lords and therefore the strengthening of the 'Catholic' vote was desirable in that House. Not surprisingly the Lords rejected Canning's Bill. He had, however, reaffirmed his interest in the general problem and had succeeded in mustering a majority in the Commons.

When he returned to the Cabinet as Foreign Secretary he found himself absorbed by many matters which seemed of more pressing importance than Ireland's troubles. Brougham in April 1823 accused him of 'monstrous truckling for the purposes of obtaining office'. The taunt was unjust and eventually Canning once more became actively involved in consideration of Irish problems. Writing on 15th February 1825 to Granville he said: 'I look upon the session till Easter as monopolised by the grievances and

---

[1] Therry, vol. 4, p. 351.　　　　　　　　　　[2] Ibid., p. 383.

distractions of Ireland.'[1] Leadership of the movement in Ireland had now passed to O'Connell, and his Catholic Association represented a formidable new force. In February 1825 the Government brought forward a motion to suppress the Association. Canning agreed with the Government's policy but at the same time remained convinced that the situation in Ireland now demanded the carrying of Catholic Emancipation; otherwise, he felt, the Union itself would be compromised. During the debate on the Suppression Act he explained his reasons for supporting Government policy. 'The tide of English wealth,' he pointed out, 'has been lately setting in strongly towards Ireland. The alarm occasioned by this Association acts at present as an obstacle to turn that tide, and to frighten from the Irish shores the industry, enterprise, and capital of England. Is it not then, Sir, I ask, the duty of Parliament to endeavour to remove this obstacle — to restore things to the course which nature and opportunity were opening; and to encourage and improve in Ireland the capacity to receive that full measure of prosperity, which will raise her, by no slow degrees, to her proper rank in the scale of nations?'[2] 'I am of the opinion,' he insisted, 'that the existence and proceedings of the Catholic Association have greatly alienated the public mind of England from the Catholic cause.'[3] He reaffirmed his own belief in the inviolability of the Church of Ireland and added: 'Let it not be inferred that I am therefore unfriendly to the Catholic Question. I peremptorily deny that inference. I am at all times ready to give the Catholic Question my best support, but I plead guilty to the charge of being irreconcilably unfriendly to the spoliation of the Protestant Church of Ireland.'[4] He then reviewed his whole previous attitude to the Catholic Question and endeavoured to prove that he had been a consistent advocate of Emancipation; he recognised that the obstacles were considerable and he urged that, mainly because of an anxiety to move too fast, much ground had been lost. 'But, Sir,' he concluded, 'the lost ground may yet be recovered. . . . With a view to that recovery, we must put down, in Ireland, faction, of whatever description; we must put down all

[1] C.G.C., vol. 1, p. 241. [2] Therry, vol. 5, p. 339.
[3] Ibid., p. 347. [4] Ibid., p. 354.

unconstitutional associations, but foremost, this Catholic Association, for which alone a stand has been made. I conjure the House
therefore to entertain and to pass this Bill; first for the suppression
of an association of which no Government worthy of the name of
a Government could tolerate the existence; and secondly, for the
advancement of the great question to which that association has
endeavoured to ally itself, an alliance of which the Catholic Question must be disencumbered before it can have fair play.'[1]

Obviously Canning found himself in a somewhat awkward
position. He detested the Catholic Association and yet the activities of the Association confirmed his opinion that Emancipation
had become an urgent question; by pressing Emancipation he
could hope to win over moderate Catholic opinion in Ireland; on
the other hand, by pressing too strongly he might only succeed
in mobilising Protestant opinion in England. Thus, while recognising the need for action, he yet felt obliged to advise a temporis-
ing policy. In retrospect he was satisfied with the debate and with
his own performance. As he wrote to Granville: 'Upon the whole
the battle has done good. It was very disagreeable and to me personally very difficult. But the result has been to the Government,
strength; to the House of Commons, credit; and to me, an intel-
ligible and assured position upon a ground hitherto doubtful and
slippery; a position in which, when the demagogues have struck
and the Opposition have exhausted themselves, I may perhaps
hereafter — but at my own time and in my own way — be enabled to do some good to Ireland, and to bring this most intractable question to a pause, if not a final settlement.'[2] On 1st March
1825 Burdett[3] moved a preliminary resolution in favour of the
Catholics and obtained a majority of thirteen. A Bill founded on
the resolution was at once introduced. On 21st April the second
reading was opposed. Canning reaffirmed his faith in Catholic
Emancipation in a major speech. 'I say, then,' he warned in his
concluding words, 'that whatever rival nation looks jealously into

[1] Therry, vol. 5, p. 385.
[2] 22nd February 1825. C.G.C., vol. 1, p. 250.
[3] Sir Francis Burdett (1770–1844). A leading radical M.P., he had twice been
imprisoned on political charges in 1810 and again in 1820.

the state of England to find a compensation for all her advantages, and a symptom of weakness amidst all her power, will fix — does fix — as if by instinct, its eyes on the state in which we keep the Catholic population of Ireland. "There," they say, "is the weakness, there is the vulnerable point of England." How sad that they should say this with so great a semblance of truth!'[1] The motion was carried by 27 votes and the Bill accordingly read a second time. On 10th May it passed the House of Commons with a majority of 21. Peel had tendered his resignation on 29th April in anticipation and it seemed that a Cabinet crisis could no longer be averted.[2] In the House of Lords the Duke of York, on presenting a petition against the Bill on 12th May, created a sensation by delivering a violent speech to support his father's opinions on the Catholic Question. The Lords rejected the Bill. A 'No Popery' agitation once again met some popular response. First Peel, and now Canning, seemed disposed to bring matters to a head. But in the Cabinet, after many discussions, moderate counsels prevailed. As late as 25th May Mrs. Arbuthnot recorded: 'Cabinet discussion of Irish Q. Nothing settled. He (W) wishes to keep everything as it is, but I doubt his keeping Mr. Peel if Canning stays.'[3] However, on 27th May she noted: 'To the surprise of everybody, when the Cabinet met, Mr. Canning, tho' evidently very much out of humour, said he did not wish to break up the Govt. on the Catholic question, and as he found he had a right to consider the subject in the Cabinet when he pleased, he should do nothing more at present!'[4] The Prime Minister was mainly responsible for patching up this truce.[5] With the help of Arbuthnot and Bathurst he successfully induced Peel to withdraw his resignation and at the same time rejected Bathurst's suggestion that Canning's resignation, if submitted, should be accepted.[6] By his attitude he rallied the Cabinet. He feared the consequences of a split on the Catholic issue. And so, after careful reflection, did Canning. He felt certain

[1] Therry, vol. 5, p. 422.
[2] See N. Gash: *Mr. Secretary Peel*, p. 417.
[3] Mrs. A., vol. 1, p. 400.
[4] Ibid., p. 401.
[5] See N. Gash: *Mr. Secretary Peel*, pp. 418–20.
[6] See p. 135 above.

that his own resignation would break up the Ministry; that would lead to a dissolution; elections, in present circumstances, would produce a 'Protestant' majority in Parliament; and so the cause of Catholic Emancipation, he concluded, would be prejudiced, rather than aided, by any gestures on his part. As he wrote on 3rd June 1825 to Granville: 'If we can get a quiet summer and autumn in Ireland and a quiet session next year in Parliament (supposing no dissolution) or a New Parliament (supposing one) in as good principles as the present, I think the cause will be gained.'[1] But, he insisted, 'quiet in Ireland was indispensable'. Any immediate dissolution would result in a 'No Popery' Parliament. If Ireland were disturbed, a 'No Popery' Parliament would emerge whenever elections were held. He concluded that there was no point in pressing the Catholic Question in the present Parliament because 'it is only by new authority that they (the Lords) can feel justified in changing their vote'. Thus only a new Parliament could secure Catholic Emancipation; but elections must be deferred until passions had had time to cool. Canning was now concerned to damp the ardour of 'Catholic' supporters on the one hand and to prevent a dissolution on the other.

In the latter task he needed to walk warily in order not to evoke too many suspicions on the part of his 'Protestant' colleagues in the Cabinet. On 5th September he wrote to Liverpool: 'I never had to deal with a more perplexing question than that on which you ask my opinion.'[2] After some prevarication he recommended postponement but proclaimed himself willing to defer his own opinion. On 12th September he recognised that '. . . if the dissolution be deferred, the discussion of the Catholic Question must be prevented', and professed himself 'ready in that case to take the task of preventing it upon myself'. 'In such a state of things,' he added, 'it seems to me that delay is the safer course. Should there be any furious religious contest now, we shall bear the blame of exciting it unprovokedly and unnecessarily. Should the like contest (or one still more furious), be produced next year, at least it will not be our fault, but that of an inevitable necessity.'[3]

[1] C.G.C., vol 1, p. 271.   [2] Ibid., p. 289.
[3] Canning to Liverpool. C.G.C., vol. 1, pp. 294–5.

Liverpool gladly accepted Canning's advice. 'I have never,' grumbled Mrs. Arbuthnot, 'known Ld Liverpool more duped by Mr. Canning in my life. . . . I am very sorry we do not dissolve this year but I daresay the feeling against Popery will be just as strong next year. . . . Mr. Canning, however, succeeding in his object is a great proof of his influence and the more provoking because the Opposition, who dreaded a dissolution, had all along said they knew Mr. Canning would save them from it.'[1] The Opposition seem to have been grateful and, by soft-pedalling on the Catholic Question, enabled Canning to redeem his promise to Liverpool.

When the Parliament of 1820 was eventually permitted 'to die of extreme old age' in 1826, feelings in England on the Catholic Question, though calmer, were still running high. 'No Popery' was a popular slogan, as Lord John Russell found when he lost his seat. In Ireland, on the other hand, O'Connell's campaign was turning into a triumph. This convinced Canning that the Catholic Question could not longer safely be left in abeyance. He considered the inevitable struggle which lay ahead with resignation rather than enthusiasm. It was generally known that Burdett would return to the attack in the House in the New Year. In the meanwhile the Duke of York tried to bring pressure on Liverpool to form an all 'Protestant' Administration; he resisted this pressure, remaining uneasily and unwillingly in office, to face a certain crisis on the Catholic Question. On 16th February 1827 he succumbed to a stroke. In the ensuing confusion, which was complicated by Canning's own poor state of health, Burdett offered to postpone raising the Catholic Question. This apparently generous offer did not suit Canning. On the contrary, he wished the Question to be brought forward and Emancipation carried in the Commons before a new Administration was formed. In the Liverpool Ministry the Catholic Question was an open one; there seemed every chance that in these circumstances a majority for Emancipation could be won. On the other hand, if the debate were postponed the Catholic Question was bound to bedevil Ministerial reconstruction and Canning as a 'Catholic' could not so

[1] 26th September 1825. Mrs. A., vol. 1, p. 414.

easily claim to lead any Ministry where the Question was left an open one. So Canning insisted that there should be no delay on account of his indisposition.

Accordingly Burdett brought forward his motion on 5th March; on 6th March Canning spoke eloquently in its favour. But, to Canning's surprise and disappointment, the motion was lost by four votes. This caused Canning to change his plans. He concluded that a pause was inevitable before the Question could be tackled again. The first essential was that he himself should succeed Liverpool. Then, once his own position as head of a new Government had been established, and after he had gained the approval of the King, he hoped to be able at length to carry Catholic Emancipation.

In the event, his road to the Premiership proved a hard one. He found no support as leader of a reconstructed Liverpool Administration. He was forced to bargain with the Whigs and, in order to satisfy the King's conscience and many of his remaining Tory supporters, he had to maintain that the Catholic Question would continue to remain an open one; because he was suspect as a 'Catholic' he had to give guarantees that 'Protestants' would be found for the Government of Ireland; the search proved difficult and aroused bitter feelings in both camps; but eventually with the choice of William Lamb as Secretary an acceptable compromise was reached. Delicate manoeuvres lay ahead. Canning was compelled to preach patience and discretion to 'Catholics' while relying on his own ascendancy with the King gradually to force the royal conscience. It is possible that, had he lived, Canning would have succeeded in welding the disparate elements of his Ministry together and, after only a show of resistance on the King's part, carried Catholic Emancipation. Certainly it had become one of his main objectives.

But even if Canning had been able to carry Emancipation it is very unlikely that he would have solved the Irish Question. Catholic Emancipation might have reconciled Ireland to the terms of the Union in 1801. By 1827 it was too late. Though Canning had throughout appreciated the importance of Catholic Emancipation, and though he manoeuvred with some dexterity, he still regarded the Irish Question as one of English expediency. This made him over-optimistic. Though he regretted delays and post-ponements, he did not believe that they were likely to prove fatal. His care for Ireland was not proof against fear of prejudicing other issues or of causing an English political crisis. He laboured cautiously and consistently but he was not passionately moved. Furthermore he assumed too easily that Emancipation would solve all problems. His knowledge of recent developments was superficial. He had no more than a hazy conception of the gravity of Ireland's economic plight, now magnified beyond danger level by a vast increase in population. In the story of Ireland, he can only claim a place among the many British statesmen with good intentions but without enough sense of urgency or direct personal knowledge.

During the last, and 'liberal', years of Liverpool's Government, Canning, in addition to his minority and abortive campaign for Catholic Emancipation, generally backed the policy of change. He approved Peel's Benthamite approach to his duties at the Home Office. One of the results was a complete revision of the Criminal Code based on the findings of Mackintosh's Committee of En-quiry. Though inspiration came from the Radicals, it was Peel who translated their ideas into Government policy. Canning took no personal share in these transactions and was only involved as a sympathetic Cabinet colleague.

With the Government's economic policy, as evolved by Robin-son and by Huskisson, he was more closely associated. Belief in the virtue and importance of the middle class was a fundamental point in his political creed. To Canning the middle class meant the financiers of the City and the leading merchants of England. His bias towards the middle class was emphasised by the pleasure he frequently took in tilting at the aristocracy and the landed in-terest. Canning was not one of them, either by birth, or by upbringing, or by his tastes. Although he had shared their educa-tional privileges, he liked to claim that he had risen by his un-aided talents and exertions. He seemed almost determined to pose as an outsider. This attitude was not merely a platform gambit. It sprang from pride and possibly from envy. But it also helps to explain Canning's predisposition in favour of commercial interests.

Apart from this psychological factor Canning had, as a disciple of Pitt, been influenced by the ideas of Adam Smith. He had not devoted any particular study to economic questions but had been satisfied to take most of Adam Smith's conclusions, as understood by Pitt, for granted. In 1810 he had served with Huskisson on the Bullion Committee and he had familiarised himself with currency problems. Following this association he developed an implicit trust in Huskisson's judgement. Through Huskisson he preserved his faith in Adam Smith and also, at the same time, acquired respect for Ricardo's views on public finance.

When Robinson replaced Vansittart as Chancellor of the Exchequer, and Huskisson was admitted to the Cabinet as President of the Board of Trade, the way was clear for widespread abolition of trade and industrial restrictions. Canning gave steady and unquestioning support in the Cabinet and occasionally, as over the silk trade, in the House. This support was particularly valuable when, as in late 1825 and early 1826, a mild economic blizzard gave colour to the complaints and criticisms of Huskisson's opponents.[1] In spite of their misgivings Huskisson succeeded in implementing a great part of his reforming programme.

This achievement, from his point of view, was offset by the threat to England's economic health which the anomalous Corn Laws continued to represent. He was convinced that change was essential and here he faced even more ignorance and prejudice. Eventually Liverpool took the matter into his own hands and won over the Cabinet to Huskisson's draft Bill, which made provision for a sliding scale of duties. Canning approved the project but he did not become directly involved in the Corn controversy until after Liverpool's stroke.

---

[1] As Mrs. Arbuthnot noted on the 10th February 1826, 'Credit is totally destroyed, the funds are today at 76 having been this time last year at 90, and every person in the City is in despair. . . . I saw Rothschild this morning, who told me the whole country would be ruined if the Ministers persisted in letting in foreign goods next July.' Mrs. A., vol. 2, p. 11.

Then he applied himself industriously to the problem and, having mastered its intricacies, devoted all his energy to promoting the Government measure. After success in committee he moved the Bill on 1st March 1827 in the House. He spoke persuasively and tactfully. With minor amendments the first reading was carried. To Canning's regret there was no time for further progress before the Ministerial crisis which finally resulted in his own Premiership.

It was therefore in different and more difficult circumstances that he resumed the Corn struggle. On 4th May 1827 he wrote to Granville: 'As sometimes happens, the storm of Parliament arises, like other storms, after a long calm and in sight of port. Such is the Corn Question at this moment; which occupies and will occupy for the next few days all my thoughts, and more than all the time I have to bestow upon it.'[1] On the 9th he again confessed: 'Corn still monopolises me.'[2] On 12th he reported with satisfaction majorities of 5 to 2 in the Lords and 3 to 1 in Commons and added that this had 'further dissipated a thousand apprehensions, and insinuations, and surmises, which the discontent of our agricultural grandees, inflamed by the treachery of Lord Lauderdale, and the miscalculating fury of Lord Grey had been raising, for the last fortnight, in town and country.'[3] His hopes were premature. When the Bill came before the Lords for its third reading the Duke of Wellington proposed an amendment. Before doing so he had been in correspondence with Huskisson; a complete misunderstanding ensued, as a result of which Wellington believed that he had got Huskisson's approval. In fact, as Goderich at once realised, the amendment destroyed the whole sense of the Bill. This he tried to explain, but Canning's personal enemies, including Grey, could not resist the opportunity and, thanks to their support, the amendment was carried against the Government. An attempt to undo the damage on report was frustrated when the Lords confirmed the amendment with an increased majority. Canning was so enraged that he doubted the Duke's good faith. 'The D. of Wellington,' he wrote to Granville, 'I am afraid, has greatly lowered his high estimation by his trickery, or dupery (I

[1] C.G.C., vol. 2, p. 49.   [2] Ibid., p. 52.   [3] Ibid., p. 53.

will not venture to pronounce which) upon the Corn Bill.'[1] To
Granville he also reported on 17th June: 'We have lost our Corn
Bill in the Lords, but I yesterday launched a new one in the H of C
which I trust will serve the present purpose and which, if the
Lords are not absolutely mad with faction, must pass that House
too.'[2] This was just a temporary expedient, as Canning explained
in the House, and involved no more than the release of currently
bonded corn. He complained that a plot had been engineered
against him and that the Duke had been used as an instrument,
but he insisted that his resolution was unshaken and that he would
bring forward the original Bill once more in the forthcoming
session. In fact he was not to meet Parliament again, and so, in
spite of all his efforts, he proved unable to settle Corn according
to Huskisson's compromise plan.

Thus, in support of Huskisson's economic policy at home, save
for his brief and unsuccessful sponsorship of the Corn Bill, Canning's role was a subsidiary one. But in his conduct of foreign
policy he gave clear indication of the importance which he
attached to commercial questions and of his lively appreciation of
the problems at issue. This interest was evident in most of his
Latin-American dispatches and in much of his correspondence
with other British representatives abroad.[3] The arts of diplomacy
were effectively mobilised; every move was calculated and every
bargain shrewd. In addition to his practical interest in current
commercial questions, Canning also exercised his mind on future
possibilities and problems. For instance, on 26th April 1825 he
wrote to Liverpool: 'I am not sure among all our thousand under-
takings whether we have an isthmus (Panama) cutting company
or not, but it will certainly be most provoking to pay toll to the
Yankees.'[4] And again on 24th June 1826, in reply to a question
from Liverpool about Columbian frontier lines, he wrote: 'I will

---

[1] Canning to Granville. 17th June 1827. C.G.C., vol. 2, p. 325.

[2] Ibid., p. 325.

[3] Even Canning's famous rhyming dispatch to Bagot contained a serious
instruction on reprisals which might be threatened if the Dutch persisted in their
refusal to sign a reciprocity treaty on lines which he had determined.

[4] C.G.C., vol. 1, p. 268.

N

take care of your memorandum for information respecting trade and the [river] Columbia. But it is not from what our trade is now, that the question is to be estimated. It is when China shall open to English as well as American Commerce that the real value of settlements on the North-West coast of America will become apparent.'[1]

In general, while regarding the promotion of commerce as a major function of British foreign policy, Canning, as has been suggested, took economic theory for granted. When winding up his budget speech on 1st June 1827, he read out a long quotation and concluded: 'These words, Sir, are Mr. Pitt's: the authority cited is Dr. Adam Smith. He clearly says, that the application of philosophy to politics is not innovation. This was in 1792, and I, Sir, am content to go back to 1792, and take those words of Mr. Pitt into my own mouth, and proclaim them to Parliament, as those which shall be the guide and pole star of my political course.'[2] The economic theories of Adam Smith, as understood by Huskisson, pointed towards drastic revision of the Corn Laws, and it seems likely that if Canning had lived, and if his Ministry had survived, he might have been led to anticipate Peel in the direction of total repeal.[3] As events transpired, however, it was his attitude towards economic questions, rather than any positive achievement, which indicated that he was in tune with the 'wind of change'.

Greville subsequently claimed that 'he was the only statesman who had the sagacity to enter into and comprehend the spirit of the times, and to put himself at the head of that movement which was no longer to be arrested. The march of Liberalism (as it is called) would not be stopped, and this he knew, and he resolved to govern and lead instead of opposing it.'[4] Greville's claim, whatever its validity, was no doubt partly based on Canning's flair for public relations. When the publication of diplomatic correspondence could serve his ends he was never slow to grasp the oppor-

[1] C.G.C., vol. 2, p. 62.

[2] Therry, vol. 4, p. 284.

[3] It might even be suggested that had Canning lived, repeal of the Corn Laws would have preceded Parliamentary Reform.

[4] 31st August 1830. GRE, vol. 2, p. 41.

tunity.[1] Professor Temperley has estimated that in his efforts to ameliorate the condition of slaves in the Colonies and to abolish the Slave Trade throughout the world, he wrote more than a thousand dispatches; most of these were published, for instance, 262 in 1825/6 and 255 in 1826/27.[2] Far from shunning publicity, he gloried in it. When speaking in the House, which he treated as a stage, he obviously was addressing, and through the Press reaching, a wider audience. He also believed in giving outside performances. As Mrs. Arbuthnot angrily noted on 14th November 1823: 'Mr. C. has been making himself more ridiculous than enough by going round the country speechifying and discussing the Acts and intentions of the Govt. This is quite a new system *among us* and excites great indignation.'[3] On 27th April 1824 she again complained: 'Mr. Canning . . . finding he makes no way with the King or the Tory party, is running a race of popularity. He went on Easter Monday to the Lord Mayor's feast . . . all these speeches at taverns will only disgust rational people who do not like to see the dignity of high office prostituted to such purposes.'[4] Canning, who had incurred royal wrath, justified his attendance at the dinner in a characteristic letter to Liverpool for submission to the King. '*The City,*' he wrote, 'may be a very inconvenient power in the state. But *there it is.* You cannot put it aside. You cannot even control it. It has been suffered to slip out of your hands; but I think it would be a good policy to endeavour, by all reasonable attentions, to recover it. I flatter myself that I have as good a right as any publick man of the present day not to be suspected of courting popularity by a compromise with Jacobinism. I have passed nearly thirty years in fighting the battle with it. I have incurred as much unpopularity, in that contest, as any man, and have braved that unpopularity as fearlessly. But I think the battle has now been fought. I think we have gained the victory. And I think it would be something like a dereliction of publick duty not to reap the full advantages of the present position of the Government; a position which it is for the interest of the King's service to strengthen, and which owes the small part of its

---

[1] See Temp, p. 315.   [2] Ibid., p. 314.
[3] Mrs. A., vol. 1, p. 275.   [4] Ibid., p. 304.

present strength to His Majesty's personal popularity.'[1] Of course Canning was not the first politician to publish departmental correspondence, or to have his speeches extensively reported in the Press, or to make frequent addresses to his constituents, or to indulge in policy pronouncements at civic banquets. But his purpose was so deliberate and his efforts so successful that his attitude seemed, to friends and enemies alike, to represent a significant innovation.

In the light of his general approach to public relations it is not surprising that Canning recognised the growing importance of the Press. As Treasurer of the Navy he had gained early experience of the duties of a Government Press officer. Writing on 30th December 1809 to Huskisson, who was then Treasurer of the Navy, he told him that it was 'of course as much his business to deny having any influence over the newspapers as it was his duty to exercise that influence'.[2] During his years out of office he wrote extensively for the new *Quarterly Review*, which was designed to break the Whig monopoly of the educated reading public. On his return to the Foreign Office, although the newspapers were generally anti-Government, he enjoyed increasingly favourable publicity. *The Times*, however, though occasionally 'borne away by the tide of public opinion', remained, as a result of an old feud, basically as 'inimical . . . as ever'.[3] But in general, as the 1827 Ministerial crisis showed, the newspapers were, as he had intended, on Canning's side.

The audience to whom Canning was appealing, via his own speeches and indirectly via Press opinion, consisted mainly of non-aristocratic men of substance such as his own Liverpool constituents. Their backing was not only a useful asset in his political manoeuvres but, as he rightly concluded, a growing necessity for any Government in the changing world of his time. It was at a farewell dinner to his Liverpool constituents, in the Lyceum room on 30th August 1822, that he eloquently defined his view of the role of public opinion in the British Constitution.

[1] Canning to Liverpool. 5th May 1824. ASP, vol. 3, no. 1163, p. 75.
[2] HUSK, p. 72.
[3] See Canning to Granville. 29th December 1826. G.C. & T., p. 556.

'What should we think of that philosopher, who, in writing, at the present day, a treatise upon naval architecture and the theory of navigation, should omit wholly from his calculation that new and mighty power — new, at least, in the application of its might — which walks the water, like a giant rejoicing in his course; — stemming alike the tempest and the tide — accelerating intercourse, shortening distances — creating, as it were, unexpected neighbourhoods, and new combinations of social and commercial relation — and giving to the fickleness of winds and the faithlessness of waves the certainty and steadiness of a highway upon the land? Such a writer, though he might describe a ship correctly, though he might show from what quarters the winds of heaven blow, would be surely an incurious and an idle spectator of the progress of nautical science, who did not see in the power of *steam* a corrective of all former calculations. So, in political science, he who, speculating on the British Constitution, should content himself with marking the distribution of acknowledged technical powers between the House of Lords, the House of Commons, and the Crown, and assigning to each their separate provinces — to the Lords their legislative authority — to the Crown its veto (how often used?) — to the House of Commons its power of stopping supplies (how often, in fact, necessary to be resorted to?) — and should think that he had thus described the British Constitution as it acts and as it is influenced in its action; but should omit from his enumeration that mighty power of public opinion, embodied in a free Press, which pervades, and checks, and perhaps, in the last resort, nearly governs the whole — such a man would, surely give but an imperfect view of the Government of England as it is now modified, and would greatly underrate the counter-acting influences against which that of the executive power has to contend.'[1] It is interesting to notice, and very typical of Canning, that this peroration came in the midst of a defence of his opposition to Parliamentary Reform; equally typical was the adroit use of the steam analogy to a Liverpool audience.

During the last five years of his life Canning consciously

[1] Therry, vol. 6, pp. 404–5.

fostered his 'liberal' reputation. It was based primarily on foreign policy, where he revelled in the role of hero to Metternich's villain; on his endeavours to reduce the Slave Trade; on his championship of Catholic Emancipation; on his support of administrative and economic reforms; on his tilting at the landed establishment; and on his advertised eagerness for public approbation.

His campaign met with considerable success. For instance, in a letter to Bagot on 30th August 1825, Lord Strangford wrote '... I hear that Canning is in high force at the Lakes. I should have liked to have seen him and Southey together. How times are changed! It is now Southey who is anti-Jacobin, and Canning who scoffs at Kings and Priests. His South American and Roman Catholic policy is more archi-liberal than anything poor Southey ever said or sang.'[1] This impression was not confined to Tories and by many progressives in the Whig party Canning was eventually accepted as a 'liberal'.

How far did he deserve the label? How far was he really in tune with the forces of change? When Prime Minister, in a moment of pique against his enemies in the Lords,[2] he made some remarks which Stapleton recorded in a memorandum. 'It is a great misfortune,' he said, 'that the Lords take so narrow a view of their present situation that they cannot see that we are on the brink of a great struggle between property and population; that such a struggle is only to be averted by the mildest and most liberal legislation. Mark my words that struggle will one day come, when probably I may be removed from the scene; but if the policy of the Newcastles and the Northumberlands is to prevail, that struggle cannot be staved off much longer.'[3] Canning could thus envisage the probability of a class war. But he never seems to have paused to consider and to investigate the causes of the danger which he apprehended. He seems, like so many of his contemporaries, to

---

[1] BAG, vol. 2, p. 292.

[2] Some of Canning's contemporaries believed that he was ready for a showdown and that he would have used his influence with the King to swamp the House of Lords. I think that he might have used the threat and that this would have proved effective — as an unwelcome expedient, not as a happy necessity.

[3] 3rd June 1827. C.G.C., vol. 2, p. 321.

have been entirely oblivious of the political and social problems
posed by the Industrial Revolution. The old England was disap-
pearing. But, although Canning used modern political methods,
he could not see any need for basic political change. To Parliamentary Reform, as a sensible if specious palliative to current
unrest, he remained resolutely opposed. His justification for this
attitude was based on a Burke mystique which, if he had subjected
it to any fresh analysis, he must have questioned. In radically
altered circumstances Canning clung blindly to a creed which,
though obviously outworn, continued to be comfortable. In
spite of all the incidental political wisdom which Burke's writings
contained, his final appraisal of the British Constitution was designed to meet a particular and transient danger. That danger, as
Canning fully recognised, had passed. The times had changed.
But, though in many ways Canning himself had contributed to
this process of change, his mind remained closed to its political
implications. Because he relied so much on the ideas of others he
was handicapped by the contemporary validity of his sources.
While he could confidently still rely on Huskisson, whether inter-
preting Adam Smith or Ricardo, as his 'man of business', Burke
had become a more dubious manual of politics in an age of industrial revolution.

As a political thinker Canning lacked vision. As an administrator, owing to a variety of circumstances, his personal contribution to Government achievements in England and Ireland
was relatively barren. If any claim is made that Canning deserves
to be ranked among England's greatest statesmen, it surely must
depend on his conduct of foreign affairs.

(ii) *Foreign Affairs: 1796–1822*

'I hope,' said Canning in a speech at Plymouth on 28th October
1823, 'that my heart beats as high for the general interest of
humanity — I hope that I have as friendly a disposition towards
the nations of the earth, as anyone who vaunts his philanthropy
most highly; but I am contented to confess, that in the conduct
of political affairs, the grand object of my contemplation is the

interest of England.'[1] At a time when memories of French conquests in the name of liberty lingered, when Metternich posed as a
European necessity, and when the Tsar was volunteering Cossacks
as Congress crusaders, Canning's realism was as pointed as a
paradox. He was, and he took pride in the admission, primarily
concerned with the interests of his own country. In this he was
not original either among Foreign Ministers or among English-
men. Concern for national interests has generally dominated
those who have tried to direct or influence the conduct of
British foreign policy. Even Cobden, who abhorred and would
gladly have abolished both armaments and diplomacy, based his
arguments on the premise that his policies were better calculated
to serve national interests than Lord Palmerston's. On the
subject of national interests in a broad sense there has generally
been a wide measure of agreement; differences have tended to be
confined to methods of serving them. Pitt and Fox were equally
concerned with the security and material prosperity of England;
they differed over the necessity, timing and execution of military
measures in support of these interests. Gladstone and Disraeli,
during their ill-informed wrangle over the Eastern Question,
betrayed their own limitations but were equally anxious to keep
England secure and prosperous. When Neville Chamberlain
sought to avert, and Winston Churchill to promote, war against
Nazi Germany their ultimate object was the same. Indeed, although Canning's quip:

> *A steady patriot of the world alone*
> *The Friend of every country but his own*

has often been levelled by one politician against another, the
charge has, in almost all cases, been an empty one. The desire to
ensure national security and to promote national prosperity,
however differently interpreted or expressed, has generally been
mutual.

Where foreign affairs were concerned Canning, like so many
of his contemporaries, was a self-styled disciple of William Pitt.
Pitt believed, conforming to established tradition, that England's

[1] Therry, vol. 4, p. 421.

security required the maintenance of a powerful Navy. The Navy's capacity to protect the British Isles against invasion was dependent not only on its strength but on strategic considerations. The most important of these was control of the Continental Channel ports. If any single European power controlled all the Continental Channel ports then, however powerful the British Navy, England could not be secure against invasion. Therefore security implied, not only the maintenance of a powerful Navy, but the existence of a balance of power on the Continent. For this reason England was concerned with European power politics.

Material prosperity, in Pitt's view, depended on overseas trade. The protection of overseas trade, just as the security of the British Isles, depended on naval force. But the Navy in this instance required to operate from far-flung bases. The acquisition of new bases, according to changing circumstances, might become an essential policy objective. Otherwise Pitt could not envisage the need for any further territorial expansion. It was, and here Pitt was more influenced by Adam Smith than by tradition, unnecessary to colonise in order to trade. War, according to Adam Smith, was the worst enemy of trade, and therefore any operations of war arising out of the Navy's protective duties almost represented a contradiction in terms; consequently Pitt shared Adam Smith's reluctance to engage in major warfare for the sake of protecting threatened commerce. Even where security was concerned he was unwilling to consider war as a weapon of policy save in face of an immediate and pressing danger.

Because Pitt believed so intensely in the material advantages of peace, he generally favoured the maintenance of the territorial *status quo* and urged respect for international treaties and agreements. As soon as he became Prime Minister, in eager anticipation of years of retrenchment and reform during which British wealth would automatically multiply, he tried as far as he could to encourage the notion that the international order was settled and in a sense legally established.

It is not surprising, in the light of these views, that the French Revolution caused him early anxiety. He feared that France's apparent state of anarchy would prove a temptation to her neighbours; if the *status quo* were disturbed and France was attacked, Frenchmen might then unite against their aggressors; their united efforts could result in victories which would threaten the balance of power. He hoped, therefore, that the Revolution would remain a purely domestic matter.

In 1790, in spite of his anxieties about France, he was more directly concerned with Russia. Catherine the Great's seizure of the Black Sea port of Oczakov from Turkey struck him as a serious potential menace to British Mediterranean trade. He was prepared to protest energetically and even, surprisingly, to contemplate the use of force. His fears, however, found no echo in the House and with many misgivings he accepted the situation; but, henceforth, he was to remain most suspicious of Russia's intentions.

His anxieties about the French Revolution revived when Austria and Prussia declared war on France. As he had anticipated, France drew strength from the struggle. French victories resulted in the conquest of the Austrian Netherlands and of Holland. There followed the opening of the Scheldt to international trade and French control of all the Channel ports. The presumed blow to British trade could have been borne but the threat to security was too direct. Reluctantly Pitt concluded that war had become a necessity. His aim was the restoration of France to her old limits, not the dismemberment of France; that, he believed, would only lead to eventual revival of a national spirit and a new French war of revenge.

As the struggle proceeded Pitt began to feel that even this limited objective was unattainable; he became prepared to accept compromises whereby some boundary might be set on French conquests and some return to order, if not the old order, achieved. Even after Napoleon's advent to power Pitt was still ready to accept a compromise peace. The negotiations which led to the Treaty of Amiens had been opened during his Premiership and it was not until the resumption of hostilities that he seems to have become convinced that no workable compromise could be achieved until Napoleon had suffered decisive military defeat. From henceforth he was resigned to long and perhaps hopeless years of war. But, even if a miracle were vouchsafed and total victory secured, Pitt did not waver in his belief that France must not be dismembered. National interests, he continued to maintain, would be best served, not by trying to destroy France, but by reducing her to her old boundaries. Once this had been achieved steps must be taken to ensure that Dutch and Belgian ports would never again fall into French hands.

Castlereagh's policy, after Napoleon's defeat, was based almost entirely on the lines laid down by Pitt. The restoration of France to her old limits, the union of Belgium and Holland (together with a subsidiary scheme of fortifications and a specific guarantee from the wartime allies), the rejection of all conquests save for some essential new maritime bases, the endeavour to parry Russian designs, all followed from Pitt's hopes and plans. Only in one particular had Pitt been influenced by considerations other than purely national interests. Inspired by Wilberforce, he believed in the abolition of the Slave Trade. And, at Vienna, Castlereagh duly canvassed, by means of bribery and cajolery, in this cause. Otherwise Castlereagh was guided at the Congress simply by consideration of national interests as determined by William Pitt.

Like Castlereagh, Canning drew his inspiration from Pitt and he entirely endorsed Pitt's conception of national interests.[1] He also accepted Pitt's views of how, in principle, those interests could best be promoted. He did not seek nor, incidentally, did he bring, any new ideas in his approach to foreign policy. It is therefore by his contribution to the conduct of policy alone that Canning's claim to statesmanship must be measured. What particular problems did he meet? How did he tackle them? Did the results of his endeavours serve the objectives for which they had been designed? Were those objectives based on sound appreciation of British interests in the light of prevailing circumstances? In order to attempt to answer these questions it is proposed to consider briefly Canning's role in the making of

---

[1] He also agreed that, apart from national interest, the abolition of the Slave Trade was the only cause which should be, when possible, simultaneously pursued.

foreign policy up to 1822 and to examine more closely the part he played during the last five years of his life.

In January 1796 Canning became Under-Secretary of State to the Foreign Minister Lord Grenville. 'I care not,' he had said to Boringdon in the previous year, 'about the internal state or Government of France one farthing — whether Republic — anarchy — monarchy — or what not — it does not signify for my argument — I only desire you to look at the Map of Europe. . . . Tell me if any statesman that ever lived on being shown that France was mistress of the Netherlands and of Holland . . . would not exclaim at once "then England *must* be at war with her".'[1] As Under-Secretary, Canning was not able to exercise any influence on the formulation of policy though obviously he gained knowledge and experience. He appreciated Pitt's motives in seeking a compromise peace but, after the breakdown of negotiations in the autumn of 1797, he was convinced, perhaps even more strongly than Pitt, that the war must be continued and must be pursued with all possible vigour. When negotiations were successfully resumed he was no longer in office and, on learning the terms of the Treaty of Amiens, he was bitterly hostile. Personal resentment against Addington and jealousy of Hawkesbury no doubt influenced, but did not cloud, his judgement. During the uneasy peace he urged preparedness for new war. 'Let us not amuse ourselves,' he reminded the House on 8th December 1802, 'with vain notions, that our greatness and our happiness as a nation are capable of being separated. . . . We have, as my honourable friend (Mr Sheridan) has well observed no refuge in littleness. We must maintain ourselves what we are, or cease to have a political existence worth preserving.'[2] Not surprisingly he welcomed the resumption of hostilities, stressing the vital importance of Malta[3] and at the same time insisting on the wider issues of the struggle. That struggle, he conveniently but understandably concluded, demanded the return of Pitt and a Ministry of All Talents. These objectives, in concert with Grenville,

---

[1] Canning recorded this conversation in his *Journal*. D.M., p. 91.
[2] Therry, vol. 2, p. 48.
[3] In a speech on 24th May 1803. Ibid., p. 87.

absorbed his whole energies. When Pitt did return, but without the War Cabinet of Canning's dreams, he somewhat ungraciously accepted the Treasuryship of the Navy.[1] Loyalty to Pitt muzzled the criticisms which frustrated ambition and genuine concern for the conduct of the war were prompting. After Pitt's death Canning lost no opportunity to belabour the Grenville coalition. 'There had not,' he reminded the House on 19th December 1806, 'been even a single warlike plan, much less any warlike achievement.'[2] Canning was itching, for personal and for patriotic motives, to direct the war; it is difficult to believe that he would not have levelled charges of mismanagement at this juncture whatever the circumstances.

In March 1807 he became Foreign Secretary in the Portland Administration and held that office until he resigned in September 1809. He regarded himself as the real head of the Government, a war leader rather than a Foreign Secretary. During this period Napoleon was almost completely successful in isolating England. The number of British diplomatic representatives was greatly reduced and there was relatively little routine office work. Canning, as he had for long insisted, was anxious to encourage every and any kind of resistance to Napoleon. He sought to establish that any opponent of the French could rely on British subsidies and support. But ways and means were difficult to find. He approved the hastily improvised expedition to the Swedish Island of Rüjen, even though by the time the British force arrived Danzig had fallen to the French and Prussian resistance had ended. Other plans to aid Russia were fatally interrupted by Russia's defeat at Friedland. It also became known that expeditions planned by the previous Government for operations in the Near East and in South America had met with disaster.

Canning felt that he must concentrate on trying to anticipate Napoleon's future moves. His most spectacular effort on these lines was the Copenhagen expedition which resulted in the seizure of the Danish Fleet. He boasted that the move had prevented 'a Northern confederacy, an invasion of Ireland, and

---

[1] See p. 76 above.
[2] Therry, vol. 2, p. 262.

the shutting of Russian ports'.[1] The boast, as regards Russian ports, was rather a wild one and Canning found it difficult to justify this high-handed and much criticised enterprise while news of the Tilsit meeting remained secret. It was, therefore, with relief that he wrote on 4th December 1807: 'The peace of Tilsit is come out. We did not want any more case for Copenhagen; but if we had this gives it to us.'[2] Canning had in fact gambled successfully on the accuracy of his intelligence sources.

His next concern was to prevent the Portuguese Fleet from falling into Napoleon's grasp. He opened negotiations with the Prince Regent of Portugal,[3] who agreed to hand over his Fleet to the British and retire to Brazil. Delays supervened and it was not until French troops had reached the suburbs of Lisbon that the Regent fulfilled his bargain.

When these sources of naval strength had been denied to Napoleon, Canning found little scope for action beyond attempting to intensify the blockade by Orders-in-Council and opening a dangerous quarrel with the United States in the process. During this period of frustration he was reduced to planning, in collaboration with Castlereagh, a new expedition to Latin America. Wellesley was to have taken command. But, when news was received of a revolt against the French in Spain, the project was abandoned.

Now, at last, there seemed to be an opportunity once again to support active resistance to Napoleon on the European Continent. Canning reacted promptly and with enthusiasm. 'We shall proceed,' he told the House of Commons, 'on the principle that any nation of Europe that starts up with a determination to oppose a Power which, whether professing insidious peace or declaring open war, is the common enemy of all nations, whatever may be the existing political relations of that nation with Great Britain, becomes instantly our essential ally.'[4] Peace between England and Spain was immediately concluded and Frere[5]

[1] *Paget Papers*, vol. 2, p. 363.
[2] G.C. & T., p. 435.
[3] Dom John. Later King John VI of Portugal.
[4] 15th June 1808. Therry, vol. 2, p. 352.
[5] John Hookham Frere, one of Canning's closest friends. See p. 28 above.

was appointed British representative to the Resistance Government. Canning strongly supported plans to send British troops
to the Peninsula. As a result of these plans Wellesley, and the
force which had been destined for Latin America, were dispatched
to Portugal. Another expeditionary force under the command of
Sir John Moore sailed for the same destination. Both Wellesley
and Moore were placed under the command of Sir Hew Dal-
rymple, the Governor-General of Gibraltar. Sir Harry Burrard
was then ordered to Portugal to take over as second in command
to Sir Hew. These arrangements, which led to some confusion,
were the responsibility of the War Office and Canning, who was
lusting to exploit the military as well as the political implications
of the Spanish revolt, began to question Castlereagh's competence
as War Minister. After the Convention of Cintra Canning, who
was absent from the Cabinet meeting which approved it but was
obviously bound by the decision reached, could not resist private
criticisms which were in fact mainly ill-informed.

Following the Erfurt meeting between Napoleon and Alexander, the two Emperors sent a peace ultimatum to George III.
This matter was clearly within the Foreign Secretary's province.
He drafted a reply expressing willingness to negotiate providing
all parties, including England's Spanish allies, were admitted to
the conference. This condition was inevitably rejected by
Napoleon. Canning then wrote to the Tsar conveying regrets
from George III that Alexander should have sanctioned 'an
usurpation unparalleled in history'.

Apart from this brief diplomatic exchange Canning's attention
remained focused on events in the Peninsula. There Moore had
now been appointed Commander-in-Chief. Frere bombarded
Canning with criticisms of Moore and Canning was compelled
to remind Frere that the disposal of British troops was the individual responsibility of the Commander-in-Chief. In Canning's
own mind, however, doubts about Moore were already firmly
lodged. Castlereagh, during a Cabinet discussion, had revealed
that Moore, before he left for Spain, had declared: 'Remember,
my lord, I protest against the expedition and foretell its failure.'
'Good God,' retorted Canning, 'and do you really mean to say

that you allowed a man entertaining such feelings with regard to the expedition to go and assume command of it.'[1] On 4th December, after the three main Spanish armies had been defeated without receiving any effective British aid, Napoleon entered Madrid and, although Moore died gloriously while his armies triumphed at Corunna, Canning blamed him for having failed to support the Spaniards. In this attitude he was surely influenced by Frere, whose differences with Moore had continued and who, after the fall of Madrid, resigned. Canning replaced him by the Marquess of Wellesley. His brother Sir Arthur Wellesley was finally, on 2nd April 1809, appointed Commander-in-Chief with Canning's full approval.

Late in the previous February Canning had replied to an Opposition motion demanding an enquiry 'into the causes, conduct and events of the last war in Spain'.[2] He endeavoured on this occasion to defend both Moore and Frere. He covered his own private doubts and criticisms in mockery of the Whig argument that 'before the assistance of this country had been given to Spain, it ought to have been ascertained whether or not the Spaniards were instigated by the monks; whether they were encouraged by the higher ranks, or animated by Popery; whether they were wedded to their ancient institutions, or disposed to shake off the oppression of their former Government; to abjure the errors of a delusive religion or prepared to foreswear the Pope and the Grand Inquisitor'. 'The Government,' Canning argued, 'felt that the Spanish nation wanted other and more aids than lectures or municipal institutions; they were content that a British army should act in Spain, though the Grand Inquisitor might have been at the head of the Spanish armies; though the people might have been attached to their ancient monarchy, and with one hand upheld Ferdinand VII, whilst with the other, they worshipped the Lady of the Pillar. To assist the patriotic efforts of the Spanish nation was the sole object, and they did not wish to inflict upon that country any change as the price of that

---

[1] G.C. & T., p. 159. This 'anecdote', Stapleton adds in a note, was told to him by Canning.

[2] See Therry, vol. 2, p. 363.

assistance. God forbid that we should ever be so intolerant, as to make conformity to our own opinion the price of our assistance to others, in their efforts for national independence; or to carry the sword in one hand, and what we might choose to call the Rights of Man in the other!'[1] So Canning proclaimed his faith in continued attempts to provide aid without strings. He also made clear his belief in Spain's capacity for further resistance. While defending the cause of Peninsular intervention he was able to forget his irritation at not having been able to control its course.

When Austria re-entered the war against Napoleon, Canning at once pressed for authority to provide immediate financial assistance and he was able to arrange for the dispatch of £250,000 in silver bars to Trieste. England and Austria were still nominally at war; by the time peace negotiatons had been concluded the battle of Wagram was over and the French were in Vienna. Nothing more could be done to help the Austrians. Their brief campaign had, however, forced Napoleon to withdraw troops from the Peninsula; this relieved pressure on Wellesley and made possible his victory at Talavera.

Fortified by this success, the War Office was now busy with various new plans. Fifteen thousand troops were assembled for a campaign against Naples and, with a contingent of Sicilians, they occupied Ischia, Procida and the castle of Scylla. Following these exploits the force was withdrawn. More serious consideration was given to a plan to capture Antwerp. Thirty-five ships of the line and forty thousand men were assembled for the Walcheren expedition. It was badly led and badly equipped. The result was total disaster.

As has been seen, ever since March 1809 Canning had been endeavouring to obtain Castlereagh's transfer from the War Ministry. The business of the Foreign Office under war conditions was ill-suited to Canning's restless energy. He could not help becoming absorbed in details of military operations and he could not help being critical of their direction. Without much difficulty he had convinced himself of Castlereagh's inadequacy and had determined that, either directly or indirectly, he must

[1] Therry, vol. 2, p. 372.

o

achieve control of the War Ministry himself. Believing that
Castlereagh's transfer was only being postponed until the conclusion of the Walcheren expedition, he assumed that the move
would follow its failure. On discovering that he had been misled,
he chose, in pursuit of the supreme power which he was seeking,
to resign.

At this point in his career there was relatively little evidence
on which his capacities as a Foreign Secretary could be fairly
judged. In the business of his own office he had given no more
than hints of his qualities and failings. His dispatches showed
confidence, clear grasp of essentials and minute attention to
detail. He was a strict disciplinarian and demanded of British
representatives rigid adherence to their instructions. Erskine's[1]
reproof and recall made Foreign Office history. There was no
doubt during Canning's term of office who should be master.
But although Canning proved that he could command authority,
there were hints that his judgement might not always be reliable.
Erskine's was a case in point. Relations with America had become
strained; this was partly due to British methods of impressment
but above all to American resentment at the Orders-in-Council.
There was every reason to use diplomatic tact in dealings with
America. Erskine was proving a most useful Ambassador. In his
negotiations he knowingly and sensibly overstepped his instructions. His castigation was hardly deserved and could certainly
have been couched in less offensive terms. His recall was bitterly
resented in America. Anglo-American relations, which had been
improving in adverse circumstances, suffered a serious blow.
Canning was rightly believed to be prejudiced against America
and this episode increased American distrust. All hope of a
settlement vanished, particularly after the arrival of Erskine's
successor, Mr. Jackson. His personality[2] was calculated to act

---

[1] David Montagu Erskine, son of Lord Erskine who had been Lord Chancellor in the previous Grenville Ministry, appointed British Minister in Washington by Fox and recalled in 1809 by Canning.

[2] He was an ultra Tory. Not long previously he had presented the ultimatum which resulted in the surrender of the Danish Fleet. He was reputed to
have relished this mission and had gained the nickname of 'Copenhagen Jackson'.
See H. C. Allen: *Great Britain and the United States*, p. 311.

as an irritant and this, combined with rigid adherence to inflexible instructions, set Anglo-American relations firmly on the course which eventually led to war.

Copenhagen had suggested the imaginative ruthlessness of a great war leader; this was emphasised by Canning's general subordination of all interests in the successful prosecution of war. If Canning's career had ended in 1809, he might have been regretted as a potential Chatham or Churchill; he would hardly have been remembered as one of England's great Foreign Secretaries.

After he resigned Canning rarely expressed opinions on foreign affairs. In 1812 he supported the Government's declaration of war against America; in July 1813 he spoke eloquently in support of the Government's vote of thanks to Wellington after the Battle of Vittoria. But, on the whole, as the tide of war turned, Canning diverted his attention to domestic questions. During the crucial time when Great Britain's peace policy was being established and while Castlereagh was at Vienna, Canning was on a mission to Portugal. He seems to have generally approved the terms of the peace settlement and he wrote on 17th March 1815 to Huskisson: 'Poland, to be sure he [Castlereagh] has not been able to save, but Saxony is arranged, not discreditably to us, and he has done a good deal upon the Slave Trade. . . . He returns, surely, with great advantages.'[1] On another occasion Canning expressed some disapproval of the allocation of Norway to Sweden. There is no evidence of other criticism.

When Canning rejoined the Government in 1816 the business of his own office was little related to the main stream of British foreign policy. In the differences which arose between the Governor-General and the Court of Directors over the wisdom of using force to consolidate British power in India Canning, partly because he deliberately sought to cultivate good relations with the Directors and partly because he respected Liverpool's fear of incurring expense, sided with the Directors.[2] Hastings'

[1] HUSK, p. 100.
[2] See C. H. Philips: *The East India Company 1784-1834*, chapter VIII. Canning's East India Policy 1816-22.

achievements were the result of his own initiative. Canning viewed Indian affairs from an English party political point of view and he lacked, in this respect, the vision which Pitt had shown.

While operations against the Marathas and the Pindaris could be regarded as an Indian internal affair, the activities of Sir Stamford Raffles, the Company's Lieutenant-Governor of Bencoolen on the Island of Sumatra, came into a different category because of resultant friction with the Dutch. In this matter Canning agreed with the Cabinet in wishing to avoid provoking Dutch susceptibilities and, through Hastings, warnings were conveyed to Sir Stamford. Undeterred by these warnings Sir Stamford Raffles in January 1819 acquired from the Sultan of Johore the settlement of Singapore which guarded the route through the Archipelago between the Indian and the China Seas. This move obviously offered new provocation to the Dutch. Hastings and the Directors were, however, fully alive to the importance of the new acquisition. Their confidence influenced Canning, who was himself at first mainly concerned by the Dutch protest and its possible repercussions. Once engaged, however, he successfully employed delaying tactics and eventually a series of general negotiations were opened with the Dutch. These were not concluded until November 1823, when Dutch financial exigencies induced them to recognise British rights in Singapore and Malacca in return for the cession of Billitan and Bencoolen. Trading rights in the Archipelago were guaranteed to merchants of both nations. The Treaty, which was in the circumstances generous to the Dutch, put an end to disputes which might have led to war and gave Great Britain considerable commercial and strategic advantages. Canning conducted the negotiations with ability and foresight; but the original conception, which had embarrassed Canning, came from Sir Stamford and was endorsed by Hastings and the Company.[1]

Apart from the work of his own office, Canning acted in the Commons as Government spokesman; thus allowing Castlereagh,

---

[1] See C. H. Philips: *The East India Company 1784–1834*, chapter VIII. Canning's East India Policy 1816–22.

the Leader of the House, more leisure to concentrate on the conduct of foreign affairs. In the Cabinet Canning seems to have specialised in foreign affairs and to have given consistent support to Castlereagh. The suggestion that he resigned because of differences over the conduct of foreign policy seems totally without foundation. As is shown by the State Paper of May 1820, Castlereagh could see as clearly as Canning where British interests diverged from those of her Continental allies. Canning may have felt, as he later manifested, less susceptibility for the notion of allied solidarity; if a policy of disengagement was inevitable, he might have moved faster and with more enthusiasm than Castlereagh but, while they remained colleagues, the issue, though anticipated, was not directly posed. They were able, therefore, to work in complete harmony.

When Canning resigned in December 1820 Castlereagh lost a useful adviser; Canning was deprived of detailed information and lost touch with Castlereagh's plans to meet current problems. At the time when Castlereagh was making his dispositions in the late summer of 1822 for a forthcoming Congress, Canning was preparing to leave for India. On 30th August, in a farewell speech to his Liverpool constituents, he referred in very general terms to current European problems.[1] 'Gentlemen,' he said, 'in the times in which we live, there is (disguise it how we may) a struggle going on — in some countries an open one, and in some a tacit struggle, between the principles of monarchy and democracy. God be praised that in that struggle we have not any part to take. God be praised, that we have long ago arrived at all the blessings that are to be derived from that which alone can end such a struggle beneficially — a compromise and intermixture of those conflicting principles. It is not, as it appears to me, the duty of this country to side with those who stand on the defensive, when they will grant nothing. England has only to maintain herself on the basis of her own solid and settled Constitution, firm unshaken — a spectatress interested in the contest only by her

---

[1] Although Canning insisted on making this farewell speech he already had good reason to believe that the Castlereagh succession would be offered to him. His references to foreign policy were deliberately calculated.

sympathies — not a partisan on either side, but, for the sake of both, a model, and ultimately perhaps an umpire. Should we be led by any false impulse of chivalrous benevolence, to participate in the struggle itself, we commit and thereby impair, our authority; we abandon the position in which we might hereafter do most good, and may bring the danger of a foreign struggle home to our own hearths and institutions.'[1]

To Canning, who now lacked inside knowledge, the situation was quite clear. England must pursue a policy of disengagement. Her own vital interests were not concerned and she could afford, amid European troubles, to enjoy the role of a spectator.

To Castlereagh the situation had not seemed so simple. On the contrary, in the weeks before his death he was obsessed by dangers which seemed to be immediately pressing. He relied on his personal influence and on his diplomatic skill to avert a major crisis. The responsibility weighed heavily upon him and he regarded the forthcoming Congress at Verona as a critical test of his own ability. In the Near East the Greek Revolution was providing Tsar Alexander with an open invitation to intervene. The Greek rising against the Turks in the Peloponnese began early in 1821. It had been occasioned partly by a move, which enjoyed a measure of Russian support, on the part of the Greek aristocracy to seize power in Roumanian Moldavia and Wallachia, and partly by the opportunity which was presented by the clash between the Sultan of Turkey and his turbulent vassal, Ali of Yanina. The rising in Roumania proved a total failure and was finally suppressed in July 1821. The Greeks in the Peloponnese, on the other hand, quite contrary to expectations, succeeded, with support from neighbouring islands, in causing considerable disruption of Turkish authority. As an early reprisal for these acts of rebellion, the Sultan ordered the execution, on 22nd April 1821, of Gregorios, the Orthodox Patriarch in Constantinople. No more spectacular provocation could have been offered to Tsar Alexander. In fact he found the situation embarrassing and, while protesting to the Sultan on the one hand, he vehemently disowned complicity with rebellion on the other. So long as the

[1] Therry, vol. 6, p. 410.

Greeks remained able to look after themselves, Alexander's aloofness, so essential to Metternich's policy, could be maintained
without too much strain. But, with the final defeat and death of
Ali of Yanina early in 1822, the Sultan was able to devote more
energy against the Greek rebels who had, by their early successes,
already established a popular legend. Their need for support then
became awkwardly apparent. Not only did the Tsar still have an
excuse for intervention, but he was now also faced with fear for
his own prestige at home if he failed to show some care for the
fate of his heroic Greek co-religionists. This threatened Russian
intervention seemed most likely to result in a Russo–Turkish
war and to the eventual establishment of Russia as a Mediterranean Power. Castlereagh, like Pitt, viewed Russian Mediterranean ambitions with alarm. He was, therefore, most anxious to
avoid any Russian action in Greece and he hoped that discussion
of the Greek Question at Verona might avert this particular
danger. There were disturbing hints that Alexander would show
forbearance in the Near East only if he were allowed the glory
of leading a crusade against revolutionaries in Spain. There, as a
result of a military *coup d'état* led by Riego in January 1820,
Ferdinand VII had been forced to restore the ultra-liberal Constitution of 1812 and was now a puppet in the hands of men who
were misgoverning almost as hopelessly as he had done since his
own return to Spain. While feigning to co-operate with his new
masters, he sought to divide them and at the same time appealed
constantly to the rest of Europe to be rescued from his bondage.
Castlereagh disliked the notion of Russian intervention in Spain
almost as much as in Greece. Metternich, who also feared the
possibility of Russian action in either sphere, was, on the other
hand, loath to give offence to Alexander, upon whom he depended
for moral support for his policies in Italy and in Germany.
Furthermore, although he cared little for the fate of Ferdinand,
the situations in Italy and Germany compelled him to oppose
Liberalism, however unreal, in Spain. In France, restless counsels,
represented flamboyantly by Chateaubriand, were abroad; there
were rumours of a bargain with Russia which would allow France
to occupy the left bank of the Rhine and there was strong pressure

for intervention in Spain. Castlereagh was anxious to avoid either joint or separate action in Spain. He disapproved of joint action because, as had been made clear in the State Paper of May 1820, England could not afford to associate herself with such a policy; in the first place she lacked the military resources to play any direct part; and secondly, it was not possible to represent to Parliament that British interests could in any way be served by suppressing revolution in Spain. Joint intervention, from which England was disassociated, would therefore have emphasised divisions between England and her Continental Allies at a time when, for other reasons, Castlereagh was most concerned to maintain a measure of co-operation. Separate action meant intervention by Russia or by France. To Russian intervention Castlereagh was fundamentally opposed. A French military adventure threatened, if unsuccessful, a revolution in France and the possible reopening of a general European struggle; on the other hand, if the adventure were a success French influence would be re-established in Spain and this could be regarded as detrimental, not only to British interests in Spain itself, but to British interests in the Spanish Colonies and in Portugal.

Castlereagh, therefore, objected to any kind of intervention in Spain and was determined, as far as possible, to avoid discussion of this topic at the Congress. He hoped that, after the Greek Question had been raised, it would be possible to turn, not to Spain itself, but to the question of the Spanish Colonies. Here British interests were directly concerned. The existing situation was most unsatisfactory. On the one hand, Great Britain was involved in constant disputes with the Spanish Government and, on the other hand, British merchants could get no redress for their grievances so long as the British Government refused recognition to the new States. In these circumstances the field was dangerously open to the United States of America. Castlereagh also feared that France might be tempted to steal a march on Great Britain and grant recognition on her own. He had by now concluded that general recognition was only a matter of time and he hoped that agreement on this subject could be reached at the Congress. The moment seemed propitious because the Continental Allies had no ties of loyalty or sympathy with the Revolutionary Government of Spain.

While Castlereagh was making his plans to attend the Congress he was handicapped by temporary loss of royal favour.[1] The King, encouraged by Countess Lieven, threatened to attend the Congress in person. Eventually, however, he allowed himself to be dissuaded and he resumed friendly relations with Castlereagh. The interlude, however, had been disquieting and Castlereagh was further hampered by his personal unpopularity, and that of the Government, in the country at large. He was, therefore, under considerable pressure when drawing up his own instructions for the Congress. The instructions themselves were incomplete but he relied on his knowledge of the participants and on the efficiency of private negotiation to fill in the gaps. He intended to visit Villèle in Paris and then to see Metternich in Vienna before the Congress opened. He hoped to persuade Villèle to agree that the Greek Question and the Spanish Colonies Question should be tackled at the Congress before any discussion about Spain itself. He proposed to make provision with Villèle for eventual recognition of the independence of the Spanish Colonies and for a joint policy on the Greek Question. Having gained French support, he planned to present Metternich with this *fait accompli* in Vienna and to gain his adherence to the agreement reached. By these manoeuvres Castlereagh hoped to put the awkward Spanish Question on ice while concentrating on a solution to the Greek and Spanish Colonies Questions, both of which touched British interests directly. He relied much on his personal influence with Metternich and on Metternich's known desire to achieve a restoration of the Concert of Europe. Concert, however, was to be restored on Anglo–Austrian rather than on Russo–Austrian lines. In fact, as Castlereagh and Metternich both knew, British and Austrian interests were basically similar. Both feared Russian power in the Near East and Russian intervention in Spain; neither had any direct interest in the internal affairs of Spain and a negotiated settlement in Latin America, while primarily a British interest, was in no way detrimental to Austria. In effect

[1] See p. 117 above.

Castlereagh was seeking to isolate Alexander. And yet he realised that Metternich could not afford to make an enemy of the Tsar. Therefore he was prepared to reserve for himself the delicate task of trying to reconcile Alexander to developments which would obviously be both unexpected and unwelcome. It was an ambitious programme. Castlereagh was fully conscious of the difficulties and he obviously dreaded the ordeal. But rightly he calculated that he was the only man who stood some chance of bringing such manoeuvres to a successful conclusion. In the event over-work and over-worry precipitated the crisis in his own health which led to a breakdown and eventual suicide.

When Canning returned to the Foreign Office he inherited problems which had faced Castlereagh, but he had little notion of how Castlereagh proposed to deal with them. Even if he had possessed this knowledge and had agreed with Castlereagh's methods, he could not, lacking the confidence of George IV, of the Cabinet, of Metternich and of Alexander, have stood any chance of pursuing his predecessor's plans with success. It was inevitable, therefore, that Canning should have started off at a disadvantage. There could hardly have been a more awkward time for a change of master at the Foreign Office.

(iii) *Foreign Affairs: 1822–27*

Canning began his second career at the Foreign Office in un-favourable circumstances. And yet, after five years, he seemed triumphantly to have tackled most of the problems which had so gravely preoccupied Castlereagh at the time of his death. The Neo-Holy Alliance, as the alignment of Russia, Austria and Prussia has been aptly described,[1] was destroyed. This alignment, which Metternich had countenanced in order to give a decent burial to Alexander's Holy Alliance dream, was based on an advertised bond of monarchical solidarity. It was designed to dominate the Congress System which had emerged from the projection of the war-time Quadruple Alliance of Great Britain, Russia, Austria and Prussia; this Alliance had also been joined by the restored Mon-

[1] By Professor Temperley. TEMP, p. 16.

archy of defeated France. Metternich calculated that, once he had
appeased Alexander in order to gain Russian support for his own
immediate ends in Germany and Italy, he would be able to avoid
Austrian dependence on Russia by making use of British and
French influence within the framework of the Congress System.
As has been seen, Castlereagh mistrusted the Neo-Holy Alliance
and hoped, with French support, to break up this alignment
while yet manoeuvring within the Congress framework, which he
was reluctant to destroy. Canning showed no such tenderness for
the framework. On the contrary, his road to the destruction of the
Neo-Holy Alliance lay through the ruins of the Congress System.
In the place of the Neo-Holy Alliance he eventually achieved a
direct agreement between Great Britain and Russia, based initially
on co-operation in the Near East, and firmly buttressed by France.
By this agreement Russian ambitions seemed to have been brought
under some measure of satisfactory control, while France was
apparently committed to following Great Britain's lead. Although
Metternich had been outwitted and although his pride was hurt,
Austrian interests, as Canning rightly calculated and as Metternich himself recognised, could best be served by accepting the
situation. Prussia at this juncture was virtually a cypher in
European power politics.[1] So the new order in Europe, with
Great Britain, Russia and France in close accord and with
Austria and Prussia as their somewhat reluctant but resigned
associates, had been established. Canning's boast that he had re-
stored Great Britain to a leading position among the Continental
Powers was not a vain one.

At the same time the question of Greek independence had been
settled in a manner which seemed likely to safeguard British com-
merical and strategic interests in the Eastern Mediterranean. The
tentative French bid for power in the Iberian Peninsula had been
checkmated by the complete restoration of British authority in
Portugal. The Spanish King himself was now urging the withdrawal of French forces from Spain. The separation of Portugal

[1] Canning deliberately ignored Prussia. As he cheerfully confessed to Granville 13th October 1825, '. . . I have even written to Berlin — for the first time I
believe this year — certainly for the last.' C.G.C., vol. 1, p. 297.

and Brazil had been successfully concluded under British auspices, and the monarchy had been preserved in Brazil. The independence of the Spanish-American Colonies had been recognised by Great Britain and no kind of interference was possible from any European power. Little gratitude to the United States was evident in any part of Latin America, where British influence seemed paramount. There were no awkward partners in Great Britain's Latin-American prospects.

The attainment of these objectives enhanced British prestige, for quite different reasons, among the rulers and the liberal intelligentsia of Europe. At home foreign policy became popular, and the interests of Great Britain, which Canning so sedulously fostered, were stamped with a warming liberal image. These achievements were secured without war and without great expenditure on armaments; force was, on occasions, threatened, but the risk, thanks to Canning's careful and calculated judgement, was minimal. Throughout he was prepared for set-backs and quick to turn even these to advantage; he seized upon the weaknesses and mistakes of others; he never failed to exploit success. Resolutely opposed to negotiation with a group of potentially hostile European Powers, he was always prepared to negotiate and bargain privately with each; co-operation was inevitably on British terms; diplomacy, in Canning's hands, proved a formidable weapon.

The pattern of this success is not very easy to follow. But, after his first somewhat faltering steps, Canning was working to rule — although not with any fixed time-table. The diplomatic manoeuvres were devious and complicated and often incomprehensible, even to his closest associates. And yet behind them there was a clear purpose. In order to promote British interests as he understood them, Canning believed that he must be in a position of ascendency at the international controls. This Bismarckian objective was manifestly achieved.

Canning's first step, on taking office in September 1822, was to confirm the interim decision that the Duke of Wellington should represent Great Britain at the forthcoming Congress and that he should be guided by the instructions which Castlereagh had prepared. On his way to Verona, where the Congress was now to assemble, the Duke met Villèle.[1] Villèle informed Wellington that a 'cordon sanitaire' of French troops was established on the Spanish border and hinted that he himself favoured French intervention. This news surprised Canning, who sent supplementary instructions to Wellington insisting that in no circumstances would Great Britain be a party to interference in Spain. Castlereagh would, of course, have agreed with this but in his conversations with Villèle he had intended, as has been seen, to reject discussion of this topic and to bring France into line with Great Britain before the opening of the Congress.

At the Congress itself confusion reigned. Metternich, dispirited by the loss of Castlereagh, feared any clash with Alexander upon whom, on the contrary, he felt even more bound to lean. Montmorency[2] and Chateaubriand,[3] the two French representatives, were at odds with one another and yet equally unwilling to follow Villèle's cautionary instructions. Chateaubriand hoped that the Congress would fail and that France would have an excuse to act alone.

In the absence of any concerted plan Spain quickly proved the main topic of discussion. Here Wellington's brief was clear and his attitude immediately isolated Great Britain. Where Castlereagh had reserved that role for Alexander, in these circumstances it was Wellington who found himself the odd man out. Finally, on 30th October, he delivered what Professor Temperley has described as his 'bombshell'.[4] In reply to French queries about the attitude of the Powers if France was obliged to recall her Minister from Madrid and if she found herself compelled to intervene by force, Wellington declared, in a memorandum, that 'such an interference appeared to be an unnecessary assumption of responsibility',[5] and he refused to commit Great Britain to any token of approval or support for any kind of intervention. Although discussion continued and some agreement on minor matters was reached, the failure of the Congress was now manifest and, with

[1] Now President of the French Council of Ministers.
[2] French Foreign Minister.
[3] French Ambassador to Prussia.
[4] TEMP, p. 67.
[5] Ibid.

England isolated, the other Powers concerted their policy in secret deliberations. On 30th November Wellington left Verona.

Canning was satisfied with Wellington's[1] conduct at the Congress, but he did foresee that it might lead to unilateral intervention on the part of France. On his way home Wellington again saw Villèle in Paris. Acting on Canning's instructions he offered British mediation in the current disputes between France and the Government of Spain. At this point the decision, which had been privately reached at Verona by the Continental Powers, to withdraw their diplomatic representatives from Spain, was made public. Metternich hoped that this moral demonstration would avert the need for any other kind of action and he had therefore supported it. France, however, did not withdraw her Minister and yet continued to threaten Spain. While Villèle sought to reassure Wellington, it became increasingly obvious that final decisions would now lie with Chateaubriand.[2] He was known to be receiving encouragement from Pozzo di Borgo, the Russian Ambassador; this encouragement was re-enforced by the veiled threat that if France did not intervene soon she would find herself obliged to grant a passage for Russian troops.

On 29th December Canning summed up the situation, in the light of British interests, in a dispatch to A'Court:[3] 'There can be no issue of a war between France and Spain that would not be disastrous in the extreme. A beaten or baffled French army, flowing back upon France would infallibly set France in revolution — a new "Iliad of woes" for Europe. The possession of the Peninsula, the occupation of it for three months by a French army is an event which cannot be contemplated but as an equally infallible source of disquietude, and some way or other ultimately of war, to this country. We are not insensible to other dangers, or rather to other miseries and misfortunes (for the danger to us, I think, is comparatively small) *that* may arise from the unchecked power of

---

[1] Though Wellington later complained to Mrs. Arbuthnot that he had not had any thanks for Verona from Liverpool or Canning. See Mrs. A., vol. 1, p. 203.

[2] He had replaced Montmorency as Foreign Minister.

[3] Sir William A'Court (Lord Heytesbury), Ambassador at Madrid.

revolution. But the attempt to check is sure to exasperate, and almost sure to fail in suppressing it. And geographically as well as morally, Spain is perhaps the country in which a revolution is most likely to burn itself out, without catching in other parts of Europe.'[1] He continued to hope that French threats would not be translated into action. Wellington, on his return from Paris, encouraged Canning in this belief, by expressing his own conviction that, in spite of Villèle's rejection of the mediation offer, peace would be maintained. This impression seemed to be confirmed by personal reassurances from Villèle to Canning. Accordingly he wrote on 3rd January 1823 in a mood of some complacency[2] to Bagot at St. Petersburg: 'I am afraid your Emperor will owe me a grudge for the issues of Verona, which has split the one and indivisible alliance into three parts, as distinct as the Constitutions of England, France and Muscovy. First there are the three absolute Crowns, who send three angry despatches to their Ministers at Madrid, with orders to come away if they do not receive submissive answers in fifteen days. Next there is France, who sends a whining despatch for her Minister, with no orders at all as to coming away. Thirdly there is *we*, who are in the course of amicable and furious correspondence with Spain — amicable as far as relates to Europe, in which quarter of the globe we defend her against invasion; furious in relation to America, where we have a squadron now employed in seeking forcible redress for grievances. . . . Villèle is a Minister of thirty years ago; no revolutionary scoundrel, but constitutionally hating England, as Choiseul or Vergennes used to hate us, and so things are getting back to a wholesome state again. Every nation for itself, and God

---

[1] G.C. & T., p. 389.

[2] The mood, in some ways prophetic, but at the time inaccurate, was captured in a letter about Canning, saying 'how he pleased his sovereign, made friends of everybody, had no enemies, had established the peace of Europe, had knocked the Holy Alliance on the head, had saved Spain, was going to protect the Greeks against both Turks and Russians, and had now nothing left to do but to save England.' The passage, read to Mrs. Villiers by Tierney, who refused to disclose the writer's name, was quoted by her in a letter of 2nd January 1823 to her son, later 4th Earl of Clarendon. *Life and Letters of the 4th Earl of Clarendon*, vol. 1, p. 35.

for us all. Only bid your Emperor be quiet, for the time for
Areopagus and the like of that, is gone by.'[1]

Canning's insular optimism was misplaced. Chateaubriand remained bent on war with Spain. He continued to receive encouragement from Pozzo di Borgo, while Metternich did not dare
to make any formal opposition. Furthermore, reports reaching
France of the attitude of George IV and of the 'Ultras' seemed
to suggest that, despite official policy, Chateaubriand could count
on some sympathetic understanding in England. As the situation
deteriorated Canning tried to prevent a clash by diplomatic
pressure. He urged moderation on the Spanish Government,
while impressing on the French how seriously Great Britain would
react to any military intervention. He failed either to influence the
Spaniards, or to impress Chateaubriand; and on 13th March 1823
the Duc d'Angoulême left Paris to command the French Army on
the frontier. War now seemed inevitable and Canning's chief
concern was to preserve a semblance of good relations with
France, while camouflaging the bitter blow to British prestige.

Accordingly on 21st March 1823 he informed Marcellus[2] that,
in the event of hostilities in Spain, England would observe neutrality; and on 31st March, in a dispatch to the French Government, he warned that this neutrality would depend on France
adhering to the three pledges which he regarded as having been
given: the pledges were that France should not establish a
permanent military occupation of Spain, appropriate any part of
the Spanish Colonies or violate the territorial integrity of Portugal.[3] On 6th April 1823 French troops crossed the border.

British policy had suffered a severe reverse. Canning, like
Castlereagh, was equally nervous of the consequences of French
defeat or victory, and he considered defeat more probable. On
20th February 1823 he had written to Bagot: 'I dread the war
much more for France than for Spain.'[4] In the House, however,
he felt obliged to express sympathy for the Spanish Government
and he declared on 14th April 1823: 'Indifference we can never
feel towards the affairs of Spain and I earnestly hope and trust

[1] BAG, vol. 2, p. 152.   [2] The French Chargé d'Affaires.
[3] BAG, vol. 2, p. 156.   [4] Ibid.

that she may come triumphantly out of the struggle.'[1] This point of view, which Canning maintained partly because it was a popular one outside Parliament and partly because in his opinion it coincided with prestige requirements, was anathema to the King and to the 'Ultras'. They regarded the struggle as an ideological one and fretted that England seemed to have detached herself from her natural allies and friends.

The success of France's military venture brought other problems, which Canning had also foreseen, in its train. The presence of French troops in Spain was in itself a humiliation for Great Britain; but more serious was the consequent threat to Portugal and the possible repercussions in Latin America. As has been seen, Canning had already defined British interests to the French and had indicated that Great Britain would fight in their defence. He relied, however, on the discretion of the French to save him from the consequences of his own warning. As far as the war in Spain was concerned his chief preoccupation was to avoid getting involved. At the same time he was anxious to conciliate liberal opinion at home by indicating sympathy for Spain, and disapproval of the Holy Alliance, without offering too much provocation to France. His attitude, though too mild to satisfy liberal opinion, thoroughly alarmed the King and the 'Ultras'. To the King, Canning wrote on 11th July 1823: 'Mr. Canning is intimately convinced that the true position of Your Majesty in the existing shock of adverse theories and of extreme opinions, is a neutral position.'[2] In order to justify this neutrality he argued in a speech at Plymouth: '. . . intimately connected as we are with Europe, it does not follow that we are, therefore, called upon to mix ourselves on every occasion with a restless meddling activity, in the concerns of nations which surround us.'[3] But non-intervention became even harder to justify, without loss of face and popularity, when the French captured Cadiz.[4] On 6th December 1823

---

[1] TEMP, p. 87.   [2] G.C. & T., p. 370.   [3] Therry, vol. 6, p. 422.

[4] King Ferdinand VII, who had been formally deposed and compelled to accompany the Spanish Constitutionalists in their retreat to Cadiz, was now liberated by the French. Against the advice of his liberators, and much to their embarrassment, he proceeded at once to revenge by way of a reign of terror.

P

Canning wrote to Granville: 'What is wanted is a positive disa-vowal of any design of retaining Cadiz, and a fixed term for the evacuation of it and other fortresses, but of Cadiz especially. This instruction is the fruit of two days' rather strong discussion. There are those among us who would rather see the French per-manently in Cadiz, than the risk of a new Spanish Revolution. But such is not the sense of the majority.'[1] Over the question of Cadiz the French returned soft answers but showed no signs of withdrawing. Short of war Canning was helpless and the Spanish situation therefore continued to represent a humiliation for Great Britain abroad and fodder for the Opposition at home.

Canning, with characteristic resilience, sought to turn defeat into victory by concentrating on other spheres. He now devoted his main energies to Portugal and Brazil, to the Spanish Colonies and to the Eastern Question. In all these cases direct British interests were at stake. Canning, however, was concerned, not only with the protection of these interests, but with the restoration of British prestige, popularity at home and the breaking up of a potentially hostile Continental alignment.

Portugal, though not the most important, was perhaps the most pressing problem because the Portuguese situation pro-vided the most immediate threat of a clash with France.

In 1820 the Regency, which had misgoverned Portugal since 1808, when the royal family had migrated to Brazil, was over-thrown by revolution. A Constitution, in the name of the King, was then proclaimed and in the summer of 1821, after many vacillations, King John eventually returned from Brazil and swore allegiance to the new Constitution. Efforts to bring Brazil under effective control of the home Government were met by a revolu-tion in Brazil and by the proclamation on 1st December 1822 of Dom Pedro[2] as Emperor. British interests in Portugal and in Brazil, therefore, became difficult to reconcile and Great Britain had little cause to be satisfied with the new 'Constitutional' Por-tuguese Government.

When in the autumn of 1822 there were rumours of an im-pending French attack against Spain, the Portuguese Government

[1] G.C. & T., p. 448.   [2] King John's eldest son.

sought for a British guarantee of protection and invoked the 1810 Treaty of Alliance. The Portuguese threatened that, if this guarantee were not forthcoming, they would ally defensively and offensively with Spain. Canning replied that the Alliance of 1810 had been annulled in 1815 and pointed out that, while England was ready to fulfil her existing treaty obligations in defending Portugal, 'the signature of an *offensive* alliance with another Power to act against a third would prevent Portugal from having the right to call on His Majesty for aid'.[1] Canning also warned the Portuguese against provoking war by any aggressive action. While there remained any hope of preventing French intervention in Spain, Canning was desperately anxious to impose restraint on Portugal and her trouble-making Government. As he later commented: 'Those Revolutionists were the scum of the earth and the Portuguese earth — fierce, rascally, thieving, ignorant ragamuffins; hating England and labouring with all their might and cunning to force and entrap us into war.'[2]

Just before the French invasion of Spain Canning made it clear, in a dispatch on 31st March 1823, that so long as Portugal preserved strict neutrality, England would defend her territorial integrity against France or any other power.[3] But he remained chiefly concerned to impose restraint on the Portuguese Government, which he continued to mistrust. His task was facilitated by the attitude of the French who, in the early stages of their campaign, were anxious to avoid giving any cause for offence to the Portuguese Government.

Domestic affairs in Portugal now changed the situation. In October 1822 the Queen had refused to take an oath of allegiance to the Constitution and had been compelled to leave the Court. She encouraged her second son, Dom Miguel, to plot against the régime. By May 1823 he had obtained sufficient army support to persuade the King to leave his capital and denounce the Constitution, though he promised to issue a new one. On 5th June John VI returned to Lisbon, now virtually a prisoner in the hands of

[1] TEMP, p. 196.
[2] Canning to Bagot. 14th July 1823. BAG, vol. 2, p. 183.
[3] TEMP, p. 196.

Dom Miguel, who was proclaimed Commander-in-Chief and assumed the functions of a military dictator. A spate of political arrests followed. In the ensuing confusion three factions emerged. The 'Absolutists', pinning their faith on Dom Miguel, wished to depose John VI and proclaim their leader King. Subserra, a sol- dier who had fought on the French side in the Napoleonic wars, proposed turning to France for guidance and protection. Palmella, who had been Portuguese Minister in London, preferred to rely on traditional British friendship and favoured a moderate Con- stitutional régime. The struggle for power resulted in a qualified victory for Palmella, who was appointed Foreign Minister in June 1823. He promptly appealed for British aid to suppress the 'reactionaries' in Portugal.[1] Though Canning was very satisfied to see Palmella, 'the best of Portuguese', in control, he was even more anxious to avoid giving any provocation to the French and, therefore, unwilling to back Palmella with any direct assistance. In view of this he rejected Palmella's appeal, but he did send a naval squadron to the Tagus and a new Minister, Thornton, to Lisbon. These half measures failed to placate liberal opinion in England and Canning was taunted for not giving his full backing to Palmella.

On 10th August 1823 Hyde de Neuville, a friend and disciple of Chateaubriand, arrived as French Ambassador in Lisbon. He dreamed of establishing French predominance throughout the Iberian Peninsula and he had no patience with the cautious tactics hitherto pursued by France in Portugal. In order to undermine Palmella's position he gave encouragement to the intrigues of Subserra and even, though less enthusiastically, to those of Dom Miguel. In the meanwhile the members of the Neo-Holy Alliance brought pressure to bear upon King John to break his promise about granting a new Constitution. On 27th October 1823 Hyde de Neuville felt his position strong enough to offer a French alliance to the House of Braganza which would include support

---

[1] During the brief spell of Dom Miguel's ascendancy Portuguese neutrality had been strained by assistance afforded to France in her blockade of the Spanish constitutionalists in Cadiz; Palmella, therefore, could represent the supression of the 'Reactionaries' as a British interest deserving of active British support.

for any attempt to recover authority in Brazil. While French influence at Lisbon thus appeared to be supplanting British, King John on 21st February 1824 endeavoured to assert himself by issuing a decree for the reassembling of the Ancient Cortes. Dom Miguel used this as an excuse to attempt a *coup d'état*. He was, however, disavowed by both de Neuville and Subserra. Nevertheless he achieved temporary success and in the panic which followed first Subserra, then Palmella, and finally King John himself, took refuge on British warships. From that vantage position King John denounced all his son's measures and Dom Miguel, suddenly losing confidence, presented abject apologies and allowed himself to be deported, in a Portuguese frigate under British and French escort, to the South of France. Palmella and Subserra were both restored to office. De Neuville, however, now enjoyed greater credit than Thornton because he had offered the support of French troops against Dom Miguel's *coup*. In order to restore the situation Palmella once again appealed for the dispatch of a British force to Portugal. This move was supported by Thornton. Canning replied furiously: 'Is it possible that you did not see the dilemma in which we were to be placed by such a demand as has been made to us, a demand equally embarrassing whether we granted or refused it?

If we refused it we must consign an old and faithful ally to ruin, or consent to an occupation of Portugal by France *against* which (however you may have reconciled yourself to it) your Government is pledged in the face of the world.

If we granted it we must either do so, *in concurrence* with France, and the Powers of the Continent; and then behold us associated with their schemes, and converts to the principles of the Holy Alliance, or we must do (as if at all we should do it) without their leave, and then who shall say to what this first step may lead?'[1] Thornton was instructed to try and persuade the King and Palmella to withdraw their request.

In the meanwhile, however, Canning felt it essential to make some kind of preparation for the gesture which he dreaded. No

[1] *F.O. Portugal 179/26.* Canning to Thornton, received 20th July 1824. TEMP, p. 202.

British troops were available but, at the Cabinet's request, the King agreed to send Hanoverians should the situation make such a step necessary. Rumours of this were reported in the Press and these rumours, by alarming the French Government, helped Canning to turn discomfiture into a minor triumph. Polignac was instructed to seek for information of England's intentions. This gave Canning an opportunity to complain of de Neuville's proceedings. The result was a disavowal of de Neuville's offer of French troops to Portugal and a reaffirmation that France had no designs to intervene in Portuguese domestic affairs. The case for sending British (or Hanoverian) troops therefore disappeared and de Neuville's stock in Portugal suffered a gratifying decline. Canning now determined to exploit his success by working for the total defeat of French influence. As a preliminary step he decided to recall Thornton, upon whom he vented the pent-up irritations which former frustrations in Portugal had engendered. He complained that Thornton had allowed himself to be inveigled into ambassadorial conferences and that he had meddled, against instructions, in the internal affairs of Portugal;[1] he even accused him of lending countenance to a revival of the Congress System. Thornton dutifully acknowledged his mistakes and was replaced by the more energetic and more astute A'Court.

Why, now that the danger of French military intervention had receded, did Canning wish to pursue a forward policy in Portugal? Writing to Liverpool on 15th October 1824 he explained: 'Portugal appears to be the chosen ground on which the Continental Alliance have resolved to fight England hand to hand, and we must be prepared to meet and defeat them, under every imagineable form of intrigue or intimidation, or be driven from the field.'[2] Apart from this general prestige point, which perhaps Canning was disposed to over-emphasise, there was the question of the continued presence of French troops in Spain; this symbol

---

[1] His real fault, of course, was to have meddled too little and too unsuccessfully. 'I am obliged to recall Thornton,' Canning confided to Granville on 17th August 1824. 'He has been cowed and cajoled till he forgot that he was Minister for England.' C.G.C., vol. 1, p. 154.

[2] G.C. & T., p. 500.

of defeat, constantly recalled by the 'liberal' Opposition, could most conveniently be offset by success in Portugal. Further justification for Canning's decision was provided by the Brazilian Question. His efforts to bring about a settlement between Portugal and Brazil were being checkmated by France and the Neo-Holy Alliance. The Portuguese Government was not only being discouraged from negotiating, but positively encouraged to resort to force. As Canning complained '. . . the Brazilian *contre-projet* is obviously calculated for failure. The intention, then, is to declare the negotiation broken off, and to prepare the expedition in the Tagus. . . . Can we suffer our squadron to remain in the Tagus, to protect (as it were) the fitting out of their expedition against Brazil? Can we withdraw that squadron — at the risk of its being replaced by a French squadron — at all? Can we do so, and leave the expedition to be fitted out under French and Russian protection, without marking our sense of the policy pursued by Portugal by a direct advance to Brazil? Can we, independently of these considerations, leave our relations with Brazil undefined much longer; the treaty being by express stipulation, revisable, at the requisition of either party, in February next? To all these questions I am disposed to answer, No; and they involve as weighty and difficult determination as ever Government was called upon to decide.'[1] Indeed, upon Brazil depended the whole of Canning's policy in Latin America. If Portugal could be induced to recognise the independence of Brazil then the main obstacle in the way of British recognition would have disappeared. Canning's general thesis that in recognising independence he was not favouring Republicanism would be supported and his campaign to convert the Cabinet to a policy of recognition in other cases would be facilitated.

The campaign against French influence did not at first proceed smoothly, and on 18th December 1824, Sir William A'Court remarked ruefully: 'You have given me no sinecure here. I have not only to struggle with the French Ambassador, but against all the existing authorities of the country, aided more or less, by the greater part of my colleagues. I stand alone in a country occupied

[1] Canning to Liverpool. 15th October 1824. G.C. & T., p. 500.

by enemies.'[1] While A'Court struggled at Lisbon, Canning finally obtained from the French Government a decision to recall de Neuville. Writing to Granville on 17th January 1825, Canning rejoiced that 'A'Court should now be able to act' and praised him for having 'done admirably in most difficult circumstances'. 'Even in case of failure,' he added, 'I shall do him justice at all times.'[2] In anticipation of final success Canning again wrote to Granville on 21st January 1825 '. . . Polignac is full of jealousy about Portugal; which is excessively foolish; because Portugal has been, and always *must* be English, so long as Europe and the world remain in anything like their present state.'[3]

In the meanwhile, strengthened by de Neuville's recall, A'Court brought heavy pressure to bear on King John, threatening even to withdraw the British Squadron unless Subserra were dismissed. Eventually, on 21st January 1825, King John responded by dismissing all his old Ministers, including Palmella. This was regarded as a triumph for A'Court and for British influence, which was now manifestly predominant at Lisbon.

One immediate and direct advantage ensued: the solution of the Brazilian Question. It had long been in suspense. During early negotiations, relations with Dom Pedro, the Emperor, had been hampered by discussions over the Slave Trade, but by the summer of 1823 agreement was reached. On 23rd September 1823 the Portuguese Minister, Villa Réal, applied for British mediation between Portugal and Brazil. He tried, however, to attach conditions; Canning rejected these. Villa Réal then suggested mediation by the Congress Powers; Canning protested that 'England would never recognize rights in the Allied Powers to intermingle in the affairs of the Colonies' and added that in such a case 'England would feel free to grant unilateral recognition'. 'If England acted otherwise,' he argued, 'it might be said that she recognized the Tribunal the Allies had wished to set up to direct the affairs of Europe, and she could not permit it to be exercised in the New World, when she had constantly pronounced against a similar supremacy in Europe.'[4] Villa Réal then proposed appealing to

[1] G.C. & T., p. 504.   [2] Ibid., p. 507.
[3] Ibid., p. 508.   [4] *F.O. Brazil 128/1*. TEMP, pp. 213–14.

Prussia and Austria. Canning was prepared to co-operate with Austria. On the question of Brazilian independence Metternich and Canning held similar views; they were equally anxious to obtain the consent of the Portuguese King and to preserve monarchical Government. In April 1824 the Brazilian Commissioners arrived in London. On 12th July 1824 a conference was held with Villa Réal and both Canning and Neumann in attendance. Canning put forward a compromise scheme but failed, in this instance, to get Austrian support. He decided to proceed alone by bringing pressure to bear on Portugal. But British influence at Lisbon was at a low ebb, and Canning made little impression, even though he now warned the Portuguese Government that England intended to recognise the independence of the Spanish Colonies and would surely follow suit in Brazil. Because Portuguese obstinacy was obviously supported by de Neuville, Canning, as has been seen, pressed for his recall and the dismissal of Subserra. Once these objectives had been secured Portuguese resistance crumbled. The Government agreed to receive Sir Charles Stuart, who was eventually accredited as their own representative and authorised to proceed to Rio with powers to treat a final settlement. He reached Rio in July 1825 and, after various French intrigues to make a separate bargain with Dom Pedro had been frustrated, was able to secure a definitive agreement, which was embodied in a Treaty signed on 29th August.[1] It was ratified at Lisbon on 20th November. Canning regretted that no effective provision had been made for the succession in Portugal, but refused, on the other hand, the suggestion that such a provision might be added if guaranteed by England. This difference clouded Anglo-Portuguese relations, but was of minor importance compared to the generally successful outcome of Canning's diplomatic initiative.

His preoccupation with Portugal and Brazil was closely tied to his interest in the Latin American Question as a whole. In a

[1] Sir Charles Stuart was less successful in his endeavours, as British Minister, to negotiate a new trade treaty with Brazil. The draft which he had approved was published in Brazil before its contents were known to Canning. He raised a number of objections and recalled Stuart. A new commercial treaty, which satisfied Canning's requirements was eventually negotiated by Stuart's successor, Robert Gordon.

memorandum circulated to the Cabinet on 15th November 1822 he insisted that 'no questions relating to Continental Europe can be more immediately and vitally important to Great Britain than those which relate to America'.[1] 'Our commerce,' he complained, 'was exposed to daily depredations in the American seas and awe of our maritime preponderancy was duly diminished.' For this Spain was largely to blame. He quoted one example. Recently the *Lord Collingwood*, a British merchant ship, had been captured by the *Panchita*, a royal Spanish privateer, and condemned in the courts of Porto Rico. As a consequence of such cases convoys were now necessary. 'Convoy in time of peace!' he protested, 'and against the attacks of a nation with which we are professedly in amity. . . .' 'Our commerce with the late Spanish Colonies,' he continued, 'is one which we either claim a right to carry on, or carry on knowing it to be illegitimate. If the former ought we to need a convoy? If the latter ought we not either to abandon the commerce or make it lawful?' The United States, Canning pointed out, had already recognised *de facto* independence. Supposing they were to occupy Cuba, the Americans would then control both shores through which Jamaican trade must pass. This was but one of the many dangers inherent in the situation. 'Let us apply,' Canning proposed, 'local remedy' and dispatch a naval force to the West Indies. This force could deal with pirates, who were operating with Spanish connivance from Cuba, and might, if necessary, effect a landing in Cuba itself to wipe out the pirate headquarters. The tacit compact with Spain 'whereby our trade was unmolested and the independence of the late Spanish Colonies was unrecognised' had been broken. While a naval force could deal with contingencies on the spot, recognition could not now be indefinitely postponed. 'The question,' Canning urged, was 'therefore one entirely of time and degree' and the situation varied 'according to the situation in each state'. As to Spain, he concluded: 'We do not take her anarchy as an offense, but she must not plead it as a privilege.' As a preliminary step towards recognition Canning planned to send civil agents to the principal ports of South America. He was strengthened in this resolve, not only by Ameri-

[1] C.G.C., vol. 1, p. 48.

can *de facto* recognition, but also because French 'commissions of enquiry' had already been despatched. Canning, however, remained anxious to avoid any head-on clash with Spain. Though he rated trading interests very high, he refused to be hustled by any pressure-group of British merchants and he continued to hope that the Spanish Government would eventually come to see reason. Only thus, he felt, was there any possibility of preserving monarchical institutions in any part of Spanish America.

As the prospect of European intervention in Spain grew Canning's irritation mounted. 'Our difficulty,' he wrote to A'Court on 3rd December 1822, 'arises from the double character in which Spain presents herself in Europe and in America; fighting for her independence in the former and in the latter exercising a tyranny, and assuming a tone of arrogance not to be endured; proposing new ties of friendship here, and there prohibiting our accustomed intercourse; holding out her European hand for charity, and with her American one picking our pockets.'[1] Canning feared that if a French invasion of Spain coincided with operations of the British West Indies Squadron, there would be 'an appearance of concert, utterly remote from the truth, indeed, but likely enough to impose upon Europe'. He begged A'Court to impress on the Spanish Government that 'the patience of our mercantile interest' was 'exhausted by the long series of injuries which they had endured'. On 29th December 1822 he again warned: 'but if they misconstrue us, if they evince distrust instead of thankfulness, and deny to us the means of satisfying England upon points of English interest; they may depend upon it, that the sins of American Spain will not only enable but compel us to remain, not only neutral, but indifferent to the fate of Spain in Europe.'[2]

The Spanish Government now finally sought to meet British grievances. Compensation was offered for British losses and plans were made to call a Convention to settle outstanding differences. Canning therefore suspended operations against the pirates and also shelved his plans to accredit consuls in Latin American ports. He thus showed that, provided specific grievances were redressed, he was willing to defer the general question of recognition

[1] G.C. & T., p. 385.   [2] Ibid., p. 389.

while the Spanish Government was itself in such immediate danger.

In the early stages of the French invasion of Spain Canning warned against French interference in Spanish America but otherwise made no further moves. French successes in Spain, however, prompted him during the summer to an essay in Anglo-American co-operation. He knew that the United States were irritated by Russian pretensions in Alaska and that, having granted *de facto* recognition in Latin America, they might be presumed to be in a mood for co-operation with Great Britain. On 16th August 1823 he proposed to Richard Rush, the American Minister, that a definite understanding should be concluded. He argued that such an understanding would restrain any possible interventionists because of 'the large share of the maritime power of the world which Great Britain and the United States held, and the consequent influence which the knowledge of their common policy, on a question involving such important maritime interests, present and future, could not fail to produce everywhere'.[1] Rush intimated that a British recognition of independence must precede an understanding. This condition Canning could not fulfil; partly because he had not yet converted the Cabinet, and partly because he still hoped that a new Spanish Government might eventually be induced to accept the situation, and thus perhaps preserve monarchical institutions, at least in some of the new States. He continued, however, to press Rush and urged that 'there had seldom been an opportunity when so small an effort of the two friendly Governments might produce so unequivocal a good and prevent such extensive calamities'.

On 25th August 1823 Canning, when proposing the health of the new American Minister to Sweden who was about to embark at Liverpool, declared that 'the force of blood again prevails, and the daughter and mother stand together against the world'.[2] Though these overtures were received with interest and satisfaction in the United States, suspicions of England and of Canning lingered. His unwillingness to recognise the independence of the

[1] D. Perkins: *The Monroe Doctrine*, p. 63.
[2] Therry, vol. 6, p. 414.

Colonies forthwith proved decisive in preventing any positive response. Instead, amid conflicting opinions, the President's message, which became known as the Monroe Doctrine, was prepared as a compromise plan which might lead to eventual co-operation. Canning's overtures and resulting reliance on the British Navy had provided the initial inspiration.

In the meantime Canning, perturbed by the imminent fall of Cadiz and by persistent rumours of French plans for intervention in Latin America, judged that he could not afford to wait for United States co-operation. This expedient, which might have prevented a European Congress, was, therefore, shelved in favour of direct diplomatic pressure on France. Canning summoned Polignac to a conference early in October 1823 and demanded information about France's attitude towards the Spanish Colonies. He stated that England would recognise independence if any attempt was made to restrict her existing trade; he then warned Polignac against any French interference by force or by menace, and in reply Polignac felt compelled to abjure any such intentions on the part of his country. When Polignac tried to parry with proposals for joint deliberations, Canning insisted that England, because of her greater interests, could not agree to be on equal footing with other Powers and in any case could not consent to joint deliberations at all unless the United States was a party to them. Polignac found himself out-manoeuvred. Canning's approach had been admirably timed. The French Minister was aware that his Government, at this juncture in the Spanish campaign, feared giving the least cause of offence to England; he had, therefore, no alternative but to give Canning all the required assurances.

These Canning now demanded in writing and, in spite of Polignac's protests, presented him with a record of their conversations. Villèle deemed it prudent to accept the Memorandum, which Polignac was loath to acknowledge. Canning's foresight in using this opportunity to gain such a declaration from the French paid handsome dividends. Although the Memorandum was not published, and then only in part, until the following March, Canning ensured that its contents became known and was thus at once able to offset the less palatable effects of the Monroe Doctrine.

England could plausibly be represented as the real guarantor of Latin-American liberty; there was documentary evidence for the Canning version of events.

On the day after Canning's conversations with Polignac had been concluded, news of the fall of Cadiz reached England.[1] The Memorandum could not serve as an immediate riposte. Accordingly, on 10th October, it was announced that Consuls had been accredited to the principal ports of Spanish America and that Commissions of Enquiry to Mexico and Columbia were to be dispatched. This gesture was followed on 28th October 1823 by a blustering speech at Plymouth which constituted Canning's public answer to Cadiz, contained a hint of the warnings to Polignac and was mainly tuned for home consumption. 'But . . . let it not be said,' he warned, 'that we cultivate peace, either because we fear, or because we are unprepared for, war. . . . Our present repose is no more a proof of our inability to act, than the state of inertness or inactivity in which I have seen those mighty masses that float in the waters above your town, is a proof that they are devoid of strength, and incapable of being fitted out for action. You will know how soon one of these stupendous masses, now reposing in their shadows in perfect stillness — how soon, upon any call of patriotism, or of necessity, it would assume the likeness of an animated thing, instinct with life and motion — how soon it would ruffle, as it were, its swelling plumage — how quickly it would put forth all its beauty and its bravery, collect its scattered elements of strength, and awaken its dormant thunder. Such as is one of these magnificent machines when springing from inaction into a display of its might — such is England herself, while apparently passive and motionless, she silently concentrates the power to be put forth on an adequate occasion.'[2] The boast was not an empty one, in that British naval strength was adequate to prevent any European intervention in Latin America. Seldom, however, has war been threatened with less risk of a bluff being called. Canning's calculated dramatic flourish served his policy on the one hand and popularised it on the other.

The Monroe Doctrine was proclaimed on 2nd December 1823,

[1] 10th October 1823.   [2] Therry, vol. 6, pp. 423-4.

but it was not known to Canning until late in the month. His reactions to the news were mixed. On the one hand, America's attitude provided a useful support to his general policy, while on the other, it threatened to rob England of some of the glory of protecting the independence of Latin America and proclaimed certain pretensions which England was not prepared unequivocally to countenance. Canning summed up his opinions of the situation in a letter of 31st December 1823 to A'Court. 'Laissez faire, et laissez venir,' he wrote, 'Pozzo may bustle and Ferdinand may swear, but sooner or later, if we are only quiet, and give no hold against us, things must go pretty much as we wish, or at least as we allow.

The Spanish American Question is, essentially, settled. There will be no Congress upon it; and things will take their own course on that continent, which cannot be otherwise than favourable to us. . . . I have no objection to Monarchy in Mexico — quite otherwise . . . Monarchy in Mexico and Monarchy in Brazil would cure the evils of universal democracy, and prevent the drawing of the line of demarcation which I most dread — America *versus* Europe.

The United States, naturally enough, aim at this division, and cherish the democracy which leads to it. . . . Mexico and they are too neighbourly to be friends. In the meantime they have aided us materially. The Congress was broken in all its limbs before, but the President's speech gives it the *coup de grâce* . . . I sounded Mr. Rush . . . as to his powers and disposition, to join in any step which we might take to prevent a hostile enterprise on the part of the European Powers against Spanish America. He had no powers; but he would have taken upon himself to join with us, if we would have begun by recognizing the Spanish American States. This we could not do, and so we went on without. But I have no doubt that his report to his Government of this *sounding* (which he probably represented as an overture) had a great share in producing the explicit declarations of the President.'[1] Canning went on to say that he was enclosing copies of the Polignac Memorandum for A'Court's use at his own discretion. He ex-

[1] G.C. & T., pp. 394-5.

plained that the Memorandum could not be published, but added: 'short of that it cannot be too generally known. Its date is most important; both in reference to the state of things which then existed, and in reference to the American speech which it so long preceded.' Thus, while recognising the value of United States support, Canning took steps to ensure that England's own credit for current and future achievement would not be diminished. He also made a discreet reply to unacceptable American pretensions in a conversation with Rush when he pointed out to him: 'If we were to be repelled from the shores of America, it would not matter to us whether that repulsion was effected by the ukase of Russia excluding us from the sea, or by the New Doctrine of the President excluding us from the land. But we cannot yield obedience to either.'[1] So, on England's behalf, Canning rejected the implications of the Monroe Doctrine. But he was anxious to avoid any public controversy on the subject. This attitude he made clear two years later in a letter to Vaughan;[2] 'The general maxim,' he wrote, 'that our interests and those of the United States are essentially the same etc. etc. is one that cannot be too readily admitted, when put forward by the United States. But we must not be the dupes of this conventional language of courtesy. The avowed pretension of the United States to put themselves at the head of the Confederacy of all the Americas, and to sway that Confederacy against Europe (Great Britain included) is *not* a pretension identified with our interests, or one that we can countenance as tolerable. It is however a pretension that there is no use in contesting in the abstract; but we must not say anything that seems to admit the principle.'[3]

Although there were important reservations to Canning's enthusiasm for the Monroe Doctrine he was, on the whole, well satisfied. As he wrote on 22nd January 1824 to Bagot: 'The effect of the ultra-liberalism of our Yankee co-operators, on the ultra-despotism of our Aix-la-Chapelle allies, gives me just the balance I wanted.'[4]

[1] H. C. Allen: *Great Britain and the United States*, p. 379.

[2] Charles R. Vaughan. British Minister to the United States (1823–35).

[3] 8th February 1826. WEB, vol. 2, no. 623, p. 542.

[4] BAG, vol. 2, p. 217. Bagot was warned not to act jointly with his American

Further attempts to persuade Canning to attend a Congress on Latin America in Paris in March were parried by a repetition of the point made in the Polignac Memorandum that he could not do so unless an American representative were also invited to attend. Such an invitation, he knew, would never be forthcoming. When the possibility of sending French troops was canvassed among the Allied Ambassadors in Paris, Chateaubriand himself took refuge in the assurances given by France in the Polignac Memorandum and, to Canning's great gratification, informed Metternich that France was formally committed to refrain from any intervention. Canning, in the meanwhile, devoted his energies to the hopeless task of once again trying to persuade the Spanish Government to negotiate directly with her former Colonies. In the hope, mainly, of preserving a monarchy in Mexico, he offered mediation. He also offered to guarantee Cuba to Spain, provided Spain would recognise the independence of her other Colonies. This offer was rejected on 3rd May 1824 and Canning concluded: 'Result of it is simply that His Majesty reserves to himself the right of taking, at his own time such steps as His Majesty may think proper, in respect to the several States of Spanish America, without further reference to the Court of Madrid.'[1]

Recognition was now Canning's deliberate policy. Reports from the British Commissioners were favourable. The Government of Spain was obviously intractable and there was no longer any cause to trouble about Spanish susceptibilities. French troops remained in Spain and continued to provide justification for a counter gesture. More than words were now needed to overcome the United States' bid for popularity. In these circumstances the interests of British merchants could claim unequivocal consideration.

Having reached his own decision, Canning still had to deal with opposition from the King and in the Cabinet. During the

---

colleague but Canning nevertheless advised him to
> Be kind and courteous to that gentleman,
> Hop in his walks and gambol in his eyes,
> Feed him with apricocks and dewberries.

[1] *F.O. Spain 185/95*. Canning to A'Court. TEMP, p. 140.

Q

summer he was busy preparing the ground. On 23rd October 1824 a particularly useful report reached him from the Commissioners in Columbia. Late in November a memorandum from Liverpool, which Canning had obviously drawn up, was circulated to the Cabinet. 'Sooner or later,' it was argued, 'we shall probably have to contend with the combined maritime power of France and the United States. The disposition of the new States is at present highly favourable to England. If we take advantage of that disposition we may establish through our influence with them a fair counterpoise to that combined maritime power. Let us not, then, throw the present golden opportunity away, which once lost may never be recovered.'[1] On 7th December 1824 the Cabinet finally agreed that the question should be decided 'without reference to the opinions of the Continental Allied Powers, that Spain need not be further consulted and that the actual recognition should be given on the merits of each individual State'.[2]

Much further pressure was required before the Cabinet would in fact agree to recognition in any specific case. Canning deliberately raised the old bogey of French ambitions, and the possible consequences of a new 'family compact' between France and Spain. In order to give colour to this danger he required Granville on 3rd December 1824 to enquire whether France would promise to evacuate her military force from Spain in a definite time. The answer, which reached England on 9th December, was, as Canning could have predicted, evasive. But it gave him the excuse to proclaim, in a memorandum circulated to the Cabinet, that 'the greatest practical question for us seems to be how, in the event of an actual incorporation of the resources of Spain with those of France, such an accession to the power of France can best be counteracted. I have no hesitation in saying that this must be by the separation of the resources of Spanish America from those of Spain.'[3] He then pressed for recognition of Mexico, arguing that an amicable connection with Mexico would oppose a powerful barrier to United States ambitions. On 14th December Liverpool and Canning recommended recognition of Buenos Aires, Mexico and Columbia, and Cabinet agreement was finally secured on the 15th.

[1] TEMP, p. 145.   [2] Ibid., p. 146.   [3] Ibid.

On 31st December 1824 a dispatch announcing this decision was sent to Spain to be read to the Spanish Foreign Minister. On 11th January 1825 the news was broken to foreign representatives in London and on 7th February a formal announcement was included in the King's Speech.

Remonstrances followed from the European Courts. Villèle, who would dearly have wished to follow England's example at once, was even more angry because he could not. Alexander was infuriated because he had identified himself with the Congress System, and the System seemed to have been snubbed. Metternich, who had borne the brunt of Canning's taunts and who had hoped, via the King and the 'Ultras', to have outwitted his enemy, resented above all the blow to his pride. Their violent reactions magnified Canning's achievement and converted an ordinary diplomatic move into the appearance of a triumph.

The recognition of *de facto* independence of three new States was not in itself a major stroke of policy, nor was it attended with any great risk. Strong in her maritime supremacy, England could, on such an issue, afford to risk any amount of European displeasure. There was no danger that moral censure could be converted into forceful retribution; nor any hint that such a policy was contemplated. Recognition was no more than an act of obvious diplomacy, which was indeed only undertaken when all other methods of achieving a solution had failed. But European anger suggested that a battle had been won, and Canning was quick to claim a victory. Though his real success was against Cabinet opposition and against the King, he gloried in a triumph over the Neo-Holy Alliance. By their complaints the partners in that Alliance endorsed his opinion. Canning had deliberately sought to raise British prestige and in this objective, thanks largely to the reactions of his opponents, he scored an unqualified success. As he had once explained to Frere: 'for "Alliance" read "England"; and you have the clue to my policy.'[1] Now he could boast results.

While Canning was thus engaged in restoring British influence in Portugal and in settling the Latin-American Question,

[1] 7th August 1823. Canning to Frere. FEST, p 259.

he pursued a cautious and waiting game in the Near East. Like Castlereagh, he inherited Pitt's suspicions of Russia. This consideration complicated the simple commercial issues which the Greek Revolution had posed. Canning was not moved by any sentimental or ideological sympathy for the Greeks in their struggle for independence. But he feared the conflict as providing an open invitation for Russian intervention. On the other hand he was not sorry that the situation caused friction between Russia and Austria. Immediately, he was anxious to avoid an armed clash between Russia and Turkey, and therefore he focused his attention on the problem of effecting a Russo–Turkish accommodation. As a first step, and as a result of the Verona Congress, Russian demands were communicated to Lord Strangford for negotiation at Constantinople. Russia required: 1. Guarantees by the Turks to the Greeks for future good government. 2. Reduction of the Turkish armed forces in the Principalities to a pre-1821 standard. 3. Removal of obstacles placed in the way of Russian Black Sea commerce.

By September 1823 Strangford considered that satisfaction had been obtained on the first point and that the other two points were likely soon to be conceded.

In the meanwhile Canning had, in March 1823, recognised the Greeks as belligerents. This was a practical step taken in the interest of British commerce. It was implicit in Castlereagh's previous attitude, and it only caused some stir because Canning was now at the helm. The other Powers could enjoy the luxury of protesting, but they had no comparable Mediterranean trade to protect. Apart from this step, Canning remained impassive during the Strangford negotiations. On 14th July 1823 he confided some of his anxieties and difficulties to Bagot. Having referred to the Tsar's moderation, he continued: 'Can it hold out against the temptation of Turkish refractoriness and of an army upon his hands pining for employment? . . . I need hardly assure you that you are not to believe anything that you hear of supposed encouragement from us to the Greeks — not one word.'[1] On the other hand he explained: 'we have not *dis*couraged the

[1] BAG, vol. 2, p. 180.

speeches and subscriptions for Greeks at home, for two reasons; first, that we have no effective means of doing so, and secondly that discouragement generally inflames an enthusiasm. But our neutrality in the quarrel is as strict and sincere as in that of Spain, and I have not uttered a wish for the Greeks, because they, right or wrong, are the assailants.' Encouragement for the Greeks was left to individuals, and particularly of course to Lord Byron. His death more than anything else popularised the Greek cause in England. Canning's chief immediate concern was the resumption of diplomatic relations between Russia and Turkey. This, and his motives, he made clear to Bagot in a letter of 20th August 1823.

'But I am as anxious as he [Metternich] can be, although not for his reasons, that the Russian Mission (*a* Russian Mission, I care not of what size or character) should be sent to Constantinople. I wish it, first, because I think that we have too much upon our hands there; 2nd, because the responsibility is enormous and the interest to *us*, I think disproportionate; 3rd, because, though S[trangfor]d has done admirably, he is vagarious and uncertain, and a single false step might spoil all; 4th, because while we are occupied wholly with Russian interests, English interests are of necessity postponed, and this begins to be found out here and to create dissatisfaction; 5th, because we exhaust our authority in pleading for Russia and may miss it when we have occasion to demand for ourselves; and lastly because, if the Emperor of Russia should go to war after all, while the negotiation is yet *in our hands*, the blame would fall on us — both at Constantinople and in England — just as surely as we are blamed in Russia for having so long deferred this desired consummation. Let but a Russian Mission get back to Constantinople, and I care not if they quarrel with the Porte on the morrow.

Care not! No — care not. Metternich cares, because a Russian war with the Porte must affect Austrian interests deeply, turn which way it will, but more, I believe, because the Emperor of Russia's army is his, Metternich's, talisman for the government of Europe. But it is not necessary to *us* either that Metternich should govern Europe, or that Austria should have leisure to meddle in everybody's affairs, being secure of her own; or, lastly, that the strength of the Austrian army should remain unbroken, and a terror to evil-doers. In short, had I been in office six months sooner than I was, so as to be in any degree master of the questions to be discussed at Verona, and had I seen as clearly as I think I do now that in the prurient and tantalised state of the Russian army some vent must be found — in short — that the Spanish war was the alternative of the Turkish — I should have preferred peace, certainly commercial peace, to any war — but deliberately the Turkish to the Spanish. Metternich's choice was, quite naturally, just the reverse. But see the consequence! The Russians have conquered Spain, so far as it is conquered, without marching; and their army is (I suppose from Metternich's present fear) as prurient as before.'[1]

In these circumstances, although the invasion of Spain had not been prevented and the Russian danger yet remained, peace in the Near East was still preferable to war. For the sake of that peace Canning could do no more than continue laborious and unpopular efforts to play the part of honest broker between Russian and Turk.

In January 1824 Alexander proposed in a memorandum that a Congress should be held to work out a solution to the Greek question on the basis that Turkey was to be required to set up three autonomous Greek principalities. This proposal was obviously not calculated to satisfy either the Greeks or the Turks, and seemed, in fact, only to serve Russian interests. Though he disapproved, Metternich was not in a position openly to oppose and felt that at any rate a Congress might procure delay. Delay was also favoured by Canning. 'Blessed is he who invented procrastination,' he remarked to Bagot, 'for it is akin to sleep.'[2] Therefore, while intending to evade the Congress, he avoided any categoric statement of this intention. On the other hand, he welcomed Alexander's decision, which was now made known, to restore a Russian Mission to Constantinople. 'The restoration of the Russian Mission to Constantinople,' he wrote to Bagot, 'is

---

[1] BAG, vol. 2, p. 197.
[2] 22nd January 1824. Ibid., p. 214.

the greatest point gained this many a day; and on the morning on which the Ambassador — or Minister — (for I will not quarrel for degrees) leaves St. Petersburgh, you may get something to drink — what you please — the liquid bubble in the inside of a frozen bottle of usquebaugh if you will — and charge it to the office. I will face out Hume himself on that article of your extraordinaries.'[1] But Canning was not prepared to allow this move on Alexander's part to bind him to attending a Congress. 'It has never,' Bagot had recently been warned, 'hitherto been understood by the British Govt. that the settlement of the Affairs of Greece was to be a condition of the re-establishment of the Russian Mission at Constantinople.'[2] Furthermore Bagot was warned that he must avoid any appearance of concert with the Allies over the Greek Question. They must not be allowed to assume that differences, 'where we do differ', were only a feint. 'There are real fundamental essential irreconcilable differences of principle,' he wrote, 'and every attempt to represent them as trifling or fictitious we must steadily repel. The times are really too big for compromise of this sort. If things were prevented from going to extremities it must be by *our* keeping a distinct middle ground between conflicting *bigotries* and staying the plague both ways.'[3]

But, in spite of these warnings, Bagot, in his endeavours to remain on good terms with the Tsar and to speed up the appointment of a Russian Ambassador to Constantinople, did attend two meetings with the Allied Ambassadors at St. Petersburg, on 17th June and 2nd July 1824, at which the Greek Question was discussed. The publication of the Tsar's January Memorandum in May gave Canning the pretext to take an independent line, and Bagot was now informed that its publication made it impossible to think of taking further steps towards the opening of a Congress on Greece. Bagot's conduct was disavowed and he received a snub.[4]

[1] 22nd January 1824. BAG, vol. 2, p. 215.
[2] Canning to Bagot. 15th January 1824. BAG, vol. 2, p. 213.
[3] Ibid. 22nd January 1824. Ibid., p. 221.
[4] 'I am sorry,' Canning wrote, 'to have to snub or snouch you, in your old age (the old age of your Embassy) for disobedience of your instructions.' BAG, vol. 2, p. 268.

On 23rd July 1824 Canning wrote to Strangford: 'Your Excellency will learn from Sir Charles Bagot's despatch that his attendance at that conference was altogether against his instructions.'[1] On 6th August Ribeaupierre's nomination as Russian Ambassador to Turkey was announced but, on various pretexts, his departure was delayed. This gave Canning a continued excuse to avoid committing himself to participation in a Congress. His reluctance was confirmed by anxiety to avoid any Congress discussion of the Latin-American Question and by the popularity of the Greek cause in liberal circles at home.

In pursuit of evasive tactics Canning repeatedly recommended discretion to his representatives. This negative attitude was infuriating to the Allies, and many efforts were made to trap representatives into the expression of opinions. On one occasion Granville proved unwary and was warned: 'Do not let Pozzo betray you into giving your opinions again. Retract the old one, if you can. Never mention the subject first, and when mentioned to you only smile, and make no confidences even as to the meaning of your smile, with your colleagues.'[2]

The Greeks, however, by presenting a protest against the Russian Memorandum, eventually forced Canning himself to express some kind of opinion. He replied as cautiously as he could; the Memorandum, he pointed out, was rejected by both parties; any hope of successful intervention was at present vain; as with Latin America, England intended to be neutral; she was connected with Turkey by ancient treaties; if she aided the Greeks she would be engaging in 'unprovoked hostilities against that power in a struggle not her own'; on the other hand the Greeks could be assured that Great Britain would not be concerned 'in any attempt (if any were in contemplation) to force upon them a plan of pacification contrary to their wishes; but she would undertake the office of mediation with Turkey, if asked by the Greeks, and if accepted by Turkey, would do her best to convey it into effect conjointly with the other Powers'.[3] Enclosing the draft of

[1] BAG, vol. 2, p. 257.
[2] Canning to Granville. 16th November 1824. G.C. & T., p. 459.
[3] C.G.C., vol. 1, p. 197.

this reply to Liverpool Canning explained his motives in a cover-ing note: '1. The letter itself is a record of our policy in the struggle. 2. The communication of it to the Porte will for ever silence all cavil there. 3. The communication of it to Russia will be at once a proof of the fairness with which we deal with her, and an indication of our determination not to be knocked into another Congress at Verona — a Congress, I mean, in which we should protest against the employment of force, but leave others at liberty to employ it as they like. 4. It is a rallying point for both Greek and Turk. 5. It hangs up the question of intervention till then.'[1]

The task of informing Metternich and Alexander of Canning's refusal to participate in any Congress on Greek affairs fell to Stratford Canning, who was travelling to St. Petersburg, via Vienna, on a special mission to the Tsar before taking up his appointment at Constantinople. Stratford Canning found Metter-nich dismayed at this categoric refusal. He was hoping that he could have used the Congress to persuade Alexander to stay his hand. On Canning's instructions his cousin informed Metternich that England could not join a Congress for the ostensible pur-pose of intervention and the real motive of preventing it. 'We must either assign to the Parliament and people of this country,' he argued, 'reasons for our conduct by which in fact it is not actuated, and must express hopes of success which in fact we do not feel; or, by declaring frankly our real motives . . . must betray the secret . . . and therewith destroy the illusion by which the Emperor of Russia has to be fortified against the warlike im-pulsion of his people. In the silent recesses of a Cabinet it may be possible to employ arguments which you do not openly avow. . . . But in the broad daylight of Parliament no British Minister could venture on a declaration by which the truth should be knowingly either altered or concealed.'[2] Canning surely took some malicious pleasure in thus using the British Constitution as an excuse to explain what was in fact his own deliberate policy. Metternich obviously derived cold comfort from this irritating explanation.

[1] 16th November 1824. C.G.C., vol. 1, p. 197.   [2] TEMP, p. 334.

Alexander, who was presumably relying on the Congress to sanction the use of force against Turkey, and who seemed, at any rate to Canning, to have betrayed this intention by his failure to send Ribeaupierre to Constantinople, made no attempt to hide his anger. 'The Cabinet of London,' he declared, 'will easily understand that His Imperial Majesty on his side regards all further deliberation between Russia and England on the relations with Turkey and on the pacification of Greece as definitely closed.'[1]

Canning now felt that he could rely on differences between the Allies to cause the failure of any Congress on Greek affairs. Writing to Granville on 10th January 1825 he commented: 'Metternich is very angry (over Latin America) and threatens Russian hostilities against Turkey — threatens us, that is, but is much more alive to the dangers for himself.'[2]

Under the shadow of Egyptian intervention in Greece a conference was finally held at St. Petersburg. It was known that the Sultan, despairing of crushing the Greeks without adequate naval power, had finally concluded a bargain with his vassal and enemy, Mohammed Ali of Egypt.[3] In return for full Egyptian military and naval support against the Greeks, Ibrahim, Mohammed Ali's son, was appointed Pasha of the Peloponnese. In July 1824 the main Egyptian expeditionary force under his command set sail from Alexandria. It was in the light of this new threat, and in a desperate gamble to checkmate Russian ambitions, that Metternich himself was reduced to proposing recognition of Greek Independence. This was rejected by Alexander, who came up against French and Austrian opposition to the use of any kind of force. As Canning had anticipated, no agreement could be reached and meetings were eventually suspended in May. In the meanwhile, relations between Alexander and Metternich had deteriorated. During a visit to Paris in April Metternich had un-

---

[1] Nesselrode to Lieven. 30th December 1824. TEMP, p. 335.

[2] C.G.C., vol. 1, p. 231.

[3] As early as 1822 the Sultan had gained some Egyptian help in return for granting Crete to Mohammed Ali. Egyptian energies had been mainly directed towards the capture of this prize.

wisely boasted of his ascendency over the Tsar. Knowledge of this confirmed Alexander's growing mistrust.

In these circumstances Canning very tentatively reopened conversations with the Russian Ambassador in London. Countess Lieven, whose friendship with Metternich was beginning to cool, and whose opinion of Canning was being revised, spoke in St. Petersburg, during a visit in June 1825, in favour of co-operation with England. Canning's changed attitude can be explained partly because he now felt that he could negotiate from strength, and partly because of the situation in Greece itself was turning sharply against the Greeks. Though their own differences had been hurriedly patched up, Ibrahim's forces were now threatening them with total disaster. On 24th September 1825 a Greek delegation had arrived in England appealing for aid and for an English candidate for the Greek throne. Canning answered by referring to his previous reply. But the possibility of successful British mediation now seemed greater; the Greeks continued to regard England as their favoured protector; the Turks trusted England more than Russia; there were slight hints that France, and even Austria, might welcome a British move. 'I begin to think,' wrote Canning on 25th October 1825, to Liverpool, 'that the time approaches when *something* must be done; but not till Austria as well as France has put into our hands the dealing — first with Russia and then with the parties to the war.'[1] And on 31st October he confided to Granville: 'What is to be done is a different thing but nothing just yet. Things are not yet ripe for our interference, for we must not (like our good allies) interfere in vain. If we act, we must finish what is to be done.'[2] On 8th November 1825, again to Granville, he wrote: '. . . Combined operation is nonsense in a case in which the principles on which we and our Allies act, are as different as the objects at which we respectively aim. Do you imagine that I should have ever settled the question between Portugal and Brazil, had I let Russia and Prussia have voices in it; or even if I had not shaken off Austria, as a co-agent, when we came to the practical issue. . . .

---

[1] G.C. & T., p. 468.   [2] Ibid., p. 446.

It is however some satisfaction to find the members of that illustrious body (the Holy Alliance) coming one by one to confess that we alone can help them out of their difficulties. So has said Lieven. So Prince Esterhazy, so today Prince Polignac; in terms more unqualified than either of the other two. The Prussian I never see.'[1] From this standpoint, gradually Canning moved towards the conclusion that 'our concert must be straightforward and single-handed with Russia herself'. 'I think,' he explained to Bathurst, 'we can arrive at such a concert quite consistently with all that we have hitherto done and said about Greece; and without abandoning an inch of the ground which we have hitherto taken.'[2] Stratford Canning was instructed to bring pressure on Turkey to accept mediation and thus avoid a Russian declaration of war. Strangford, on the other hand, was sent to Russia with no more definite mandate than that he should flatter the Russians, welcome and transmit any overtures made, but continue to avoid discussion of any joint Allied intervention. This brief was galling to Strangford, who preferred active to passive diplomacy and who rightly suspected that Canning was using him as a dummy while he kept the real controls in his own hands.

In the meanwhile, on her return from Russia, Countess Lieven told Canning that the Tsar was anxious to co-operate with England over Greece but that the initiative must appear to come from England. If no agreement was reached Alexander would be compelled to resort to force in the spring. In these circumstances Canning began to consider the possible use of force, in co-operation with Russia, as a means of saving the Greeks and preventing a Russo–Turkish war. He was, however, still determined to avoid the impression of being a party to any 'Congress' policy and he was, therefore, annoyed at reports that Strangford had tried to bring the French and Austrian ambassadors into discussion with Nesselrode and that he had even suggested a formula which would allow Russia to go to war if Turkey remained obdurate. After disavowing Strangford, Canning, undeterred by news of Tsar Alexander's death, continued his own conversations with

[1] G.C. & T., p. 466.　　　　[2] 7th December 1825. BATH, p. 397.

the Lievens and determined to pursue his objective of a direct agreement with Russia.

Accordingly, on 12th January 1826, Canning informed Lieven that he proposed to send the Duke of Wellington on a congratulatory visit to the new Tsar. The Ambassador received the news with 'tears of pleasure'. To Granville Canning explained: 'The Duke of Wellington would not have done for any purpose of mine a twelve month ago. No more would confidence with Russia but now, the "Ultra" system being dissolved by the carrying of every point which they opposed, the elements of that system have become agreeable for good purpose. I hope to save Greece through the agency of the Russian name on the fears of Turkey without a war which the Duke of Wellington is the fittest man to deprecate. . . . De plus . . . the Duke of Wellington is the only agent by whom I could suppress and extinguish Strangford.' Canning added that when the Mission was proposed the King expressed doubts about the effects on the Duke's health, but agreed that he should be approached. 'The Duke,' Canning commented, 'not only accepted, but *jumped* as I foresaw he would at my proposal. "Never better in my life", "ready to set out in a week" and the like expressions of alertness, leave no doubt in my mind that the selection of *another* person would have done his health more prejudice, than all the frosts or thaws of the hyperborean regions can do it.'[1] During his visit to Russia Wellington was to propose Anglo–Russian co-operation over the Greek Question. Force was only to be used if Ibrahim's supposed plans were carried into effect. Otherwise, even if attempts to settle the Greek Question failed, Russia would still have no mandate for military intervention. When Wellington, who did not understand the full purport of his Mission, opened discussion on these lines with Nicholas he made little headway. Nicholas was wary and suspicious; he said he regarded the Greeks as rebels and he turned discussion to Serbia and the Principalities. During the conversations he even sent an ultimatum to Turkey and it seemed as if Russia and England were at cross purposes after all. Lieven, however, then arrived opportunely at St.

[1] 13th January 1826. G.C. & T., pp. 470, 471.

Petersburg. He understood Canning's wishes far more clearly than Wellington. Thanks to his presence Wellington was cajoled into signing a Protocol which went further in defining Anglo–Russian co-operation over the Greek Question than even Canning had proposed or believed possible. As Countess Lieven wrote: 'By us the question was presented to the Duke in a new light. It was not the Revolution which we patronised; we wished to stop the insurrection, to control the movement; we wished to establish in Greece the conservation of order; for it was proved that the Turks were powerless, that we desired a regular state of things, a hierarchical discipline, all of which sounded well in the ears of the Duke of Wellington.'[1] The Duke had in effect been made the dupe of Canning and of the Lievens. He later spent much time trying to deny the importance of the document which he had signed.

In fact the Anglo–Russian alignment, which the Protocol implied, constituted a diplomatic revolution. Its premature disclosure, due to Russian indiscretions which were perhaps calculated, caused Canning some displeasure. He had counted on an interval in which to negotiate on the same subject separately with France and with Austria; he also wished to prepare opinion in England. However, these disadvantages were easily outweighed by the effects of Russia's altered attitude towards Spain and Portugal. From England's point of view Russia had become, in these spheres, a benevolent neutral.

The rapprochement with France over the Greek Question was finally established during Canning's visit to Paris in September 1826. It was facilitated by the romantic pro-Hellenism of the French King and by the realisation, on the part of his Ministers, that French commercial interests were also at stake. When Canning had an audience with Charles X the King announced: 'I am ready to go farther than you are ready to go. I mean I would concur in *co-ercing* the Porte if she is obstinate.'[2] Villèle promised that France would co-operate with the provisions of the Protocol, but as Canning wrote: 'his language on this point was much less

[1] Lieven MSS. TEMP, p. 355.
[2] Canning to the King. 22nd September 1826. ASP, vol. 3, no. 1253, p. 159.

enthusiastick than that of H.M.C. Majesty had been; nor was there any mixture of that *crusading* spirit which generally prevails among friends of the Greeks — nor any reference whatever to Epaminondas or Themistocles, in the other general topicks of declamation. M. Villèle's view of the matter was a sober practical view (such as is taken by your Majesty's Government) founded on the danger, as well as disgrace to all Europe, of leaving such a war as now desolates the Archipelago to take its course; multiplying piracies against the trade of all commercial nations and tending to exhaust both parties to the war so effectually that both may at any moment become an easy prey to the ambition of Russia. It is upon this last point that M. Villèle feels most strongly. The only two points in the Protocol upon which he made any objection were 1st the declaration that England could not undertake to guarantee the arrangement between Turkey and Greece; which he feared would leave the whole question in the hands of Russia. 2ndly the want, as he thought, of a sufficient security against the extension of hostilities, which might grow out of a failure of the negotiations at Akkermann, to Greece. . . . The discussion ended in Mr. Canning's suggestion to Mr. Villèle that if France thought further security against the aggrandisement of Russia indispensable, nothing could be easier than for France to propose the conversion of the Protocol into a Treaty, whereby the arrangement to be effected under the Protocol would be placed, if not formally under the *guarantee*, under the superintendence of all the parties to that arrangement, and the pledges of disinterestedness given in the Protocol by Russia to England *alone*, would become common to all the other Powers. With this suggestion M. Villèle appeared well contented.'[1] When France thus associated herself with the provisions of the Protocol Metternich was left, with his Prussian satellite, as a forlorn representative of the old Alliance.

But though the manoeuvre clearly represented a defeat for Metternich, Canning probably (and no doubt deliberately) exaggerated the difference between the new agreement and the Congress System. In fact it could be argued that he was simply

[1] Canning to the King. 1st October 1826. ASP, vol. 3, no. 1256, p. 165.

rebuilding a European concert to deal with Near Eastern affairs, with Russia and England, instead of Russia, Austria and France, at the centre of the stage, while England hovered in the wings. But even though an old formula was merely being refurbished, diplomacy is often a matter of *nuance* and Canning's new concert could claim many advantages, from a British point of view, over the old.

In the meanwhile, though the Greek Question remained unsolved, there was now a working arrangement with Russia. The Latin-American Question was settled to England's entire satisfaction. British influence was paramount in Portugal. Though French troops were still in Spain, her advice in that country was not heeded and Villèle was clearly angling for England's favour. Canning's policy was popular at home and its popularity was welcome to the King. British prestige was generally high. Though Canning had deliberately exaggerated his difficulties and made much capital over his triumphs, the picture, as he presented it, was at least plausible. He was ready to face further developments in the Near East from a position of vantage.

But, before tackling this problem, he met a new crisis in Portugal which tested the validity of his previous successes and in fact set a seal upon them.

In March 1826 King John VI died. His son Dom Pedro, the Emperor of Brazil, decided that his own daughter, Donna Maria, aged eight, should succeed to the Portuguese throne. She was to marry her uncle Dom Miguel[1] and the Regency was to be entrusted to Dom Pedro's sister, Donna Maria Isabella. He himself would remain Emperor of Brazil. He also announced his decision to endow Portugal with a Constitution. This news did not reach Europe until late June. Metternich was enraged and the absolutist Government of Spain infuriated. Canning was annoyed but argued that Sovereigns could do what they pleased and denied, with a clear conscience, that England had had any part in influencing Dom Pedro. The Allied Ambassadors in Paris agreed to take no action. Spain was advised to remain quiet. On the

[1] After Papal dispensation had been obtained. Dom Miguel was Dom Pedro's brother and the younger son of King John. See p. 217 above.

other hand, if the Portuguese attempted any intervention in Spain, France and Austria promised to provide support against the aggressor. For his part Canning reminded Esterhazy that Great Britain had obligations to Portugal which the Spanish Government would do well to remember. To Countess Lieven, obviously for transmission to Metternich, he remarked: 'I don't know why M. de Metternich imagines that I like Constitutional Governments. Unquestionably, as an English Minister, it is not my place to oppose them; but as a matter of taste, I should much prefer to do without them. It would be much easier for me to influence or to rule a monarchical cabinet, or a despotic one, or anything else you like. The proof is that new America gives me a hundred times more trouble than old Europe.'[1]

The danger of a clash between Spain and the new régime in Portugal was soon underlined by a specific dispute. Portuguese deserters had taken refuge in Spain. The Portuguese Government had requested their return. The Spanish Government, on Austrian and French advice, had refused to comply with this request. Portugal interpreted the refusal as an unfriendly act and suspected that the deserters, with Spanish aid, were planning to overthrow the régime by force.

In the light of this situation Canning began to consider ways and means of bringing pressure to bear on Spain. As a first step he decided to visit Paris. Shortly after his arrival, in a long letter to Liverpool, he commented on the advantages of having undertaken the trip: 'You see, I am not idle here; and upon the whole perhaps time would be gained by moving the Foreign Office hither during the Summer — one is so much nearer every field of diplomatic action.'[2] On 21st September 1826 he had an audience with Charles X, and during the next month, while he remained in Paris, he had numerous conversations with the King, with Villèle and with Pozzo di Borgo. Villèle assured Canning that he had personally been opposed to French intervention in Spain, that he had resigned himself to it in preference to European intervention and that the only reason French troops were not

[1] Lieven to Metternich. 14th July 1826. L., p. 309.
[2] C.G.C., vol. 2, p. 133.

R

now being withdrawn was to exercise some kind of restraint on the King of Spain where Portugal was concerned. Certainly France had no desire to encourage Spain in her designs against the Portuguese Government. Canning, however, mistrustful of de Moustier's[1] attitude on the spot, urged that categoric instructions should be sent to him to advise the Spanish Government to return the Portuguese deserters. On 9th October 1826 Canning reported to the King that 'he had obtained from the French Govt., after discussions with M. Villèle and M. Damas, an instruction to M. de Moustier, the terms of which were so peremptory as *almost* to amount to a recall, if he failed to overcome his C.My's resistance'.[2] Previously Canning had threatened to recall Frederick Lamb from Madrid unless the Spanish Government agreed to the return of the Portuguese deserters. He had also been speculating on possibilities of direct action against Spain, and on 6th October confided to Liverpool: 'One single word I must add, in the deepest secrecy. God forbid war; but if Spain will have it, ought we not to think of Havannah? Where else can we strike a blow? and what blow could be so effectual? it would settle all better than half a dozen Peninsular campaigns.'[3] Now, as a result of the latest instructions to de Moustier, it seemed that the Spanish Government had decided to give way and Canning, as he wrote to the King, had 'every reason to be satisfied with the assistance which he has received from the French Government'.

Though one danger seemed to have been averted, Canning now became anxious about the situation in Portugal itself. As he wrote on 16th October 1826 to Liverpool: 'The intelligence is disagreeable. *Very bad* elections; in the ultra liberal sense ... this is very untoward but we are to thank Vienna and Madrid for it.'[4] Realising that the Cortes, when they met, would be in an ebullient mood, Canning was concerned that Dom Miguel should not give an excuse for violence by withholding his oath to the new Constitution. Metternich had finally been induced to advise Dom Miguel to take the oath and Dom Miguel had now done so. But

---

[1] The French Ambassador.
[2] ASP, vol. 3, no. 1258, p. 172.
[3] C.G.C., vol. 2, p. 144.
[4] G.C. & T., p. 527.

Metternich apparently tried to keep the matter secret and Canning sent a special messenger with the news to Lisbon. It arrived, in fact, just in time for the opening of the Cortes. One further danger, therefore, seemed to have been successfully overcome.

Writing to Liverpool from Paris on 16th October, Canning claimed that his visit had been most opportune and added: 'I have been able to assure myself, to absolute conviction, that had the Government been rightly understood here in 1822 the invasion of Spain would never have taken place. In this faith I shall die.'[1] Certainly he had every reason to be satisfied with the present attitude of the French Ministers and he could, with some justice, claim that personal contact had paid handsome dividends.

On the other hand, he was over-sanguine in his hopes regarding Spain. In spite of wise counsels from Paris, and even up to a point from Vienna, the Portuguese deserters were not returned and the Spanish Government's attitude remained provocative. In November Portugal appealed to England for help and on 3rd December 1826 Palmella offered evidence of incursions from Spain into Portuguese territory. On 8th December Canning was convinced that Portuguese deserters, armed and equipped in Spain, were across the Portuguese borders and that there was 'not an hour to lose in doing our duty by Portugal'.[2] With complete confidence in his own timing, Canning was ready to use the occasion for a flourish of trumpets. On 12th December he announced in the House that troops were on their march for embarkation. 'Let us fly to the aid of Portugal,' he urged, 'by whomsoever attacked; because it is our duty to do so; and let us cease our interference where that duty ends. We go to Portugal, not to rule, not to dictate, not to prescribe Constitutions — but to defend and preserve the independence of an Ally. We go to plant the standard of England on the well known heights of Lisbon. Where that standard is planted, foreign dominion shall not come!'[3] In his reply to the Opposition speakers, Canning referred to the presence of French troops in Spain and admitted that their entry had been a blow to British pride. However, he dramatically continued: 'Contemplating Spain, such as her

[1] G.C. & T., p. 528.   [2] Ibid., p. 542.   [3] Therry, vol. 6, p. 92.

ancestors had known her, I resolved that if France had Spain, it should not be Spain with the Indies. I called the New World into existence to redress the balance of the Old.'[1] Seldom has an answer been given with so much pleasure and so much calculated effect.

The sending of British troops to Portugal stopped Spanish intervention. Canning's dramatic speech delighted the House of Commons and publicised the prestige victories claimed by its author. Mrs. Arbuthnot commented bitterly: 'All the army are charmed by this appearance of warlike action and I daresay the whole nation would be delighted if we had a war. We certainly are a strange people and *très inconséquent* for, notwithstanding all our complaints of our debt and distress, we shall send out these troops without the slightest difficulty and everybody will be pleased.'[2] In fact neither the dispatch of troops nor the speech involved any serious risks. But both were galling to French pride at a time when French Ministers were striving their hardest to play the game according to Canning's wishes. He was fully alive to the realities of this situation and on 14th December 1826 he wrote to Granville: 'So far as I am personally concerned, I cannot regret the extremity to which I was driven; for if I know anything of the House of Commons from thirty-three years experience of it or if I may trust to what reaches me in report of feelings out-of-doors, the declaration of the obvious but unsuspected truth that "I called the New World into existence to redress the balance of the Old" has been far more grateful to English ears and to English feelings ten thousand times, than would have been the most satisfactory announcement of the intention of the French Government to withdraw its army from Spain.

Personally for Villèle I am sorry, because I am afraid I shall have brought both his Oppositions upon his back. But that is no fault of mine. The fault is in the position itself, from which, if he is wise, he will extricate himself at the first opportunity. A good opportunity will arise when, after the settlement of the dispute between Portugal and Spain, we withdraw our troops from Lisbon. But once there, he must not expect that we will,

---

[1] Therry, vol. 6, p. 111.
[2] 12th December 1826. Mrs. A., vol. 2, p. 63.

under any circumstances, withdraw them leaving the French army in Spain . . . the decision of the House of Commons was quite as enthusiastic for active exertion now as it was in 1823 for passive neutrality.'[1]

Privately, through Granville, Canning made every effort to comfort the French Ministers and he was relieved at their satisfactory response. On 29th December 1826 he wrote gratefully to Granville: 'Damas is a saint . . . and Villèle an angel.'[2] Certainly they had been sorely tried by Canning.

On 2nd April 1827 he reported complacently to George IV: 'The King of Spain proposes 1st to reduce his army — on condition 2ndly that Portugal shall discontinue her armaments — 3rdly that the *French* shall withdraw their army from Spain and 4th England hers from Lisbon simultaneously.

This is the very consummation to which Mr. Canning has always ventured to look forward, as the *proof of the sum*, in respect to the interference on behalf of Portugal. But Mr. Canning confesses that it is beyond his hopes that the *proposal* of it should come from Madrid.'[3]

Once the crisis in the Iberian Peninsula had been settled to Canning's satisfaction, he returned, with confidence, to the problems of the Near East. The Convention of Ackerman, signed in early October 1826, had seemed to settle outstanding Russian grievances against Turkey. The Sultan granted a measure of autonomy to Wallachia and Moldavia and reaffirmed the virtual independence which had been accorded to Serbia. He also agreed to compensate Russia for losses suffered from the depredations of the Barbary corsairs and to permit free Russian navigation in the Black Sea. The negotiations initiated by Strangford had therefore finally come to a successful conclusion. The Greek problem remained. While in Paris, as has been seen, Canning obtained Villèle's approval of the Protocol and suggested to him that French initiative might convert this Anglo–Russian agreement into a more general Treaty. Accordingly, on 22nd November 1826, Canning communicated the Protocol to all the Powers, and Villèle

[1] G.C. & T., pp. 546–7. [2] Ibid., p. 555.
[3] ASP, vol. 3, no. 1300, p. 213.

took his cue by proposing a Treaty. Damas offered a first draft on
10th January 1827. The provisions depended on Austrian and
Prussian adherence; they consisted of an offer of simultaneous
mediation on the basis of limited independence for Greece; the
boundary question was to be settled by a conference between
Turkey and the Allied Powers; in case Turkey refused mediation
the signatories would accredit commercial agents to Greece.
Granville and Pozzo proposed a new draft where dependence on
Austrian and Prussian agreement was no longer implied. Canning and Lieven agreed with this, but Lieven was anxious that
provision should be made for bringing more pressure to bear on
Turkey. The Tsar was now known to be making military and
naval preparations, and on 21st February 1827 Lieven proposed
that, if Turkish obstinacy persisted beyond an agreed limit, then
the Treaty signatories should reunite their naval squadrons to prevent 'all aid of men, arms, or ships, whether Egyptian or Turkish,
from reaching Greece or the Archipelago'.[1]

In the light of the Tsar's war plans, and of the desperate plight
of the Greeks, Canning was convinced that a threat of force must
now be included in the Treaty if the Greeks were to be saved and
unilateral Russian intervention prevented. He had difficulty in
converting the Cabinet, and particularly the Duke of Wellington,
to this point of view, and indeed it was not until some weeks after
the formation of his own Ministry that he was able to obtain
agreement. On 22nd May 1827 a Russo–British draft, containing
a secret article on possible use of force, was forwarded to Paris.
Damas, after some discussion, offered to sign the Treaty provided it was first submitted to Austria and to Prussia. Metternich
sought to impose delay by evading a reply but, under heavy
pressure from England and Russia, he eventually rejected it on
16th June and his lead, as expected, was followed by Prussia. On
6th July 1827 England, Russia and France signed the Treaty.[2] The
secret article, as finally framed, provided that if the Turks, or the
Greeks, did not accept an armistice within one month after
receiving the Treaty, then the contracting parties would interpose

---

[1] *F.O. Russia /168*. TEMP, p. 398.
[2] It became known as the Treaty of London.

between the belligerents; instructions to this effect were immediately to be sent to the Admirals of the Allied squadrons in the Mediterranean. After signature, on Canning's initiative, the period of grace was reduced from one month to a fortnight. Polignac somewhat reluctantly accepted this amendment on 24th July. In seeking it Canning was probably influenced by the news, which reached England on 7th July, that Turkey had totally rejected British mediation offered on the basis of the Protocol. The firmest pressure would therefore presumably be required to move Turkish intransigence. But although Canning now clearly envisaged forcible Allied intervention, he devised one further plan which might have compelled Turkey's acceptance of the terms offered without the need of any sanctions. On 14th July 1827 Major Cradock, an official at the Paris Embassy, was sent on a secret mission to Mohammed Ali to warn him of the possibility of Allied naval intervention and to recommend a declaration of Egyptian neutrality. Referring to this matter and to the premature disclosure of the Treaty, including its secret article in *The Times* of 13th July, Canning wrote to Granville: 'Cradock turns out to be an old acquaintance of the Pasha of Egypt; and therefore the fittest person that could have been selected for the Commission. If the Pasha's fleet has not sailed before Cradock reaches him I flatter myself it will remain in port.

The Treaty is, after all its delays and difficulties, satisfactorily adjusted. Its premature publicity is, however, very unfortunate: I am inclined to suspect Polignac's Chancery of the breach of confidence; in great part from the eagerness with which, Dudley tells me, Polignac shows to throw the blame upon this Office. The misfortune is, nevertheless, not without its consolation. The notoriety of the provisions of the Treaty baffles misrepresentation, and leaves Austria only the choice to join or not to join, in the face of the world, a concert which all the world generally approves.'[1]

In the event Cradock's mission proved a failure and the Turks could continue to rely on Egyptian arms in Greece. News of the Treaty reached Constantinople on 8th August, the day Canning died. The Turks refused to accept an armistice and, after a

[1] 13th July 1827. *Granville MSS.* TEMP, p. 403.

fortnight's delay, the provisions of the secret article therefore became applicable. Their interpretation depended much on the Admirals on the spot and particularly on Admiral Codrington. The Battle of Navarino was the result. The Egyptian and Turkish Fleets were destroyed and the situation saved for the Greeks.

This form of intervention, however fortuitously undertaken, stemmed from Canning's policy. To the Duke of Wellington it was 'an untoward event', but there seems little doubt that Canning would have welcomed it in very different terms. Under Wellington an attempt was made to put Canning's Near-Eastern policy into reverse. In the confusion which followed Russia finally went to war with Turkey, while Great Britain looked on, alarmed, bewildered and impotent. If Constantinople remained Turkish this was due more to Russian hesitations than to any manifestation of British policy. Though Canning had helped to achieve Greek independence, his real objective had been the prevention of a Russo–Turkish war and the dangers to Great Britain's position in the Eastern Mediterranean which such a war implied. Canning's admirers have, therefore, argued that his successors failed to understand his policy and by their vacillations helped to provoke the situation which he had striven so hard to avoid. There seems no doubt that the two succeeding Ministries, deprived of his guidance, drifted where the Eastern Question was concerned rather helplessly off the tracks. On the other hand it is, of course, impossible to prove that he would have succeeded where they failed. But it can be suggested that the notion of co-operating with Russia in order to restrain her seemed a promising one. In 1840 Lord Palmerston, in 1844 Lord Aberdeen and in 1897 Lord Salisbury made attempts to revert to his idea.[1] None of these attempts showed more than ephemeral success. Perhaps the best opportunity was lost with Canning's death.

If Portugal and Greece provoked the last serious problems which faced Canning, he continued until his death to devote a great part of his attention to the New World. After the major

---

[1] The Anglo–Russian Entente of 1907 and the Treaty signed during the 1914 War which allocated Constantinople to Russia were expedients born of new pressures and cannot be included in the same category.

question of recognition had been solved, Canning considered that relations with the new States must be cultivated with jealousy and with care. He kept up an immense correspondence with the British representatives on the spot and he attempted, usually with success, to direct their activities down to the most minute details. Their task was to promote good will, to maintain British influence and to protect British commercial interests. They were hampered by the obstinacy of Spain, by the intrigues of France and of the United States, by internal political controversies and by rivalry and quarrels among the new States themselves. They were helped by the disposition of almost all leading Latin-American politicians to look towards Great Britain for support and advice. This disposition, however, added much to the labours of the British representatives and was often, in itself, a source of difficulty and embarrassment. Canning's main efforts were directed towards achieving an armistice between Spain and her former Colonies, preserving the Island of Cuba for Spain and settling the dispute between Brazil and the Argentine over the Banda Oriental. The Spanish problem proved insoluble. In October 1826 it seemed possible that Villele, by threatening to withdraw French troops from Spain, might have succeeded in bringing the required pressure to bear; Canning had suggested the idea and Villèle's response was encouraging, but, in the event, he was unable to get the required backing from Charles X; after this attempt, which was the culmination of many previous endeavours, Canning seems to have resigned himself to allowing time to take care of Spanish folly. The fate of Cuba was of particular concern to the United States; ambition was tempered with prudence and interest dictated that the Spanish *status quo* should be preserved. France also, but less justifiably, covetous had reached a similar conclusion. Canning therefore, although he sometimes chose to be suspicious, had little cause to fear either American or French designs. On the other hand, Mexico and Columbia both threatened, unless Spain recognised their own independence, to 'liberate' Cuba; the threat was not a very serious one but the situation was so delicate that Canning was inevitably apprehensive. He did not wish to dictate policy to the new States nor was he prepared to make any guarantees to Spain. His difficulties were resolved by the United States. They took the initiative in warning off Mexico and Columbia; knowledge of this was subsequently officially transmitted to Spain. Canning was sarcastic about American clumsiness in thus depriving Mexico and Columbia of a means of bringing pressure to bear on Spain; but this gave him an opportunity to score at the expense of North-American prestige in Latin America, while the Cuban question had been settled to his entire satisfaction. However, although Cuba gave him no further cause for concern, he himself, as has been seen, did consider the possibility of British intervention as a reprisal against Spain at the height of the Portuguese crisis. In the dispute between Brazil and the Argentine over the Banda Oriental, which led to hostilities in 1825, Great Britain was inevitably affected; anxious to be on good terms with both Governments, and recognising particular obligations to Brazil, Canning was also faced with the unwelcome fact that British commerce on the River Plate was, as a result of the quarrel, brought to a complete standstill. He endeavoured, through his representatives, to mediate and, although no agreement was reached in his lifetime, he did achieve a suspension of hostilities and the prevention of much unnecessary bloodshed; the negotiations which he had helped to initiate led in 1828 to the creation of independent Uruguay and the restoration of peace between Brazil and the Argentine.

Underlying Canning's preoccupation with these practical problems was his determination to countenance no rivals in Latin America's favours. French endeavours were relatively easy to block; the United States were more formidable competitors. Against them Canning deployed all the forces of combative diplomacy. He entered the lists with evident relish. Long-acquired prejudice, reprisal for the Monroe Doctrine and current differences on other scores[1] no doubt all played their part in giving him spirit for the fight. The Panama Congress, which had focused his mistrust and suspicion, became his chosen battlefield. He

---

[1] There had been a dispute over the Maine and Oregon boundaries and, as a result of commercial differences, the British West Indian ports were in July 1826 closed absolutely to American ships by an Order-in-Council.

warned the British representative that 'any project for putting the United States of North America at the head of an American Confederation as against Europe would be highly displeasing to your Government'.[1] In the event only Columbia, Mexico, Central America and Peru represented the new States at the Congress. The American representative arrived late and Dawkins, the British representative, had an easy task in preventing any notion of United States leadership. Furthermore, he squashed any suggestion that the Latin-American States should join the United States in protest against British principles of maritime warfare; the United State's effort to gain support in this longstanding dispute was turned against them when Dawkins, using evidence carefully supplied by Canning, showed how the American representative at Madrid had taken credit for stopping Mexican and Columbian designs on Cuba. At the end of the Congress Dawkins was able to report that the influence of the United States in Latin America was not to be feared. Canning seemed to have won a complete victory. But he held the trump cards, and it may be wondered whether the cause required so much exertion. Relations with the United States undoubtedly suffered, and it is significant that they improved rapidly after his death. Perhaps in his dealings with the Americas Canning's priorities were somewhat blurred.

At the time the luxury of such miscalculation was both popular and safe. It only served to underline the international status of England which Canning, Metternich's crucifier,[2] had so deliberately and so flamboyantly magnified.

(iv) *Conclusion*

In his last tenure of the Foreign Office, and during his brief Premiership, Canning set himself certain tasks and carried them out to his own entire satisfaction. The old Congress System was

[1] Canning to Dawkins. 18th March 1826. WEB, no. 212, vol. 1, p. 404.

[2] 'Mr. Canning is my Crucifier,' Metternich confessed, late in 1826, in a letter to his son. *Memoirs of Prince Metternich 1815–1829* ed. Prince Richard Metternich. Trans. Mrs. Napier, vol. 4, p. 297.

destroyed and a new alignment of England, Russia and France created. The humiliation caused by French penetration in Spain was blotted out by the triumph of British influence in Portugal, and the way was opened for simultaneous withdrawal of troops. The independence of Brazil had been secured and one Monarchy was preserved in the New World. After the United States, Great Britain had been the first to recognise the independence of any Latin-American States. They considered themselves mainly beholden to Great Britain and to Canning[1] for their safety; they looked towards Great Britain rather than to the United States for their future protection. Greek independence, without apparent risk of a Russo–Turkish war and the consequent disruption of the Turkish Empire, seemed guaranteed; furthermore, the new Greek State seemed likely to be more grateful to Great Britain than to any other power. British interests in all parts of the world were secure and British prestige was in the ascendant. Among liberals abroad Canning's name was revered and British interests were closely identified with those of humanity. Even if liberals in England still suspected Canning's political principles, they had come to join, together with the King and many Tories, in admiration of his foreign policy. In his aim to make his policy popular Canning had been eminently successful.

For these achievements he had relied largely on personal ability and exertion. By sheer industry and agility of mind he managed to keep the whole conduct of foreign policy under his immediate and direct control. He wrote or dictated almost every communication made to British representatives abroad. He was responsible for all contact with foreign diplomats. The burden was immense, but far from seeking to devolve any responsibility, Canning insisted on carrying the whole load.[2] At the Foreign

---

[1] Sentiment in Latin America has remained very faithful to Canning's memory. The statues erected in his honour and the streets named after him in their main cities act as a continual reminder.

[2] Also, of course, he was Leader of the House and, as he wrote to Frere (7th August 1823. FEST, p. 260): 'The two functions of For. Sec. and Leader of the H. of C. are too much for any man — and ought not to be united; though I of course would rather die under them than separate them, or consent to have separation in my person.'

Office he effected a few minor reforms and economies and obtained some greater measure of clerical assistance. Otherwise, in
spite of a vastly increasing colume of business, the old system
remained unchanged. Any policy once determined could be pursued everywhere and in all its ramifications with a single voice.
In the hands of a perfectionist such as Canning the operation of
this system demanded enormous labour, but the unity of purpose
achieved was impressive.

While Canning remained so effectively at the controls he demanded unquestioning obedience as well as efficiency from his
representatives abroad. He did not hesitate to criticise his closest
friends; though reprimands varied in tone, they were administered
without distinction for persons.[1] This strict discipline, though
often much resented by its victims, helped to confirm the co-
ordination which Canning was so successful in maintaining.
When communications were so slow and diplomatic representatives, buttressed by privilege, so accustomed to independence, his
achievement was little short of a *tour de force*.

Although Canning thus jealously controlled every move of his
department, he could be both circumspect and patient. 'Oh that
people could learn,' he once wrote to Granville, 'that doing
nothing is often a measure, and full as important a one, as the
most diligent activity; and that clever people could reconcile it
to themselves to own, that they have no instructions when they
have none.'[2] Of course it was easier for Canning, at the controls,
to mark time than for Ambassadors who were only imperfectly
acquainted with his intentions. And yet the successes achieved by
judicious inaction also represented a victory over his own
temperament. In his dealings with Metternich and with Alexander,
as well as with his colleagues and with George IV, he showed
that he could, when necessary, play a waiting game.

Hard work, strict discipline and patience played their part;
but Canning also owed much to his outstanding personality and
charm. This gained him the devotion of his own small staff and
of many British representatives abroad. It was not without effect

[1] See pp. 49, 50 above.
[2] 3rd January 1825. G.C. & T., p. 609.

on foreign diplomats in England and during his visit to Paris in the Autumn of 1826 he exercised something of a spell over Villèle and Damas.

By his own efforts and personality Canning achieved his objectives. Did he set himself a difficult task? On the whole the answer is: no. It suited him for obvious reasons to magnify the difficulties. But from 1822 to 1827 England's security was at no time seriously threatened and the issues at stake could hardly be considered vital. His measure as a statesman cannot be estimated by the magnitude of difficulties which faced him; it must depend on the validity of his assessment of British interests in the relatively favourable circumstances which prevailed.

Was his judgement sound? He claimed credit for destroying the Congress System; this self-imposed task proved popular; its necessity where British interests were concerned is more open to question. In spite of many reservations Canning allowed great importance to the affairs of the Iberian Peninsula; defeats and triumphs, however, proved almost equally ephemeral; while British naval superiority was so pronounced, and provided Gibraltar remained in British hands, the politics of Spain and of Portugal were not perhaps as relevant to national interests as even Canning, for all his reservations, believed. Where Latin America was concerned, recognition of the independence of the new States was an obvious commercial interest; this had been apparent to Castlereagh and he had made it clear as early as 1817 that British recognition was only a matter of time and negotiation; had Castlereagh lived the result might have been achieved more quickly but surely in less dramatic circumstances; Canning converted a routine operation into a splendid publicity campaign. He gained the good will of the New World. The advantages, in terms of commerce, can easily be exaggerated. England alone could supply the manufactures which Latin America required; she did not need to solicit for trade. Nor was cajolery required to persuade the new States to look towards London in their search for capital; it was the natural money market, and many British investors paid heavily for the privilege of speculation in Latin America. Good will was not of great practical significance when all the world was competing to obtain British goods and capital. In terms of power politics the winning of Latin-American friend-ship could only be regarded as a very long-term interest; though Canning justifiably might have assumed that progress would have proved more rapid than has been the case. But, while it may be allowed that the material advantages of good will could have been over-estimated, ties of friendship are always in themselves worth establishing and they seldom prove a totally barren heritage. The good effects of Canning's policy in Latin America are not yet spent. On the other hand, however, it must be remembered that good will was achieved in a spirit of rivalry with the United States. Canning did nothing to dispel that notion. On the contrary, he boasted of having outmanoeuvred a competitor. He was prejudiced against the United States. Many years previously he had written to Bagot: 'I am afraid, indeed, that the question is not so much how you will treat them as how they will treat you, and that the hardest lesson which a British Minister has to learn in America is not what to do, but what to bear.'[1] This attitude was typical. It is perhaps not unfair to suggest that long-term British interests would have been better served by a little more sympathetic understanding on Canning's part. But in his own day he could afford the luxury of a certain calculated perversity. Mastery of the seas was England's essential concern and here no challenge was immediately likely from the United States. With the defeat of Napoleon, the French bogey had been laid. Danger could now only threaten in the Eastern Mediterranean from Russia. Perhaps, like many British statesmen before and after, Canning was too sensitive to this threat. But his method of meeting it was imaginative and sound. Direct co-operation with Russia was probably the best means of exercising a restraining influence on Russian ambitions which, after a successful clash with Turkey, might threaten to run riot. It was also perhaps true that the price of achieving such co-operation within the frame-work of the Congress System would have been too heavy; though Castlereagh might have operated in this framework, Canning could not. Therefore it can be argued that he was wise

[1] 14th July 1815. BAG, vol. 2, p. 5.

to dissociate himself from joint discussions and to wait until the moment was opportune to create another system of co-operation on terms more of his own choosing. Possibly he exaggerated the difference, but it can be claimed that the lines on which he was proceeding in the Near East seemed well suited to serve British interests. There was some danger of Russian hegemony in the Eastern Mediterranean. This could have threatened British trade and communications. Canning was right to guard against it, and the methods he eventually adopted were well adapted to the realities of the situation. His understanding of power politics was seldom more directly expressed than when, in his great speech in the House on 12th December 1826, he asked: 'Is the balance of power a fixed and unalterable standard? Or is it not a standard perpetually varying, as civilization advances, and as new nations spring up, and take their place among established political communities? The balance of power a century and a half ago was to be adjusted between France and Spain, the Netherlands, Austria, and England. Some years after that again, Prussia became not only a substantive, but a preponderating monarchy — thus while the balance of power continued in principle the same, the means of adjusting it became more varied and enlarged. They became enlarged, in proportion to the increased number of considerable states — in proportion, I may say, to the number of weights which might be shifted into the one or other scale. To look to the policy of Europe, in the times of William and Anne, for the purpose of regulating the balance of power in Europe at the present day, is to disregard the progress of events, and to confuse dates and facts which throw a reciprocal light on each other.'[1]

If, with some reservations, it can be agreed that Canning's appreciation of specific British interests was a sound one, his general preoccupation with prestige poses another question. There is no doubt that he achieved his objective in maintaining and raising British prestige. What is the value of prestige? Prestige is like credit on an international exchange. When prestige is high it can serve in lieu of power; but, as Canning

[1] Therry, vol. 6, p. 109.

fully appreciated, the power must exist in reserve. Attempts to rely on prestige, when power is absent, quickly destroy its currency value. When, however, prestige is accompanied by power, it can serve national interests; but even then the pursuit of prestige is not without attendant dangers. Though Canning raised the voice of England in international councils, and though he often succeeded in presenting his country as a champion of popular causes, these prestige victories inevitably aroused jealousies and resentments. There is a reverse side to the prestige medal. While Canning, often cunningly, identified British interests with those of Latin Americans, Greeks or Portuguese, and thus gave to his boasts a moral veneer, his superior attitudes were at times a source of gratuitous offence. There are tactical advantages in posturing but, as was seen with Palmerston, the incidental damage can be extensive. Canning boasted with patriotic purpose; sometimes perhaps he also boasted too loudly.

Canning took pride in trying to serve his own country. Should a statesman be judged according to any other criterion? Canning privately scorned those who claimed to serve humanity. He was not interested in the fate of other peoples. He regarded Continental ideological disputes as a conflict of bigotries. Though he was prepared to make use of the badge of freedom in his diplomatic battles, he never seriously took sides. Only where the abolition of the Slave Trade was concerned did Canning show any tenderness for a cause not directly linked to England's security and prosperity. In general, save by accident, Canning was never a friend to any people not his own. For those who cannot accept a standard of unadulterated patriotism, Canning must fall short of greatness.

Otherwise, on the record of his conduct of foreign affairs during the last five years of his life, he surely earned the epithet. He showed a sound appreciation of British interests and he served them with imagination and ability. During a time when British naval power was unchallenged and no serious crises threatened, he achieved useful objectives with a minimum of risk and a maximum of publicity. He greatly enhanced British prestige at a cheap rate. Had any more vital emergency arisen, there are

s

good reasons for believing that his quality would not have been found wanting; but the times were relatively quiet, and although he made the most of his opportunities, he did not, like Louis XIV, fall into the trap of seeking glory for its own sake. On the contrary, he possessed what Sorel regards as the true mark of statesmanship: 'le tacte des choses possibles'. He was also a remarkable departmental chief. The evidence for his claim to a place, which perhaps only Castlereagh can rival, among the greatest of England's Foreign Secretaries, lies at least as much in the details of his enormous routine correspondence with British representatives abroad, and particularly in Latin America, as in his more spectacular diplomatic triumphs. He was a master-craftsman, as well as an artist, in foreign affairs.

As a man Canning possessed exceptional talents. These were entirely devoted to politics. In many ways he seemed to be travelling with the 'wind of change'. But his appreciations tended to be superficial. It was as an administrator rather than as a prophet that the quality of his mind emerged. His record as Foreign Secretary between 1822 and 1827 stands as a classic example of professional expertise. The intelligence, which he did not even try to conceal and which so often hampered his political prospects, was happily harnessed to practical realities. 'To us,' wrote Miss Martineau, speaking for the generation which followed Canning, 'he is the thoughtful calm earnest quiet statesman, sending forth from his office the most sensible and business-like dispatches as free from pomp and noise as if they were a message from some pure intelligence.'[1] The tone was fulsome but her instinct just. Canning ranks among the few who have successfully applied genius to politics.

[1] Martineau: *History of the Peace*, vol. 2, p. 146.

BIBLIOGRAPHY

Allen, H. C.	*Great Britain and the United States* (1954)
Arbuthnot	*The Correspondence of Charles*, ed. A. Aspinall (Camden 3rd Series, LXV, 1941)
Arbuthnot	*The Journal of Mrs*, ed. F. Bamford and the Duke of Wellington, 2 vols. (1950)
Aspinall, A.	*The Formation of Canning's Ministry* (Camden 3rd Series, LIX, 1937)
,,	*Lord Brougham and the Whig Party* (1927)
,,	*Politics and the Press 1780–1850* (1949)
Bagot, Josceline	*George Canning and his Friends*, 2 vols. (1909)
Bathurst	*Report on Manuscripts of Earl* (Hist. MSS Commission 1923)
Belfield, E. M. G.	*The Annals of the Addington Family* (1959)
Briggs, A.	*The Age of Improvement* (1959)
Brock, W. R.	*Lord Liverpool and Liberal Toryism, 1820–1827* (1941)
Canning's Speeches	ed. R. Therry, 6 vols. (1828)
Canning, G.	*Some Official Correspondence of*, ed. E. J. Stapleton, 2 vols. (1888)
Chateaubriand	*Correspondence de*, ed. Compte Marcellus, 2 vols. (Paris 1858)
Chateaubriand et Hyde de Neuville	*Correspondence Inédite de*, ed. Marie Durry (Paris 1929)
Cobban, A.	*The Debate on the French Revolution 1789–1800* (1950)
Colchester	*The Diary and Correspondence of Charles Abbot, Lord*, ed. Lord Colchester, 3 vols. (1861)
Connell, K. H.	*The Population of Ireland* (1950)

Crawley, C. W. — *The Question of Greek Independence* (1930)

Creevey Papers — *The*, ed. Sir H. Maxwell (1923)

Creevey's — *Life and Times*, ed. J. Gore (1934)

Croker — *The Correspondence and Diaries of J. W.*, ed. L. J. Jenning, 3 vols. (1884)

Fay, C. R. — *Huskisson and His Age* (1951)

„ — *From Adam Smith to the Present Day* (1928)

Feiling, Sir Keith G. — *The Second Tory Party* (1938)

Festing, G. — *John Hookham Frere and his Friends* (1899)

Gash, N. — *Mr. Secretary Peel* (1961)

Gayer, A. D., Rostow, W. W. and Schwartz, A. — *Growth and Fluctuations of the British Economy 1780–1850* (1953)

George IV — *The Letters of King*, ed. A. Aspinall, 3 vols. (1938)

Gower, Lord Granville Leveson — *Private Correspondence of, 1781–1821*, ed. Castalia Countess Granville, 2 vols. (1916)

Granville — *Letters of Harriet, Countess, 1810–1845*, ed. The Hon. F. Leveson Gower, 2 vols. (1894)

Greville — *Memoirs, The*, ed. L. Strachey and R. Fulford. 7 vols. (1938)

Hobhouse — *The Diary of Henry*, ed. A. Aspinall (1947)

Holland, Lady — *Letters to her son 1821–1845*, ed. the Earl of Ilchester (1946)

Humphreys, R. A. — *British Consular Reports on the Trade and Politics of Latin America 1824–1826* (Camden 3rd Series, LXIII, 1940)

Huskisson — *Papers, The*, ed. Lewis Melville (1931)

Hyde, H. M. — *The Rise of Castlereagh* (1933)

Kissinger, H. — *A World Restored* (1957)

La Gorce, Pierre de — *Louis XVIII* (Paris, 1926)

„   „ — *Charles X* (Paris 1928)

Joll, J. — *Great Britain and Europe* (1950)

Lane–Poole, S.	*The Life of Stratford de Redcliffe*, 2 vols. (1888)
Leigh, I.	*Castlereagh* (1951)
Lieven	*The Private Letters of Princess Lieven to Prince Metternich 1820–1826*, ed. P. Quennell (Albermarle Library edition 1948)
Lieven	*Letters of Dorothea, Princess, 1812–1834.* ed. L. G. Robinson (1902)
Maccoby, S.	*English Radicalism 1786–1832* (1955)
Marcellus, Comte	*Souvenirs Diplomatiques* (Paris 1858)
McDowell, R. B.	*Public Opinion and Government Policy in Ireland 1801–1846* (1952)
Marshall, Dorothy	*The Rise of George Canning* (1938)
Martin, Sir Theodore	*A Life of Lord Lyndhurst* (1884)
Martineau, Harriet	*A History of the Peace*, 7 vols. (1877)
New, Chester, W.	*The Life of Henry Brougham to 1830* (1961)
Newton, J.	*The Early Days of George Canning* (1828)
Patterson, M. W.	*Sir Francis Burdett and his Times*, 2 vols. (1931)
Peel, Sir Robert	*From his Private Papers*, ed. C. S. Parker, 3 vols. (1891–99)
Pemberton, W. Baring	*Lord Palmerston* (1954)
Perkins, Q. D.	*The Monroe Doctrine 1823–1826* (1927)
Petrie, Sir Charles	*George Canning* (2nd Edition 1946)
,, ,,	*Lord Liverpool* (1954)
,, ,,	*Wellington* (1956)
Philips, C. H.	*The East India Company 1784–1834* (1940)
Pirenne, Jacques-Henri	*La Sainte Alliance* (Neuchatel, 1946)
Reynolds, J. A.	*The Catholic Emancipation Crises in Ireland 1750–1845* (1954)
Roberts, M.	*The Whig Party 1807–1812* (1939)
Rose, J. Holland	*Pitt and Napoleon* (1912)
,, ,,	*Napoleonic Studies* (1904)
Rose	*The Diaries and Correspondence of the Rt. Hon. George*, ed. L. V. Harcourt, 2 vols. (1860)
Sanders, Lloyd	*The Holland House Circle* (1908)

Schenk, H. G.	*The Aftermath of the Napoleonic Wars* (1947)
Seton-Watson, R. W.	*Britain in Europe 1789–1914* (1937)
Stapleton, A. G.	*The Political Life of George Canning*, 3 vols. (1831)
,,	*George Canning and his Times* (1859)
Temperley, Sir Harold	*The Foreign Policy of George Canning 1822–1827* (1925)
,, ,,	*Life of Canning* (1905)
Temperley and Penson	*Foundations of British Foreign Policy from Pitt to Salisbury* (1938)
Turbeville, A. S.	*The House of Lords in the Age of Reform* (1958)
Twiss, H.	*Life Lord Chancellor Eldon*, 3 vols. (1844)
Walpole, Spencer	*Life of the Rt. Hon. Spencer Perceval*, 2 vols. (1874)
Watson, J. Steven	*The Reign of George III* (1960)
Webb, R. K.	*Harriet Martineau* (1960)
Webster, Sir Charles	*British Diplomacy 1813–1815* (1921)
,, ,,	*The Congress of Vienna* (1919)
,, ,,	*The Foreign Policy of Castlereagh 1812–1815* (1931)
,, ,,	*The Foreign Policy of Castlereagh 1815–1822* (2nd Edition. 1934)
,, ,,	*Britain and the Independence of Latin America 1812–1830*. Select Documents from the Foreign Office Archives, 2 vols. (1938)
Wellesley	*Papers, The*, 2 vols. (1914)
Wellington's New Dispatches	*1819–1832*, ed. Duke of Wellington, 8 vols. (1867–1880)
White, R. J.	*Waterloo to Peterloo* (1957)
Woodhouse, C. M.	*The Greek War of Independence* (1952)
Yonge, C. D.	*Life and Administration of the 2nd Earl of Liverpool*. 3 vols. (1868)

Note: I have, save in the case of a few recent publications, omitted works of general reference.

INDEX

γ